Plan S for Shock

Science. Shock. Solution. Speed.

Robert-Jan Smits and Rachael Pells

]u[

ubiquity press
London

Published by
Ubiquity Press Ltd.
Unit 322–323
Whitechapel Technology Centre
75 Whitechapel Road
London E1 1DU
www.ubiquitypress.com

Text © Robert-Jan Smits and Rachael Pells 2022

First published 2022

Cover design by Kirsten Weijs

Print and digital versions typeset by Siliconchips Services Ltd.

ISBN (Paperback): 978-1-914481-16-1
ISBN (PDF): 978-1-914481-17-8
ISBN (EPUB): 978-1-914481-18-5
ISBN (Mobi): 978-1-914481-19-2

DOI: https://doi.org/10.5334/bcq

This work is licensed under the Creative Commons Attribution-NonCommercial 4.0 International License (unless stated otherwise within the content of the work). To view a copy of this license, visit https://creativecommons.org/licenses/by-nc/4.0/ or send a letter to Creative Commons, 444 Castro Street, Suite 900, Mountain View, California, 94041, USA. This license allows sharing and copying any part of the work for personal use, providing author attribution is clearly stated. This license prohibits commercial use of the material.

The full text of this book has been peer-reviewed to ensure high academic standards. For full review policies, see http://www.ubiquitypress.com/

Suggested citation:
Smits, R-J, and Pells, R. 2022. *Plan S for Shock: Science. Shock. Solution. Speed.* London: Ubiquity Press. DOI: https://doi.org/10.5334/bcq. License: CC-BY-NC

To read the free, open access version of this book online, visit https://doi.org/10.5334/bcq or scan this QR code with your mobile device:

Contents

Acknowledgements	vii
Foreword	ix
Introduction	xi
Part One	**1**
1.1 Welcome to the world of academic publishing	5
1.2 What exactly is open access anyway?	7
A note on licensing	9
1.3 Why OA?	9
Reason 1: It's the principle	9
Reason 2: It makes economic sense	11
Reason 3: It makes research more accessible – which benefits society	13
Reason 4: Open access makes the research process faster and more efficient	14
Reason 5: Open access improves the quality and trustability of research	16
Reason 6: It's in the public interest	18
Reason 7: It makes research more inclusive	21
Reason 8: It allows for inclusiveness and connectivity	24
Reason 9: It helps the Global South	24
Reason 10: Academic research was always intended to be open	26
1.4 Academic publishing: a brief history	27
History repeating	29
Publishing becomes big business	30
1.5 The internet and OA: the early pioneers	32
The European campaign	36
A new era for academic publishing	36
1.6 The Wellcome Trust and Gates Foundation pave the way for OA	37
1.7 The Finch Report: taking OA to a political level	42
1.8 Brussels gets involved; the momentum picks up	43

1.9	Slow progress: the move towards OA stagnates	46
	Reason 1: Big business, big financial interests and demanding shareholders	47
	Hybrids: a halfway house	52
	Reason 2: Obsession with 'impact factor'	53
	Reason 3: Lip service to DORA	57
	Reason 4: Resistance to change; reluctance to take action	61
1.10	Time for a radical intervention	63

Part Two   65

2.1	The open access envoy	65
2.2	Forming a plan	67
2.3	The impact on smaller publishers	70
2.4	Warning bells	72
2.5	Gaining allies	75
2.6	The European tour	77
2.7	Support arrives from the universities	80
2.8	Gaining support from the younger generation of researchers	82
2.9	Compromises, compromises	84
2.10	The Coalition is born	85
2.11	The first setbacks	87
2.12	Putting the Science Europe face on; Plan S makes its first headlines	94
	September 2018: The launch	95
2.13	To the movies	99
2.14	October 2018: the US road trip	102
2.15	You win some, you lose some	106
	A breakdown of the common criticisms to Plan S	108
	APCs and the quality debate	110
	Lack of global awareness/coordination	112
	An attack on academic freedom?	113
2.16	Towards a Plan S implementation guidance	116
2.17	Berlin 2018: a radical intervention	118
	China shocks the world at OA2020 in Berlin	120
	Transforming the narrative	121
2.18	Celebrating rebels	122

2.19 Berlin take two: entering the lion's den	123
2.20 Latin America speaks out	124
2.21 Big interest from big players … and another withdrawal	127
2.22 The goodbye	129

Part Three — 131

3.1 Changing the narrative	131
1. Transformative agreements: a valid solution?	132
A mixed reception	134
2. New publishing platforms	138
3. Copyright reigns supreme …	139
… But publishers won't give up copyright without a fight	142
3.2 Reimagining publisher business models	144
The big five today: appetite for change?	146
The fall of publisher power	153
3.3 The future of academic publishing	155
Idea 1: Journals will be dead	155
Idea 2: Articles will be dead – well, almost	158
Idea 3: New technologies will lead the way …	161
… If data is made open	161
Idea 4: Attitudes towards cost will change …	163
… And journals will have to get creative …	164
… But not all will survive	165
3.4 Navigating the data-led future	167
The role of funders and institutions	168
Managing academic data	170
Europe's role in protecting academic data	171
The impact of Covid	174
Putting power back into the hands of experts	178
3.5 Plan S as a continued source of debate	179
No silver bullet	180
Changing the culture in academia with each new generation	182
Money remains a sticking point	185
The final word on hybrids	186

Looking beyond the APC model	188
Will the US make a move on OA?	188
3.6 Open science: the new normal	191
3.7 Taking stock of the legacy	192
Epilogue: Seven Lessons Learned	**197**
1. Make a plan	198
2. Seek out allies	198
3. Listen to your peers	198
4. Communicate, and stay in the news	199
5. Engage with your opponents	199
6. Learn to be resilient	199
7. Know when it is done; plan an exit	199
Index	**201**

Acknowledgements

The authors would like to sincerely thank everyone who has given their time to contribute towards this book. For some this meant several hours of interviews; for others it was the painful task of digging through documents from several years ago to provide sources, figures or background information. Thank you for your valuable insights and patience.

All the publishers mentioned in the text were contacted with a request for an interview and given the right to respond to content. A special thanks to those who chose to respond.

We would especially like to thank Frederick Fenter, Lia Noce, Agata Zaza and the rest of the team at Frontiers, without whom this book would not have been possible. Frontiers paid for Rachael's time spent writing the book, but had no influence over its content or editorial direction.

Finally, this book was written with the intention of prompting debate as part of the continuing conversations happening around open access, and we welcome readers' comments and observations.

Foreword

Scientific publication has undergone a significant transformation as a result of our now universal dependence on electronic communication. In order to survive, publishers and journals have increasingly turned away from print in favour of online access. With the advent of online publication, the speed of dissemination and wide access to research findings has challenged the traditional business model of subscription. Scientific societies and commercial publishers have struggled to maintain control of their copyrighted work in the face of easy access to preprint archives and wide dissemination of pdf copies of publications that previously were held behind paywalls available only to subscribers.

A relatively new model, open access, where the author pays for wide and immediate dissemination of their work, has challenged the hegemony of the subscription model. In open access, the true costs, and profits, of publication are made transparent as the author is directly responsible for the full expense. The advantages of open access are obvious and have become apparent to all with the immediate and open disclosure of Covid-19-related publications made available by commercial and not-for-profit publishers during the pandemic. But to many scholars in research subject areas or geographic locations where the expense of open access may be prohibitive, the downside of this model is also obvious. For the model to be adopted internationally, some form of subsidy must be developed at the level of the publisher or the institutional sponsor.

In spite of the advantages of open access, the model has been slow to take hold, primarily because of opposition from commercial publishers and certain large scientific societies where the financial gains from the subscription model has produced a huge profit incentive. The most selective scientific journals wield considerable influence among scholars who seek career advancement on the strength of publication in brand name journals such as *Nature, Science* and in the life sciences, *Cell*. The power of branding has been enhanced by the use of an alluringly simple metric, the Journal Impact Factor, which is advertised as a measure of the quality of individual research articles published by a selective journal. Unfortunately, this number, which was created to be used by librarians to help guide the selection of journals for subscription, has been promoted by commercial concerns to be used as a measure of scholarship where in fact it is more of an indication of the popularity and timeliness of an individual contribution.

The issues of open access and measures of journal impact are addressed head-on in this book by Robert-Jan Smits and Rachael Pells. Ms Pells and Mr Smits present the issues from both sides with particular emphasis on the efforts of formal and informal groups of scholars and academic leaders who seek to promote the adoption of open access by all publishers. Among these groups, a particularly successful organisation, cOAlition S (https://www.coalition-s.org), has advanced the cause with the promotion of Plan S, an effort to encourage all government and private funding agencies to move forward to adopt open access for the publication of all supported research. Plan S calls for a gradual but deliberate shift away from the subscription model. As a result of these efforts, several major private funding agencies such as the Wellcome Trust, the Gates foundation and the Howard Hughes Medical Institute have adopted the guidelines of Plan S. No doubt in response to the pressure applied by these and other funding agencies, a number of commercial publishers have agreed to transition to fully open access models in the years ahead.

At the same time, journals have been challenged to adopt other measures of scientific impact and to eschew the use of such simple metrics as impact factor. Ms Pells and Mr Smits describe the role of a group of journal editors who developed a Declaration of Research Assessment (DORA; https://sfdora.org) to encourage all in the business of research dissemination to view scholarship more broadly with a mission to "To advance practical and robust approaches to research assessment globally".

With all these efforts, it remains in the control of individual scholars and their institutions who assess research achievement, to adapt to the changes motivated by open access. The power of journal brand name and false measures of impact remain deeply embedded in the culture of scientific publication. This book offers a compelling look at how the necessary changes may advance.

Randy Schekman
Department of Molecular and Cell Biology
Howard Hughes Medical Institute
University of California, Berkeley

Introduction

If global crises have taught us anything, it is that access to information is king. At the time of writing this book, we are slowly coming out of a pandemic that has directly claimed around five and a half million lives, and indirectly millions more. Covid-19 has thrown communities and economies into freefall. The one thing that feels certain at a time like this is the need for certainty: by way of facts and figures; reassurances about what is happening to the world around us; knowledge that allows experts to find the best solutions to bring us out of the crisis.

When news of the mysterious and contagious new virus spread across China around the 2019–20 New Year, world health authorities were quick to raise the alarm. Researchers around the globe raced to find a vaccine, their pace made possible by the prompt decision from scientists in China to share the genetic code of the disease. They made the information open – in sharing the secrets of the problem, the problem was tackled by thousands more international colleagues.

Governments, too, have shifted in attitudes towards making the results of publicly funded research free – search 'Covid-19' and you will be able to read the latest peer-reviewed findings on a virus that we knew nothing of until 2020. The shared crisis we now face has shone a spotlight on our ability as a species to club together and find solutions to benefit everyone, and it is a really positive story.

In decades to come, when the pandemic becomes a memory and not a lived experience, the idea that such information was not always freely and easily accessible will seem crazy. It might sound crazy to you even now. But despite all the lessons learned during this crisis – and from the many previous global

---

How to cite this book chapter:
Smits, R-J. and Pells, R. 2022. *Plan S for Shock: Science. Shock. Solution. Speed.* Pp. xi–xiii. London: Ubiquity Press. DOI: https://doi.org/10.5334/bcq.a. License: CC-BY-NC

health and economic crises – we are still living in a world where access to expert research is not guaranteed. Today, as many as two thirds[1] of academic research papers are hidden behind a paywall: those are the health findings, the social reflections and philosophies, possible cures for illnesses and solutions to the threats presented by climate change, the clues that already exist to improve our quality of life.

One of the clearest examples of this in recent times was illustrated in an open letter published by the *New York Times* in 2015. In 'Yes, We Were Warned about Ebola'[2] a group of senior health researchers including the chief medical officer of Liberia wrote that the devastating spread of Ebola could have been prevented. In fact, they pointed out, the epidemic had been predicted way back in 1982 – but the relevant research was published in a subscription-only journal with limited readership. Not enough people had access to the information to learn about it or conduct the necessary further research to work towards preventing the problem.

It will likely be several years before we can come to understand the true extent of the disruption, chaos and trauma caused by the Covid-19 pandemic, but it is important we learn from our mistakes. If we can bring together stakeholders from across continents and industries to agree to make the results of Covid-19 research freely available – and we did manage it extremely quickly – why can the same not be done for research into climate change, cancer research, social inequality and food security? All these issues and more will continue to present major challenges to human health and the future of our planet over the coming decades.

Crucial to communities' social and economic recovery will be ease of access to the increasing body of multidisciplinary research surrounding this global crisis – from the scientific immunology reports to studies into social care and justice. Whether or not Covid-19 will be the final push needed to break the publishing cycle, only time will tell. In the meantime, it is vital that free access to information is safeguarded – more than this, that the output of research funded by the public for the public good is available for the public to read.

This is a book about a bold initiative that helped to expose a broken system, an initiative that set out to flip an archaic academic publishing model on its head. Each year, taxpayers contribute over $2 trillion[3] towards the world's

---

[1] European Commission. *Trends for open access to publications*. European Commission; 2019. Retrieved from https://ec.europa.eu/info/research-and-innovation/strategy/goals-research-and-innovation-policy/open-science/open-science-monitor/trends-open-access-publications_en.

[2] Dahn B, Mussah V, Nutt C. Yes, we were warned about Ebola. *New York Times*, 7 April 2015. Retrieved from https://www.nytimes.com/2015/04/08/opinion/yes-we-were-warned-about-ebola.html (accessed 13 March 2021).

[3] Worldbank.org. *Research and development expenditure (% of GDP) | Data*. World Bank; 2019. Retrieved from https://data.worldbank.org/indicator/GB.XPD.RSDV.GD.ZS (accessed 13 March 2021).

research and development, helping to produce around 2.5 million scholarly articles per year – and taxpayers have access to just a fraction of that output. Meanwhile, commercial publishers are turning that public funding into private profit: in 2017, the five largest academic publishing houses boasted a turnover of $19bn.[4] It is a public scandal that rarely receives the mainstream public attention it deserves.

Plan S was founded on the principles that scientific publications resulting from research funded by public grants must be published immediately and in fully compliant open access journals or platforms for all to read. For 30 years, publishers and researchers alike have agreed that these principles – making research 'open access' – should be adhered to. But progress has been slow. Tired of waiting for publishers to comply with the transition towards making journals open, Robert-Jan Smits dared to propose a plan that would shock the sector into action.

Since it was first unveiled, on 4 September 2018, Plan S has received backing from 27 signatories and counting. Additional spoken commitments towards making research open extend almost as far, with statements of intent from the likes of India, China and a number of Latin American and African countries made in recent months. But the real impact of Plan S, it could be said, is the positive change seen in the attitudes of researchers, academic leaders, funders and other decision makers themselves.

This book does not set out to be an academic scholarly work. It is a record, told from the perspective of Robert-Jan Smits, the architect of Plan S, about the story of the open access movement and Plan S more specifically. At the same time, we have approached the writing of this book as a piece of journalism: methodically, with an open mind and seeking to include as many voices as possible from those who were also involved and have an interest in the academic publishing system.

Sometimes it was not possible to include all the perspectives we would have liked – and it is a sad fact that both academic publishing and the world of European policymaking are still dominated by men. But there are so many more people working tirelessly behind the scenes to improve the research system for all. To all those who have fought for open access, we are grateful, and dedicate this book.

---

[4] Solomon N. The profits from publishing: authors' perspective. *The Bookseller*; 2018. Retrieved from https://www.thebookseller.com/blogs/profits-publishing-authors-perspective-743226 (accessed 13 March 2021). See also: Buranyi S. Is the staggeringly profitable business of scientific publishing bad for science? *The Guardian*, 27 June 2017. Retrieved from https://www.theguardian.com/science/2017/jun/27/profitable-business-scientific-publishing-bad-for-science (accessed 13 March 2021).

Part One

Pam Callaway had been feeling unwell for some time, but even after plenty of tests her doctors were not sure what to diagnose. 'At first they thought my elevated heart rate was due to a medication side effect, so they took me off it,' she recalls. 'Then, when I came back in, still feeling off and short of breath, they manually checked for blood clots in my legs but didn't find any.'

Pam did in fact have a blood clot so large that it was eventually spotted on a chest X-ray. 'Typically, something that shows up in the lungs like that, coupled with shortness of breath, is diagnosed as pneumonia, so they gave me antibiotics,' she says. 'Three days later, I was so short of breath that I called 911 in a panic, saying I couldn't breathe. They asked if I was having a panic attack, well – I got so mad that I started stomping across the living room and promptly passed out.'

By this time, Pam's husband, Tom, was on his way back from work. 'I came home and there was an ambulance and she was being loaded into it,' he says. 'I felt incredibly helpless … a feeling that was reinforced as time passed.'

Pam had suffered a pulmonary embolism – a blockage in an artery in her lungs – a life-threatening condition that came on 'suddenly, unexpectedly'. All her tests came back inconclusive, with future tests contradicting the results of previous tests; no one could say why she had a pulmonary embolism or what caused it. 'You can't fix something when you don't know what's broken. It could have been her birth control, it could have been genetics, it could be a blood disease or a disorder, but no one was sure. The only consistent thing we kept hearing was that she was statistically at a greater risk of having another one,' says Tom.

'It was extraordinarily frustrating to not have any conclusive answers,' Pam adds. 'I wanted to know what my risk was for another blood clot, and what to tell my family about their risk. I wanted to know everything about the tests, the mechanism of blood clotting, and why this was happening. My haematologist spent a lot of time talking to me about what was known, but, in my case, he could only explain how the blood clots form and not why.'

How to cite this book chapter:
Smits, R-J. and Pells, R. 2022. *Plan S for Shock: Science. Shock. Solution. Speed.* Pp. 1–64. London: Ubiquity Press. DOI: https://doi.org/10.5334/bcq.b. License: CC-BY-NC

Desperate to find some answers, Pam and Tom set about searching for academic research papers online from their home in North Carolina in the hope that they might learn more about Pam's condition. 'I'm a smart guy,' says Tom, 'and, while I'm not a doctor or scientist, I thought, if I could see what researchers were discovering, it might open up more options for her.

'Science is a series of incremental discoveries. I didn't expect to find a paper that had "this is the reason that Pam got sick and here is how to fix it" bured inside of it, but I wanted to be able to ask informed questions to experts about things they may not have considered. Was there a genetic factor that we could test for?'

It was not long before the Callaways came up against a problem: most of the research papers they wanted to read were stuck behind a paywall. 'The paywalls just teased us,' says Tom. 'They'd show us an abstract that seemed like it would be a factor we could ask about, but we couldn't be sure. We certainly couldn't afford to buy them to find out – the medical expenses were already a burden on us, even with insurance,' he adds, far too familiar with the challenges of US healthcare costs.

Tom works in open-source software, which he explains is 'software where the source code is open for everyone to see, modify, remix and so on'. It was therefore 'especially frustrating to come against all of this valuable medical "source code" and not be able to see it. I wanted to fix the bug that was in her source code, and all of these tools and datasets were locked up in a glass display case. It sucks to feel helpless, and then have that reinforced by a paywall.'

Sadly, the Callaways' story is by no means unique. We live in a world dominated by smart technology and search engine algorithms that make information available to us at the push of a button. At the same time, it is estimated that at least two thirds of the world's publicly funded research, and an even higher majority of the world's total research content,[5] is hidden from view behind a paywall. These paywalls are blocking quite literally millions of people from accessing the information they want or need – that might be in order to learn more about themselves or a loved one's health condition, or simply to further their education or understanding of the world. But there are plenty of other reasons – some obvious, some less so – as to why free access to scientific information benefits all of us. We'll explore some of them in this chapter, but first: a brief introduction to the world of academic publishing.

Research findings, for the uninitiated, are predominantly published in some form of article, or academic paper – which more often than not are collated as part of an academic journal specialising in a particular subject. The publishing of those papers is most often handled by a publishing company, which requires a fee for their work. So far, so simple.

---

[5] European Commission. *Trends for open access to publications*. European Commission; n.d. Retrieved from https://ec.europa.eu/info/research-and-innovation/strategy/goals-research-and-innovation-policy/open-science/open-science-monitor/trends-open-access-publications_en.

The short explanation for why the academic system exists this way is because, centuries ago, scholarly societies began to outsource the distribution of their scientific work to external publishers. Before the advent of the internet, the distribution of physical paper copies was the only way to disseminate scientific knowledge – but researchers had to concede the ownership of the intellectual property of their own work in exchange for the service of distribution.

Over time, these publishers also took it upon themselves to decide the rules of the game: pricing, copyright and access to content have all become factors crucial to the publication process, but are ultimately out of the control of the researchers whose work is published.

Today, many of these publishers operate independently as large, commercial businesses with their own financial agendas to adhere to – the cost of publishing must be covered somehow, ideally for them in a way that suits their business models. As a consequence, publication through these organisations is typically paid for on a subscription basis – hence the term 'subscription journal'.

A subscription-based journal requires its readers to pay for the content they wish to read. In the digital world, this translates into a paywall for non-subscribing readers, much in the same way one might choose to subscribe to their favourite magazine or a pay-to-access news site.

The introduction of the subscription model for academic journals allowed the costs of publishing to be shared across thousands of institutions, which proved effective for a long time. The disruptive technology of the internet should have turned this world upside down, allowing the same information to be validated and distributed at a fraction of the original cost. But its invention also presented a problem for publishers, who wanted to maintain their revenue stream as they moved (slowly) to this new technology. How could they ensure that quality content – the paid-for distribution of which had been so easy to control in printed form – was not stolen from them by being free online? The result was the paywall: a barrier to licensed content on large platforms, that requires access to be paid for, most often with annual subscriptions.

For most academic scholars, the cost of this access tends to be handled by their university library or research institution, the managers of which will typically review subscriptions periodically, signing contracts with the suppliers of the journals they wish their library to stock or have online access to for the coming year. The financial burden is therefore invisible to the average scholar, who can (in theory) log into their library portal to access the papers they want, or perhaps make a request for access to one they do not already have through the librarians themselves.[6]

---

[6] While most larger research universities and institutions (particularly in the Global North) will have bulk-style subscriptions to most of the big 'hitters', it is worth noting that this is not a given – the scholar's library might not necessarily subscribe to the journal that contains the paper the scholar wants access to.

University libraries (the biggest journal subscribers) will almost always pay an agreed sum for all the journals they wish to access as part of a larger subscription deal. These deals are individually agreed upon and shrouded in secrecy – publishers often requiring libraries to sign a non-disclosure agreement (NDA) upon agreement of the price. At any rate, these costs quoted are largely irrelevant – the price here is indicative and is intended to give librarians a sense of why their annual platform subscription costs millions for the bundle. But more on this suspicious state of affairs later on.

The back catalogue tends to be provided as part of the 'value' of the electronic subscription. In the past, libraries bought physical copies, which were then the property of the library (which could sell them on, for example). When the platform bundle came along, the model switched to licensed access to content, which locked the libraries into the 'big deal' bundles forever, if they wanted to maintain access to existing scientific literature.

Given the distance between the typical researcher and the burden of negotiating access, it is easy to see how, for decades, this existing subscription-based access culture has quietly ticked on without too much question. Researchers are by default passionate about their own subject, whether that be art history or astrophysics, and will dedicate most of their working (and non-working) hours to that effect. Spending time thinking about something so dry and bureaucratic as library budgets and subscriptions is unlikely to be a priority. But the fact that the consumer of services is so separate from the person tasked with negotiating and paying for it provides an additional advantage to the publisher.

Non-academic readers, meanwhile, endure a tougher time if they wish to have access to a piece of scholarly writing or the latest scientific findings. It is true that lay readers like Pam and Tom Callaway can access the content of many of these subscription journals, but only if they are willing to pay a great deal of money. The cost of full access to just one prestigious medical journal will often creep into the tens of thousands – a price list for 2019 from the academic publishing company Elsevier quotes a year's subscription to the journal of *Advanced Drug Delivery Reviews* at $11,283, for example.[7] A subscription to the full back catalogue of articles is no doubt out of the question for most readers.

Meanwhile, many publishers will allow individuals to download a copy of a paper on a pay-per-view basis. But what if the purchased paper doesn't offer the answers the reader had hoped for? Even a modest survey of the existing literature on any subject will require accessing hundreds if not thousands of articles. At one point, Pam admits she 'considered paying the ridiculous sums of money required to gain access'. But, as Tom adds, 'The risk was definitely real that we were looking at something that wasn't useful, and the cost per download made it functionally impossible to dig deeper.'

A typical scientific paper published behind the paywall of a journal website hosted by Elsevier, for example (the largest and most dominant academic

---

[7] Elsevier.com. *Print price list*. Elsevier; 2021. Retrieved from https://www.elsevier.com/books-and-journals/journal-pricing/print-price-list (accessed 13 March 2021).

publisher) will, at the time of writing, incur a one-off download cost of around $39.99. The lay researcher curious about their own health condition cannot typically afford to download more than a handful of those papers before facing a very large bill. And why should they, when in all likelihood their taxes have gone towards paying for that research in the first place? It is an injustice that continues to fuel the fire of campaigners.

In practice, most academic authors will respond to an email request from any interested stranger or colleague asking them to share their published paper or 'preprint'[8] with them for free – why would they not, when what most researchers want is for more people to engage with their work? Publishers may not like it, but even they cannot control a casual email conversation between two individuals on an informal basis.

Regardless, a barrier still remains in that, in order to request a paper from an author, the interested reader still has to be able to find that paper – or, rather, stumble across it and wonder whether or not it might be worthwhile. And, in a case of one human being versus the internet, that in itself can be a daunting and frustrating endeavour.

1.1 Welcome to the world of academic publishing

One may be forgiven for imagining that a positive to take from the subscription journal culture might be that researchers are unburdened, given that the cost is placed on the reader and not the authors of the published paper themselves. This is a useful illusion for commercial publishers but is not necessarily the case.

Imagine you are a researcher. First, you must go through the admin of applying for a grant. That grant, you hope, will provide you with the money to investigate a particularly exciting idea, which you know has the potential to further human knowledge, and potentially benefit the world around you. You receive the grant: fantastic! You spend the next few months, possibly years, researching the topic and eventually come out the other side with some findings ready to share with the world.

You write a paper. Now you have a dilemma – where to publish it? Clearly, you want to submit your precious work to the most prestigious, well-known academic journal that you can. A journal that, if your paper is accepted, will score you plenty of points for credibility among the big names in science, ultimately helping you climb the ladder towards promotion. For in the world of academia lies a toxic cycle: many funders will assess your future grant applications based

---

[8] In academic publishing, a preprint is a finished version of a paper that is shared online before it has been peer-reviewed. Authors may choose to do this to get their work out there as soon as possible, given that the peer review and journal submission process can take several weeks or months. What is also interesting is that sharing of preprints has become an unofficial form of copyrighting a piece of work in itself – by putting the work online for all to see, the author has created a public record of the findings with their name on.

on which outlet you are successfully published in, and your university or research centre will assess your performance and appraisal using the same metric.

Oh, but there is a catch – if you choose to publish in that famously prestigious journal, only a tiny proportion of people will ever become aware of your work, let alone read it. Sure, you could be a big fish, but you would be left in a very small pond. Your work would be underappreciated and underutilised by the vast majority of the planet. Most people would never know about it, because they do not know about or have access to that journal. Some may even go on to do the same experiments and learn the same things over and over again, without you.[9]

Or how about a compromise – we can open up your paper to the wider global community to read after an embargo period of a few months. How does that sound? While you are left mulling that over, could you hand over a few thousand euros for the privilege? And no, you cannot retain the rights to your work in the meantime. You might not even be allowed to read it yourself online if your library does not subscribe to it – unless you want to pay us again for access to your own paper, of course.

To those real-life researchers who are still reading, step away from the keyboard – clearly this is an oversimplified explanation of the academic publishing process, and the wider publishing ecosystem is as complex in its business models as it is vast. But that, in a nutshell, is what is happening in our academic sector every day, all over the world.

Why does that matter, you might ask? For one thing, it matters because it is your taxes – your money – that are paying for this system (the majority of research is funded by governments, and therefore by the public) and so it is ultimately your money that is lining the pockets of an exploitative, multi-billion-dollar industry. Meanwhile, let's not forget, an estimated 72 per cent of the world's research remains hidden to the majority of readers behind a paywall.[10] You have essentially purchased something at great expense that you are not allowed to look at.

It does not have to be this way. Since the birth of the World Wide Web, academics have been pushing for the utilisation of the internet to make research free and easy to access, share and read – because they can, because they want their work to be seen, and because it benefits everyone to do so. Today, thousands do publish their work online, for free, for all to read; this is known as open access publishing. And yet the progress towards open access has been

---

[9] Another issue is accessibility and reusability, beyond awareness. There is another catch here – the publisher, to protect its commercial interests, restricts access to only paying clients and refuses to allow the data and results to be optimised for inclusion in big data projects, thus significantly reducing the value of the results to those who paid for the work, i.e. the vast majority of society. Tom Callaway will never see it, but neither will the AI-driven algorithms that are tackling the biggest challenges of our generation.

[10] Piwowar H, Priem J, Larivière V, Alperin JP, Matthias L, Norlander B, et al. The state of OA: a large-scale analysis of the prevalence and impact of Open Access articles. *PeerJ*. 2018; 6: e4375–e. doi: https://doi.org/10.7717/peerj.4375 (accessed 13 March 2021).

slow – only a tiny proportion of the world's research is available in this way. In this section, we are going to investigate why.

1.2 What exactly is open access anyway?

To a non-academic reader, the phrase 'open access' might sound both generic and unfamiliar – but it is a concept we are all familiar with. Wikipedia is considered by many to be the original open access (OA) platform: its content is free to read, without exception, for anyone around the world who has access to the internet.[11]

As is to be expected in an industry of world-class thinkers, academics will debate the exact definition and scope of what it means to be 'open', but in his 2012 book *Open Access*[12] the very brilliant Harvard University philosopher and OA advocate Peter Suber offered the following helpful definition:

> Open access literature is digital, online, free of charge, and free of most copyright and licensing restrictions.

Simply put, open access is the term used to describe academic research, books, video, audio and other data that is not kept behind a paywall. With this in mind, OA principles can just about be applied to any medium of content, but the open access movement we will be talking about in this book largely applies to peer-reviewed academic literature: that is, research that has traditionally been formally reviewed, edited and published in academic journals.

'Open access is a kind of access,' says Suber. 'The term applies just as much to non-academic content as to academic content. But it's used for academic content far more than for non-academic content, and for good reason.'

As with most of the content we consume on a daily basis, the advent of the internet has changed the way in which academic papers can be published and shared. Where traditional, non-open access journals cover the cost of publishing – that is, the cost of hiring editorial staff, printing costs or website hosts, for example – by implementing access tolls such as subscriptions, copyright licences and/or pay-per-view charges, OA journals are characterised by a

---

[11] It should of course be noted that not every country's government is on board with the ease of accessing information brought about by the internet. Wikipedia is currently blocked in China; other autocratic countries including Saudi Arabia, Iran and Tunisia have blocked citizens' access to the website for shorter periods in recent years. A number of western governments have also been accused of censorship for banning access to particular Wikipedia sites. Wikipedia itself can be highly subjective and biased in its reporting. It is not peer-reviewed, but a large proportion of it is controlled by a small group of people. Sanger L. *Wikipedia is badly biased*. Larry Sanger Blog; 2021. Retrieved from https://larrysanger.org/2020/05/wikipedia-is-badly-biased (accessed 13 March 2021).

[12] Suber P. 1. What is open access? In *Open access*. 1st ed. 2019. DOI: https://doi.org/10.7551/mitpress/9286.001.0001.

newer set of funding models that do not require the reader to pay to read the journal's contents. How they do that varies from platform to platform, but, by definition, all OA journals allow their published papers to be shared online and downloadable in full, for free, through one of the following routes:

Green OA: Authors self-archive their work, often by posting a preprint (the original manuscript submitted to a journal without revisions) or a postprint (the accepted manuscript by the journal with revisions from peer and editor review) on an OA repository. This method of publishing is free for both authors and readers, and is growing in popularity for that reason – but it has not always been approved of by subscription-charging journal publishers, who might argue that their business model depends upon having control over, or first showing of, a piece of work.

Gold OA: A commonly used publishing model among commercial and non-commercially published OA journals, the gold route usually asks the author to pay a fee (known as an article processing charge, or APC) to have their work made immediately OA on a publishing platform. The idea is that the cost of running the journal no longer depends on the reader but is covered by the researcher's own funding grant or institution.

The challenge here is that there is no standard price, and largely no regulation of APCs, which results in some publishers demanding very large amounts of money from authors for the privilege of publishing OA. How much a publisher charges is not necessarily related to how prestigious a journal is – but prestige is often used as an excuse by some of the publishers charging very high APCs.

Diamond OA: For most authors the holy grail of publishing, this model is essentially the same as gold in that a finished paper is made immediately OA, but with no overt charge to the author. This model requires some creative thinking from publishers in sourcing the costs of running the journal from elsewhere – but it is certainly possible, and even the norm in some parts of the world. Some of these journals are subsidised by an academic institution or by the publisher's other fee-paying journals, for example. Others make it work through advertising revenue, endowments or volunteer work on behalf of the journal's editors and publishers.

It is worth noting here that there is some disagreement over whether or not diamond or platinum should be separated into their own categories – many OA advocates do not like the terms because they believe this confuses a business model with the way that it works. For example, diamond OA could be included within gold OA – it is the same thing but without the APCs. For the purposes of this book, separating the terms is helpful at least in terms of differentiating between models that require publishing charges paid for by the author and those that do not.

According to Lars Bjørnshauge, director of the Directory of Open Access Journals (DOAJ) (https://doaj.org), it is a common misconception that diamond OA journals are few and far between. 'It really frustrates me that people – namely, publishers and those who are wary of full open access – dismiss diamond as something that is not really happening, but it is the most commonly used mode for journals,' he says. 'In some parts of the world, like Latin America it's actually the norm and has been that way for many decades.'

Data presented by the group Research Consulting shows that, as of mid-2020, around 4,090 gold access journals had been recorded around the globe. This number is dwarfed by the comparative number of diamond access journals at that time (9,848) but it is worth noting that gold still prevails in terms of the number of articles published overall (522,018 gold OA articles were published in 2019, compared with 332,000 diamond).[13]

The ratio of gold vs diamond varies between global regions, but diamond journals still prevail across each global region when broken down. As Bjørnshauge states, Latin America sails far ahead in terms of diamond: the same dataset shows that by mid-2020 the region had 2,535 diamond journals compared with 149 gold. Europe, meanwhile, had nearly double the number of diamond platforms as gold (4,205 vs 2,423). The means to publish through diamond are certainly there, and yet the figures suggest some barriers remain in terms of authors opting more often for the gold route. But more on this to come.

A note on licensing

Crucially, pure OA research is published using a **CC BY licence** – the Creative Commons 'Attribution' licence, which allows others to download, distribute, edit and build upon the published content as long as the original author is credited. The use of this licence means that the author and not the publisher, funding body or anyone else, maintains ownership of their work. The content can be included in databases for text and data mining. It also prevents a third party from withholding the research or setting arbitrary rules over how many times it can be used or shared – sadly still a common practice among larger commercial publishers.

1.3 Why OA?

Reason 1: It's the principle

First and foremost, making research open is a matter of principle. Central to that argument is the simple fact that a significant proportion of it ($2.27 trillion USD, according to World Bank figures for 2018[14]) is paid for by public

---

[13] Ficarra V, Johnson R, van der Graaf M. Gold and diamond open access journals landscape. *Research Consulting*; 2020. Retrieved from https://www.research-consulting.com/an-interactive-look-at-the-gold-and-diamond-journals-landscape (accessed 13 March 2021).

[14] Worldbank.org. *Research and development expenditure (% of GDP) | Data*. World Bank; 2019. Retrieved from https://data.worldbank.org/indicator/GB.XPD.RSDV.GD.ZS (accessed 13 March 2021).

funding. It is your money, the taxpayer's money, and you should therefore have the automatic right to read it. This is a stance taken (to varying degrees) by a number of prominent thinkers – including public funding leaders, policymakers, independent researchers and advocates. Yet, some people may well argue that their taxes fund other sectors including public transport, museums[15] and culture, too; why then are these services not freely accessible? What separates research, and how can one 'free access' exist without the other?

To this, Martin Eve, co-founder of the Open Library of Humanities and an outspoken advocate of OA policy in the UK, points out that 'education and research have long been considered eleemosynary in character. Public education is specifically seen as a valid charitable object or activity in the UK and elsewhere, so it is already viewed as "different" to other services.' Public libraries, for instance, are universally free to access for this reason: they exist not only as hubs for local communities but as educational resources. The cost of running them is largely considered to be worth it for the betterment of public education.

Stephen Curry, a structural biologist, assistant provost for equality, diversity and inclusion at Imperial College London, and chair of the Declaration on Research Assessment (DORA), personally believes there is 'no qualitative difference' between making research and making other public services free to access, 'just a quantitative one that is linked to market operation.'

'Governments subsidise transport and the arts because they see these activities as a public good and recognise that the free market will not deliver them in ways affordable to the population at large ... governments also subsidise academic research, though in this case it funds these activities fully,' he explains. 'There is not currently a market mechanism to provide affordable access to all publicly funded research – even university libraries struggle to pay all the subscriptions – so open access is a way of making a public good widely available.'

At the same time, Eve cautions that 'OA should apply to research, however it is funded'. One of the prime challenges of the argument over taxpayer access is that there will always be people who do not want to pay taxes, and do not want taxes to pay for anything, 'while others see the scope as infinitely extensible,' says Eve. 'I believe we should, instead, focus on the public good argument of all research, rather than saying "it was funded by governments so it should be open".' In any case, it's worth remembering that not all research is publicly funded, after all – a small percentage is hosted and organised by private companies who might have a vested interest in getting a tech product out, for instance, or a pharmaceutical drug. Most OA advocates believe that private research should also be in the public domain.

A key factor here is that governments have not historically been incentivised to set about making all research free for public access because the returns on their investment in research and development (R&D) are less immediate

---

[15] In some countries, including the UK, museums and galleries are of course free to access already. But this is sadly not the norm across Europe.

than with other services such as public transport. It can take decades for the benefits of a piece of research to be felt in the 'real world' – which not only makes it difficult for policymakers to directly link the value of investment to outcomes but adds to the sense of separation between research publications and the public good.[16]

Reason 2: It makes economic sense

There is also a strong financial case to be made for making research OA. In the current system, the public purse is paying three times for academic research. The first time is for the research itself (through publicly funded grants, for example) and the second is for the salaries of the professors who carry out that research (at public state-funded institutions, at least) and also volunteer their time for free to assist with the peer review process.[17]

Finally, the public purse also pays for the upkeep of the academic libraries, which in turn pay the fees of the subscription journals to access the very same literature their institution paid to produce in the first place. And, if that is not enough to boil your blood, consider that these subscription journals are generating a profit from your taxpayer money in the region of €25bn each year.

The industry is dominated by five major commercial players: Elsevier, Springer Nature, Wiley, Taylor & Francis and the American Chemical Society (ACS). An annual digital subscription to Elsevier, the largest of the commercial publishing houses, comes in at an average of $10,702 per customer.

The reported operating profit for Elsevier for 2019 came in at £2,101m, up 7 per cent on the previous year (£1,964).[18] Company profits fell to £1,525m in 2020, however, with most of the decline coming from its events sector, which has suffered the effects of the Covid-19 pandemic. And yet, overall revenues for the year ending 31 December 2020 were still recorded at £2,692m, compared with £2,637m in 2019 and £2,538m in 2018. 'In 2020 … subscription sales generated 76 per cent of revenue, transactional sales 23 per cent and advertising 1

---

[16] This subject is explained further in Paula Stephan's 2012 book *How Economics Shapes Science*: Stephan P. *How economics shapes science*. Cambridge, MA: Harvard University Press; 2012.
[17] The process known as 'peer review' means the evaluation of scientific, academic or professional work by others working in the same field. It is common practice for experts to peer review a paper in their field by another author before the paper is approved for publication.
[18] Relx.com. *Results for the year to December 2019*. Relx; 2020. Retrieved from https://www.relx.com/media/press-releases/year-2020/relx-2019-results (accessed 13 March 2021).

per cent,' the financial statement said, proposing a 3 per cent increase in shareholder dividends.[19]

Profit margins are consistently high, breaking 37.2 per cent in 2019 – a rise of 2 per cent on the previous year.[20] To put that into perspective, Google's profit margin for 2020 was around 19 per cent (Depersio, 2020).[21] Walmart, another of the biggest companies in the world, has an operating profit margin of 2.78 per cent.[22] Not only are the profit margins of the big five publishers unjustified; they are truly bizarre when compared to other, arguably similar industries. Take, for example, magazine publishing: to make a working, marketable product, a mainstream magazine publisher must cover a multitude of costs. Authors must be commissioned and paid accordingly, a team of editors must be employed and time must be spent working through the content before publication. A magazine publisher must also pay to market and distribute its final product. All these costs combined result in a profit margin of 12–15 per cent, if it is very lucky in the current publishing climate.[23]

Academic publishers like Elsevier, meanwhile, have somehow cultivated a system whereby many of these costs are non-existent – or, rather, they are passed on to the community the journals are designed to serve. Academic authors publishing their research are paid in most cases by their academic institution (which in Europe most often means they are paid a salary by the public purse). The journal publishers do not need to offer them a cash incentive to

---

[19] Relx.com. *Results for the year to December 2020*. Relx; 2021. Retrieved from https://www.relx.com/~/media/Files/R/RELX-Group/documents/press-releases/2021/results-2020-pressrelease.pdf (accessed 13 March 2021).

[20] Lem P. *Elsevier profits up again in 2019*. Research Professional News; 2020. Retrieved from https://www.researchprofessionalnews.com/rr-news-europe-infrastructure-2020-2-elsevier-profits-up-again-in-2019 (accessed 14 March 2021).

[21] Depersio G. *Google's 5 key financial ratios (GOOG)*. Investopedia; 2020. Retrieved from https://www.investopedia.com/articles/markets/021316/googles-5-key-financial-ratios-goog.asp#:~:text=Google's%20operating%20margin%20is%2019,end%20of%20March%2031%2C%202020 (accessed 13 March 2021).

[22] Macrotrends.net. *Walmart operating margin 2006-2021 | WMT*. Macro Trends; 2021. Retrieved from https://www.macrotrends.net/stocks/charts/WMT/walmart/operating-margin (accessed 13 March 2021).

[23] Solomon N. The profits from publishing: authors' perspective. *The Bookseller*; 2018. Retrieved from https://www.thebookseller.com/blogs/profits-publishing-authors-perspective-743226 (accessed 13 March 2021). See also: Buranyi S. Is the staggeringly profitable business of scientific publishing bad for science? *The Guardian*, 27 June 2017. Retrieved from https://www.theguardian.com/science/2017/jun/27/profitable-business-scientific-publishing-bad-for-science (accessed 13 March 2021).

publish with them because the scholars are in it for the prestige – they know that the real prizes are the potential future grants, salary rises and promotions that the recognition of publishing in this journal will afford them.

On top of this, the bulk of labour – the editorial checks and evaluation of the work – is done by fellow academics on a voluntary basis known as peer review. Larger journals may pay their professional editors a salary, but smaller journals and those run by learned societies will often rely solely on voluntary contributions.

Ask almost anyone working in OA policy and publishing what they make of this set-up and they will reliably respond with their own nationally influenced metaphor. As Jean-Claude Burgelman, professor of open science policy at the Free University of Brussels, puts it, he is Belgian – 'and Belgians like food ... It's like, I grow my vegetables and my cows and what have you, I prepare them, I cultivate them, I harvest them. Then I go to the restaurant and make the food, I lay the table out for everyone. Then when I want to eat it, the owner of the restaurant tells me I must pay him? It doesn't make sense.'

Reason 3: It makes research more accessible – which benefits society

The money being spent is a clear injustice in the eyes of active campaigners as well as those researchers trapped inside the system. But it is not the only reason why research should be made open. If what is paid for by the taxpayer can be made accessible in a transparent and easy to access way, it also benefits society as a whole. In short, removing price barriers to articles means more people are able to read useful and informative scientific content.

Similarly, removing copyright barriers means the content of research is not owned by a commercial entity but by the public. The authors, their universities, research institutions and other stakeholders are free to share the information however and wherever they like, including by adding knowledge to AI-driven applications that are addressing major societal challenges.

For universities themselves, this practice opens up a world of opportunities. Take, for example, teaching curricula: course leaders have more freedom in the textbooks and reading lists they set because they are not limited to what their library can afford to purchase. Students can access more information and ultimately enjoy a broader education through the ability to read widely in and around their field.

Sticking research behind a paywall, therefore, is counterproductive to these aims. In fact, there are many people who argue that paywalls are actively damaging to the natural evolution and geography of research, as well as the ability for a field to diversify.

Brian Nosek, co-founder and executive director of the US non-profit Center for Open Science, explains this predicament well. When he took a trip to Belgrade in 2013 to give a lecture at a university there, he was struck by the disproportionately high number of students he met who were choosing to specialise in his own particular field of psychology. 'It was because there was a tendency in my field for the researchers to post preprints of their work online – they literally chose the subject because they could access it. It blew my mind,' he says.

Suber tells a similar story: 'I picked my graduate school in part because its library was especially strong in the philosopher on whom I thought I'd write my dissertation. I ended up writing on a different philosopher and liking the school anyway. But I still remember taking that level of library access into account.'

It is worth noting that, while paywalls certainly have an influence on researcher and subject choice in this way, there is no evidence thus far of specialisations diminishing to the point of dying out as a consequence of research being stuck behind paywalls. For one thing, today's students have a greater number of tools to hand – it is increasingly common practice for researchers to publish a preprint online in the first instance, but there are also a growing number of pirate websites, the most famous example being Sci-Hub, which takes PDFs of paywalled research and republishes them illegally in the name of the public good.

It is, however, entirely likely that some subjects will have lost specialist subject journals for this reason: i.e. if a subject is too small to be profitable for a commercial entity, it is not within the publisher's interests to keep it going. The specialism will be merged with another, or scrapped entirely.[24]

Reason 4: Open access makes the research process faster and more efficient

It is a simple fact that, if research papers are made free to view online and download, more people – researchers, policymakers, curious amateurs, whoever – will read them. This means the findings of the research are disseminated wider, sparking new ideas, connections and revelations.

A 2020 study led by the Association of Universities in the Netherlands (VSNU) together with the Dutch University Libraries and the National Library consortium (UKB) found a noticeable advantage for journal content being openly accessible in terms of overall usage and attention gained. Their analysis, which drew from around 36,800 academic documents from Springer Nature journal websites, found that research published in fully OA publications received 2.7 times as many downloads on average than those behind a paywall.[25]

---

[24] This topic is explored further in Part Three, 'The future of academic publishing'.

[25] Wirsching H, Penny D, Lucraft M, Franssen J, Vanderfeesten M, van Wesenbeeck A, Jansen D. Open for all: Exploring the reach of open access content to non-academic audiences. *Zenodo*; 30 November 2020. DOI: http://doi.org/10.5281/zenodo.4143313.

At the time of writing, Stan Gielen leads the Dutch Research Council (NWO), the Netherlands' largest research funding body, but before that he had a long scientific career in biophysics. 'I did my PhD in 1980, and in those days there was no way to share information digitally – email didn't even exist yet,' he recalls. 'But I got a lot of requests from scientists who were interested in my data. And typically what I did was get a floppy disk or something like that with data and post it.'

While Gielen admits he did have his ideas stolen from him in this way – twice, in fact – he never felt any regret or hesitation in sharing with colleagues from afar. 'On average it was profitable, because sometimes people came back to me and asked me questions about my own data, which was a nice surprise. Their perception of my data was really helpful,' he adds. 'Quite often they led to a slightly different interpretation and even new experiments, new publications together with new collaborators. So it was very beneficial for my career.'

A sometimes-overlooked challenge presented by paywalls is that they prevent even the most established researchers from furthering their own knowledge of a particular subject. Lack of access to existing information adds to the risk of experts wasting their own time and talent pursuing the same scientific questions over and over.

It should be said that repetition of research in itself is not a bad thing – there is a growing focus in some circles on the reproducibility of research, for example, whereby organised groups are actively replicating past experiments to determine the validity of the results presented by older research papers.[26] But if researchers are oblivious to the fact their particular question has already been investigated multiple times – even that their predecessors have been met with dead ends – then they are effectively working in silos, contributing to a negative research culture that is counterproductive to collaboration and joint discovery.

The very fact research can now exist in a digital format (for instance PDF files), Suber believes, should help to resolve many of these issues. 'With the internet, we have the ability to share work perfectly – that is, perfect copies of work,' he explains. 'Even in the age of print you couldn't make a perfect copy of a work; there were small differences.'

Those small differences – a typo, a printing error, torn or crumbled paper for example – would not often matter when it came to reading the information the paper held, but they are important to note, nonetheless, since printed materials cannot be easily rectified in the same way as online content. Each printed copy of a piece of work also costs paper, ink and time. Where once academics would have had to write to a fellow researcher to ask them to send a printed copy of their work by post, today any interested individual has the ability to share perfect digital copies at zero marginal cost, or, as Suber puts it, 'I share with you the same set of bits that I share with someone else and you receive identical copies.'

---

[26] See more at https://www.cos.io.

'It still costs whatever it costs to write a long manuscript,' he adds, 'it's laborious, time-consuming, someone has to pay for that time ... but, once you've finished that, the new copy cost is zero. You can share a perfect copy with anyone who has an internet connection.' For the early adopters of email and connecting through research via the web, 'that was a quantitative change so large that it created a qualitative change,' Suber says. 'In this way, it is easy to separate the OA online research movement as significantly different to highly accessible print literature' – for instance, the free newspapers handed out to you at the train station.

Nosek agrees: 'Before the internet, the whole process took weeks. Now anyone can email an author, get an immediate response and have a downloaded version within minutes.' But with this improved speed and visibility comes an added, arguably more important benefit of OA in that it 'supports the improvement of research quality and reproducibility greatly,' he says.

Reason 5: Open access improves the quality and trustability of research

As Marcus Munafo, a professor of biological psychology at the University of Bristol and outspoken OA advocate puts it, 'the mere fact you are sharing data means you will check it more times than you would have before'. In other words, with the growth of OA, the academic community becomes increasingly self-regulatory – information is more readily available for scrutiny among peers who will quickly point out any hint of a mistake or poor quality control. But, more than this, the act of sharing academic work and data openly enforces positive research practices by the authors themselves.

In an article titled 'Five Selfish Reasons to Work Reproducibly,'[27] the Cambridge University biologist Florian Marcowitz addressed his fellow researchers by writing: 'Your most important collaborator is yourself from five years ago – and that person doesn't answer emails.' It is a quote that Munafo refers to frequently when making the case for openness to colleagues and stakeholders during his own public appearances and policy work. 'What Marcowitz means is that humans are fallible,' he says. 'I have colleagues like this who, even six months ago, all the variables were listed in their head until they've sent the paper off for publication. But when they need to go back to their own data they can't make sense of it.' Remember, for instance, revising for your school or college exams: it is impossible to store all of that information learned in the long term – in all likelihood, most of it will disappear from your mind once you leave the exam hall.

'So if you are in the habit of sharing your data, what that forces you to do is label your variables clearly, to have a data dictionary, to have a metadata[28] file

---

[27] Markowetz F. Five selfish reasons to work reproducibly. *Genome Biol.* 2015; *16*: 274. DOI: https://doi.org/10.1186/s13059-015-0850-7.

[28] A metadata file is a set of data that describes and gives information about other data, for instance the tools and approaches used to conduct a particular project or experiment. The Oxford University Press's Oxford Languages tool

that explains the basis of the experiment, and so on. Which means that not only can anyone else go back and check your data but you can go back and make sense of it years and years into the future,' says Munafo.[29]

The links between quality of research and accessibility have historically been contested, since there is no simple way of measuring this: the number of times an article is downloaded does not signify that the research is particularly good or impactful; it may simply be the only investigation of its kind that is easily accessible online, or it may have a particularly headline-grabbing title. But the argument that OA and open data specifically sit in keeping with good research practices is growing in strength by the day.

From his own experience leading reproducibility projects through the Center for Open Science, among others, Nosek strongly believes that efficiency and transparency are 'an important implication of open research. If researchers spend time sharing data, materials, and code and no one ever looks at it, then the extra work could actually reduce research efficiency,' he explains.

While no one has yet conducted the 'perfect study' to show how much a particular field has accelerated on account of its openness, 'there is a good deal of indirect evidence,' he adds, citing examples from his own work. His network's Open Science Framework,[30] for example, has around 300,000 registered users who produce content by posting and sharing research on the database. 'The number of consumers viewing and downloading material from the website is 10 times that,' Nosek says. 'For example, in 2019 alone, there were 16.3 million downloads of files shared on OSF. This doesn't directly indicate what people are doing with it, of course.'

There are also a number of individual projects that demonstrate neatly how sharing data can spawn additional research that would not otherwise be possible. For example, Project Implicit,[31] an independent non-profit OA resource with participating researchers from about a dozen universities, posts most of the data it collects from its more than one million participants per year for any researcher to reuse. According to its project leaders, who track the reuse of data using Google alerts, this in itself has spawned upwards of 100 papers

---

describes a data dictionary as 'a set of information describing the contents, format, and structure of a database and the relationship between its elements, used to control access to and manipulation of the database'.

[29] This idea is expanded upon in 'A Manifesto for Reproducible Science': Munafò M, Nosek B, Bishop D, et al. A manifesto for reproducible science. *Nat Hum Behav.* 2017; 1: 0021. DOI: https://doi.org/10.1038/s41562-016-0021.

[30] The OSF is a free, open-source web application that connects and supports the research workflow, enabling scientists to increase the efficiency and effectiveness of their research. Researchers use OSF to collaborate, document, archive, share and register research projects, materials and data. OSF is the flagship product of the non-profit Center for Open Science (http://osf.io/).

[31] Implicit.harvard.edu. 2021. Retrieved from http://implicit.harvard.edu (accessed 13 March 2021).

by researchers who would not otherwise have the resources to collect the data themselves. These additional authors have also used the same data to investigate questions that the researchers operating Project Implicit would not have had time or thought to study themselves.

Another example is the Centre for Open Science's Reproducibility Project: Psychology,[32] which Nosek was also involved with. 'More than 20 papers have reused the data of our replication studies to critique and examine new questions that were not studied in the original paper. This has been a boon to advancing understanding about replication,' he says.

In a separate report for Jisc, a UK digital academic resource network, open access is listed as a key element of encouraging best practice within the research and publishing industries. According to Liam Earney, executive director of digital resources at Jisc, this mention was in reference to a now-common understanding among policymakers that open access is 'the foundation for all other good research practices to be built upon'. The report (*Digital Tools and Services to Support Research Replicability and Verifiability*,[33] published October 2018) was written in part to address the issue of reproducibility in science, and Earney personally believes that 'OA is a prerequisite for achieving that sort of change in mindset which puts reproducibility at the forefront of scientists minds'.

'It's not that you can't have reproducibility with a paywalled journal, but I think that, once you've taken that step towards having OA as the default, things around transparency and processes become much more important,' he explains. 'Increasingly I hear people say "we want to get OA done so we can move onto the interesting stuff around reproducibility". If you haven't got OA then you are going to struggle with everything else you want to achieve – to have the conduct of science be accountable and robust.'

Reason 6: It's in the public interest

Some of the most emotive arguments in favour of OA come from the so-called common reader. Two decades after Pam suffered her pulmonary embolism, the Callaways are still waiting for clues as to why. 'Knowing anything at all about my actual risk of another blood clot would go a long way to inform decisions about future health care,' says Pam. 'If someone was doing research that looked relevant, I'd want to read it and possibly contact them, and offer to help.'

---

[32] Open Science Collaboration. Estimating the reproducibility of psychological science. *Science*. 2015; *349*(6251): aac4716. DOI: https://doi.org/ 10.1126 /science.aac4716.

[33] *Digital tools and services to support research replicability and verifiability.* Jisc; 2018. Retrieved from https://repository.jisc.ac.uk/7055/1/Digital _tools_and_services_to_support_research_replicability_and_verifiability .pdf (accessed 13 March 2021).

'I also would have liked to have known more before we had kids,' she adds. 'Sometimes the doctors themselves aren't aware of research, or give me conflicting answers, and in those cases it helps to have access to the research myself.'

'It's just become part of our life,' says Tom. 'I've said "she has a history of PE" to more doctors than I can count. Every weird pain or issue breathing makes us jump to that conclusion until we can rule it out.' The answers may or may not already exist somewhere in the ether, hidden behind a paywall.

There are positive stories of progress to be found, too. In December 2002, a Belfast teenager made world headlines after his father, Don Simms, won him the legal right to access an experimental drug after reading about it in an academic paper. Jonathan Simms had been diagnosed with variant Creutzfeldt-Jakob disease (vCJD), a distressing and fatal neurodegenerative condition that gives sufferers an average of one year to live. After receiving the drug pentosan polysulphate, however, Jonathan lived for another 10 years, defying all medical expectations. The legal decision opened doors to treatment for other patients – and all because one lay reader had gained access to medical research papers.[34]

It is important to note that this happened in spite of the paywalls put up by academic publishers, and was by no means helped by these companies. The Simms case was made possible thanks to a network of similarly affected patient advocates who had come together to share knowledge, contacting authors directly to ask questions in an attempt to take the matter of furthering understanding of the disease into their own hands.

Graham Steel, a UK publishing consultant, led one such patient advocacy group around the same time that the Simms case was happening. For Steel, too, the need to access scientific information was deeply personal: his brother Richard had died from vCJD at the age of just 33. Working as an insurance claims handler at the time, Steel had no connection to the academic world, but began to share relevant research papers and news snippets with other family members of vCJD patients through the website of a charity he had become involved in.

'This was in 2001 when I started to read research papers,' he says, 'It was all quite confusing to the average person, but I found that most of the time if I emailed the corresponding author and asked them to explain some of it they would happily oblige.

'At this time I'd never seen a whole paper online, I'd only seen abstracts, so, when I found my first open access paper on the subject, it completely threw me to realise not everything was paywalled. That was the best part of two decades ago now and not a huge amount has changed.'

Steel began to gather papers – some OA, some shared with him by the authors themselves – and distributed copies to family groups who he felt might

---

[34] Read more here: Dyer O. Family finds hospital willing to give experimental CJD treatment. *BMJ*. 2003; *326*(7379): 8. DOI: https://doi.org/10.1136/bmj.326.7379.8/a.

Introducing DASH

Harvard University's open access database, known as Digital Access to Scholarship at Harvard, or DASH,[35] is a 52,000-article strong open access repository hosted by the university library's Office for Scholarly Communication.[36] A few years back, Suber and his Harvard colleagues decided to set up a way of recording who was downloading papers, to create an interactive map of examples showing who benefits from OA and why.

Visitors to the DASH site are invited to fill in a short contact form detailing how and why the OA resource had helped them that day. The contact is by no means compulsory, but several thousand people have submitted their responses nonetheless, and the library team has collated these voluntary responses into an interactive map on the DASH site (according to Suber, the repository team receives an average of about five responses every day).

Click on any country in the world and a personal anecdote will pop up. One student accessing the site from Venezuela writes: 'Thank you for creating and maintaining this initiative. I am unable to buy books from overseas because of the tight control over currency exchange in Venezuela. I am grateful for the opportunity to access material I can cite for my undergraduate thesis.'

A self-described 'grateful researcher' in Nepal gives similar reasons: 'academic institutions and individuals [here] rarely get enough financial funding for an internet connection, let alone paid access to journals'.

A parent in the US explains their reason for accessing an article was that they were 'answering a question for my children about nature vs nurture, and was trying to access quality information on the subject'. Then there is the sadly common theme of patients seeking answers to health concerns: 'I [have a] history of breast cancer,' a user writes. 'I learned about early recurrence of breast cancer for the first time ... via open access Harvard. The day I found this website, I benefited personally immediately from it. Thank you for posting the entire article, not just the abstract. It was most informative and worthwhile to me and I will do my best to pass it on to other patients who may also benefit from this.'

---

[35] Dash.harvard.edu. *Your Story Matters* | *DASH Stories*. Harvard DASH; 2021. Retrieved from https://dash.harvard.edu/stories (accessed 13 March 2021).

[36] The OSC is the website where Harvard scholars post all their finished work. Because the principles follow OA, anyone around the world can read and share the papers.

> Another US user writes candidly: 'I made an embarrassing social gaffe, and I needed to understand why people behave like this ... I'm learning more about why I make mistakes like this, and how I can prevent them from happening again.'

be interested in reading them. 'To be honest, it didn't occur to me at the time I might be breaking some copyright law,' he admits. 'To me, this was valuable information that could really help a family who were going through something terrible, who wanted to understand a bit more about this disease we didn't know much about.' Luckily, nobody ever challenged him on it.

There are countless other examples of how access to research – scientific or otherwise – impacts positively on people's lives. From LGBT+ communities living in fear in Saudi Arabia to artists living remotely in the Scottish Outer Hebrides, being able to read the work of experts in a world saturated with 'fake news' and political agendas puts some degree of power back in the hands of individual citizens and can reassure the reader they are not alone.

Reason 7: It makes research more inclusive

Something that should seem quite obvious but is nonetheless often forgotten by the powers that be in the academic publishing world is that the general public contributes heavily towards research, too. A study into the impact and scale of 'citizen science' by researchers in the US and Canada (published in the journal *Information Science Frontiers*) suggests that public participation is 'a booming hobby for online participants worldwide and a growing trend in science'.

Public volunteers may be asked by scientists – through online advertising or on television or social media, perhaps – to contribute to studies by observing the diversity of plants and animals in their garden, for example. Other research projects have benefited from public contributions to transcribing literature or historical texts, mapping cultural or geographic objects, and cataloguing distant galaxies with home telescopes.

According to the *Information Science Frontiers* paper, more than two million people are estimated to be engaged in major citizen science projects in biodiversity research alone, 'contributing up to $2.5 billion of in-kind value annually (Theobald et al. 2015). As of 2009, the public was already providing 86 per cent of biological survey data in Europe (Schmeller et al. 2009).'[37]

---

[37] Lukyanenko R, Wiggins A, Rosser HK. Citizen science: An information quality research frontier. *Inf Syst Front.* 2020; *22*: 961–983. DOI: https://doi.org/10.1007/s10796-019-09915-z.

Separately, a lot of medical research depends on the willingness of patients to be studied and personal data to be recorded over a long period of time. In short, without public contributions in one form or another, much of our scientific understanding would be very limited. To assume these citizen scientists have no interest in seeing the results is one thing, but to actively prevent them from accessing their own contributions to science – even after paying for it through their taxes – is truly bizarre. Pam Callaway, for example, is very enthusiastic about the potential to help scientists further their research into her unusual condition, and once donated blood towards a broader medical study. But she says she 'never got to see the results'.

According to Stan Gielen, this is part of the rationale behind his funding body's decision to introduce its open access Incentive Fund in 2010 – a scheme set up to finance open access publications and activities that bring attention to open access during academic conferences. 'We all acknowledge that team science is important. We also recognise that citizen science is important, and there are many examples of this,' he explains. 'In the Netherlands we have volunteers in the biology sector who every weekend and count birds, fish or insects – and they make a great contribution to science. The same goes in astronomy. And I think it's an asset for science – but it's also having citizens participate in research contributes to a greater awareness of the impact and relevance of science for our society. It's completely fair therefore that those volunteers, those citizens, have free access to the results that they need to do their job, paid for by their taxes, and even that they have access to their own papers that they are contributing towards.'

OA content is proven to reach a broader and more diverse audience than that which lies behind a paywall: the VSNU/UKB study suggests as many as 43 per cent of the readers of OA publications work outside the research domain. As such, OA is democratising access to the results of publicly funded research by making it available to society as a whole.[38]

> **Beware the common reader as a red herring**
>
> Cases like the Simms family's provide undeniable evidence against any existing, snobbish suggestion that non-experts are not worthy of access to research. Believe it or not, the argument still pops up among researchers and in comments from commercial publishers that the average

---

[38] Wirsching H, Penny D, Lucraft M, Franssen J, Vanderfeesten M, van Wesenbeeck A, Jansen D. Open for all: Exploring the reach of open access content to non-academic audiences. *Zenodo*; 30 November 2020. DOI: http://doi.org/10.5281/zenodo.4143313.

reader would be overwhelmed or too confused by jargon to grasp an understanding of the latest scientific information that is out there.

'It's possible having too much information would cause more uncertainty, especially if the information is still experimental,' Pam Callaway reflects, 'but in cases like mine, where the established medical knowledge can provide nothing beyond the generic advice, it would be helpful to have any additional information, and to read any research that might impact me personally. Between me and my doctor, we'd figure out what it means.'

It is an argument Graham Steel is also very familiar with: 'There is a danger of becoming what's called a "cyberchondriac" – patients read up on their symptoms on Google and feed it to their doctors … but the doctors I've spoken to are very used to that,' he says. In his view, there is a much more 'fundamental problem' that needs to be addressed: putting research behind a paywall does not stop the information being out there; it merely makes the facts more obscure. As he explains, 'you can always read a research paper's title and abstract, but the abstract doesn't tell the whole story – better to let people have the whole paper so they don't make wrong assumptions about the findings'.

'There's a lot of misinformation that's put out there, but I would say let the readers decide,' he adds. 'The same applies whether research is open or closed – so you might as well give it to them in full.'

Others make the case that publishers and researchers should assist in the translation of their academic work to mainstream audiences – talking to the mainstream media about their findings, offering candid breakdowns of their research on personal blogs and social media, even taking part in patient advocacy, Q&A sessions and online webinars – and thus benefiting stakeholders on every side.

With these valid arguments aside, it is important to make clear that the campaign for OA is not solely made on behalf of the lay reader. In fact, says Suber, 'it's a known trick that publishers like to depict OA to be all about the lay readers so that they can make the claim in their patronising counterargument that lay readers don't care – and in this way, so that they can slip through the assumption that researchers already have adequate access. I believe it's a side step and made in bad faith by publishers, because researchers do not have adequate access – in some parts of the world, researchers barely have access at all.'

Suber describes his feelings on OA for lay readers as 'two-sided,' therefore. 'OA does benefit lay readers and there are a very large number of

(Continued)

> them who really do care to read peer-reviewed research. On the other hand, the primary mission of OA is to provide research to researchers, and it's researchers who are doing this for themselves.'
>
> Suber's point is that OA is not just for one group of readers or the other: there is no need to choose. 'It would even be more expensive to build the apparatus needed to give access to academics and deny it to everyone else,' he adds.[39]

Reason 8: It allows for inclusiveness and connectivity

If the Covid-19 pandemic has shown us anything about the contemporary world, it is how much our societies rely on the internet to stay connected to one another. It has also demonstrated the value of being able to access content at the click of a button – and that is just as true of research.

According to Martin Eve, scholars in humanities subjects in particular faced a problem at the beginning of the pandemic for the simple fact that so much humanities research lies in big, fat, printed tomes. With the closure of physical libraries during local and national Covid-19 lockdowns, Eve notes, 'we suddenly had people unable to do their research in the humanities disciplines because most of what they wanted to access was sat on a shelf in a closed university library in print.' Take into account the additional challenge of how costly these printed books can be to get hold of, and it suddenly seems antiquated that such content often is not easily available in digital form. Even when they are, subscription paywalls can be difficult to navigate outside campus grounds.

But it is not just an issue during pandemic times, he cautions: 'There are whole swathes of people who are permanently housebound, or for whom it is not possible to get to a library – and these people have no possibility of looking at this work at all without OA. It's an equality issue.'

Reason 9: It helps the Global South

Paywalls remain a major barrier to progress in developing countries, especially those where resources and public funding for research are limited. That researchers working in areas of sub-Saharan Africa, for example, cannot afford to access all the information they need only widens the knowledge, education and participation gap for those countries – and puts researchers at a further

---

[39] More on this subject in Suber's book: Suber P. 1. What is open access? In *Open Access* (1st ed.). 2019. DOI: https://doi.org/10.7551/mitpress/9286.001.0001 p.119.

disadvantage when it comes to competing for highly competitive international grants and other opportunities.

To this end, not only has the growth of the commercial publishing industry excluded research taking place in developing countries but by some measures it is actively damaging it. Rafael Mitchell, a Bristol University lecturer in education, helped to establish the African Education Research Database (AERD),[40] a project cataloguing research by African-based academics. Through his work, he says, he has come to understand the sheer scale of the paywall barrier in this part of the world – primarily in that researchers who do publish in globally recognised journals are sometimes unable to access even their own work. Inevitably, this comes down to money, and the sheer cost of subscriptions to closed-access journals, but in some parts of the region institutions have poor internet access on top of that. 'Some lecturers will even pay for their own internet via mobile networks that charge by the megabyte,' he explains.

Publishing bodies do often provide free or reduced-rate access for institutions in the developing world. Likewise, public funders and charities in Europe, North America and other wealthy parts of the globe are increasingly proactive in supporting access to collaborations with researchers in the Global South – the UK government's Global Challenges Research Fund being a good example.

But, according to Mitchell, there is often a lack of knowledge about these kinds of schemes among sub-Saharan institutions. 'Even some of the top Pan-African organisations have no institutional access to paywalled research – which, incidentally, is also the case for many international NGOs.'

He is also sceptical of the level of support boasted by larger publishers: 'The problem is these subscription discounts do exist for low-income countries, but it is not automated – the library or consortia have to go through a procedure to request the discount, assuming they know it exists and can navigate the bureaucracy involved. We're talking about institutions operating in regions where sometimes access to the internet but also digital literacy is limited.'

The idea that commercial publishers do enough to support publishing industries of developing nations is something that Randy Sheckman, scientific director of the ASAP (Aligning Science Across Parkinson's) foundation[41] and former editor of the journal *eLife*, contests enormously. When editing *PNAS*[42]

---

[40] The African Education Research Database is an online resource cataloguing education publications by African-based scholars, developed through a collaboration between Education Sub-Saharan Africa (ESSA) and the Research for Equitable Access and Learning (REAL) Centre at the Faculty of Education, University of Cambridge. See more: Essa-africa.org. 2021. African Education Research Database. Retrieved from https://essa-africa.org/AERD (accessed 13 March 2021).
[41] See more at https://parkinsonsroadmap.org.
[42] *PNAS* is the acronym for the rather extravagantly titled journal *Proceedings of the National Academy of Sciences of the United States of America*.

a few years ago, he says, 'I asked my librarian, "what's the cost per download in the entire University of California system?" For the PNAS catalogue, it was 4 cents per download. For Elsevier journals it was a dollar per download. Then I found out that as I went around the world, other institutions were being ripped off even worse. In Argentina – poor Argentina with a science budget that was slashed years ago – they were paying USD5 per download for access to Elsevier papers. That these companies agree fair rates for developing countries is baloney.'

For Helena Asamoah-Hassan, executive director of the African Library and Information Associations and Institutions (AfLIA), it is the cost of publishing itself that presents the biggest challenge to scholars in the region. 'Most researchers are not able to access funding support, so they do the research on their own,' she explains. In her experience, OA is helping to give African scholars the greater visibility they deserve: 'It has really opened the gate for researchers to work together globally. It's easier to collaborate with researchers elsewhere in the world, which makes it easier for African researchers to be seen. This in turn improves the rankings[43] for African institutions, their prospects and financial sustainability.'

Reason 10: Academic research was always intended to be open

There is another, oft-overlooked argument as to why research should be OA by default: it was always intended to be that way. Believe it or not, academic literature was never created with money or profit in mind. From the very beginnings of academic scholarship, research was published by individuals with the sole purpose of sharing important findings about the world with a wider audience. Likewise, the World Wide Web and modern internet as we know it were invented with the purpose of making it easier and faster to share information between scientists.

To better understand the sometimes-strained contemporary relationship between the academic sector and publisher, it helps to consider the origins of journal publishing itself.

---

[43] While not always popular, university rankings are an increasingly common tool for comparing the quality and reputation of learning institutions worldwide. In most rankings, the research influence of a university is measured by the number of times that work by an academic at that university is cited by another scholar.

See more: THE World University Rankings explained. *THE Student*; 2018. Retrieved from https://www.timeshighereducation.com/student/advice/world-university-rankings-explained (accessed 13 March 2021).

1.4 Academic publishing: a brief history

In 17th-century Europe, scholarly pursuits were less of a profession and more a pastime of the curious, if privileged few. As such, academic journals took their name because they began life as just that: a collection of personal reflections and philosophical musings by the landed noble gentry. It was not until 1665 that the world's first recognisable scholarly journals appeared in their early forms: the *Philosophical Transactions of the Royal Society of London* and the *Journal des Sçavans*, launched in London and Paris, respectively.

The London title – known affectionately as *Phil Trans* – was published by Henry Oldenburg (c.1619–77), the first secretary of Royal Society in London, and is still going today. Oldenburg acted as its publisher and editor, compiling musings from personal letters sent between scholarly associates as well as excerpts from published pamphlets, books and reviews.

This was an era very different to the one in which we live now: scholarly matters were almost exclusively reserved for the rich, white male upper classes, who had the education and leisure time to be interested. As the demand for journals expanded, it made sense therefore that a small financial contribution should be made for those wanting access to go towards the cost of producing pamphlets – they could easily afford it.

The printing of *Phil Trans* was arranged through the British Royal Society – in those days a meeting space for London's most highly regarded polymaths – which had its own printer. But it was Oldenburg himself who took responsibility for editing and shaping the pamphlet's content – effectively becoming the first journal 'editor' as we would recognise it today. In fact, he took some liberties that would raise eyebrows over editorial bias in the modern academic world.

Originally from Germany, Oldenburg was well connected to the scholarly endeavours taking place across Europe and edited and translated some of the letters accordingly. 'Oldenburg would be transforming the content, sometimes summarising it or cutting out some elements,' explains Louisiane Ferlier, digital resources manager for the Royal Society. 'But it was also his journal because he was the one receiving these letters – so he is the nexus, the centre of a really large correspondence network.'

Other editors followed in Oldenburg's footsteps to curate the journal, says Ferlier, but the editorial process became gradually more shared over time, with society members giving their own inputs and suggestions for publication by the 18th century. 'Bit by bit, the fellows became more involved in saying what should be published, in forwarding more letters – and that's progressive. It becomes more of a community-based journal in a way that you would nearly recognise it today. With committees looking at specific topics, you have meetings at the Royal Society where those articles are read and the decision to publish or not publish is taken,' she explains.

It is this process that Aileen Fyfe refers to as the 'pre-history of peer review'. A science historian at the University of St Andrews, Fyfe has spent several years investigating the history of the world's oldest running journals as part of a wider project with the Royal Society. Studying the history of academic publishing in this way offers 'a really valuable source of perspective on contemporary issues in scholarly publishing – whether that's the way in which research is evaluated and financed or otherwise,' she says.

'It's clear to me that learned societies play a very important and special role in academic publishing,' she continues. 'Part of that is historical, but part of that is also their connection to communities of scholars.' Learned societies could therefore be seen as the guardians and sponsors of research and scholarly publication.

By the 18th and 19th centuries, journals were being published in increasingly niche fields, and by the 20th century laying claim to a learned society plus a subject-specific journal had become a marker of the existence of an academic discipline, Fyfe explains.

The key thing to note here is that, historically, publishing was something scholarly societies embraced as part of their mission – but it was always not their main activity. Likewise, the purpose of academic publishing was not to make money. 'It might be difficult for us to imagine now, but in the 18th and 19th century it was taken for granted that the production and circulation of research couldn't possibly be funded by sales,' says Fyfe. Rather, the extra money required to continue printing, as well as the existence of the societies, was provided through goodwill on top of the small payments received by their readership.

Learned societies were not limited to the UK – they expanded through Europe and beyond, with some recorded in the US, South Africa and South America by 1908. These societies worked by subsidising the sharing of work, making it available to users for free through a library system. Meanwhile, similar arrangements were taking place across Europe, often linked to universities but at times independent of the academy, too. Brill, the Dutch international academic publisher, was founded in 1683 in Leiden – at that time under the name of Luchtmans, after bookseller and founder Jordaan Luchtmans. The company started life primarily as a bookshop and binder, with Luchtmans repairing older books as well as auctioning private collections on the side.

Luchtmans is considered to be one of the first academic publishers in Europe for his early interest in printing copies of scholarly works shared with him – a commemorative book issued by Brill to mark the publisher's 325th anniversary details a 1685 print of the *Historia Generalis Insectorum*, an illustrated microscopic study of insects by the entomologist Jan Swammerdam, who had died five years earlier. Competition for ownership of scholarly literature like it became an increasing focus for publishers like Luchtmans, whose customers consisted of several high-profile scholars associated with the neighbouring Leiden

University. The gradual availability and affordability of printing presses allowed these booksellers to turn the redistribution of academic papers into a business.

History repeating

On reflection, the 18th- and 19th-century scholarly community's efforts to share and promote their work could be seen as the original open access. They wanted people other than themselves to know more about the world they were discovering, and the printing press allowed them to widen that access – albeit within a relatively small, privileged circle.

Copies of the UK's Royal Society journals were sent to public libraries in some of the large industrial cities, but 'the wider public was expected to learn about the contents of the publications through third-party reporting, commenting and reprinting,' Fyfe explains. 'The argument that researchers should make their work publicly available, as a form of giving back to the taxpayers who funded them, is a far more recent development. Even when the Royal Society was presenting the argument for government funding of scientific publications in the 1890s, it focused on supporting the advance of scientific knowledge by aiding the circulation of knowledge among researchers.'

The rapid growth of universities, libraries, and trained scientists created a context that required the Society to professionalise the publication of the proceedings. Even so, the concept of making money from their work was never a consideration, in part because these scholars were not short of money (while scholarship had expanded to include the middle classes by the late 19th century, it was not a privilege yet enjoyed by poorer people). But from the moment learned societies began to start charging a contribution towards the printing process, they were unknowingly outlining a new path for academia – trapping themselves in a web of cost and profit that continues to this day.

By the end of the 19th century, 'the financial challenges of funding the Royal Society's increasingly ambitious, generous and international vision for the circulation of printed knowledge were already apparent,' says Fyfe. For the next half-century, the Society struggled to find ways to keep this vision alive, slashing the provision of free and exchange copies, and seeking additional sources of external funding. 'In the world of print-on-paper publication, the Society's commitment to the non-commercial circulation of knowledge was ultimately defeated by scale,' Fyfe adds.[44]

---

[44] Further reading on open access and the circulation of research: Fyfe A. The Royal Society and the Noncommercial Circulation of Knowledge. In: Eve M, Gray, J. (eds.) *Reassembling scholarly communications: Histories, infrastructures, and global politics of open access.* MIT Press; 2020. Retrieved from https://watermark.silverchair.com (accessed 13 March 2021).

Publishing becomes big business

With the aftermath of World War Two came an urgent need for increased productivity, innovation and fresh scientific output to boost the global economy and raise standards of living. The British government, like many others, recognised that some sort of intervention – an incentivised push – would be required to kick-start academic publishing and protect the county's place as a competitive hub for research. They were concerned that society publishing was not getting the job done: activity was too slow, with many of the most renowned journals struggling with backlogs of work on account of lack of money and resources.

Commercialisation offered a solution to the problem, and so it came to be that the UK's respected old-school publishing house Butterworths[45] (now owned by Elsevier) was partnered with the renowned German publisher Springer, which had some experience of this and would teach Butterworths how to turn journals into profit.

In 1951, the infamous media mogul Robert Maxwell offered £13,000 (about €462,000 today) for shares of both Butterworths and Springer, giving him control of the company. The new venture was named Pergamon Press; 40 years later, in 1991, Maxwell reportedly sold the company to Elsevier for £440 million.[46]

In an article published in the Wiley journal *Learned Publishing* in 2002,[47] Brian Cox, a former subscriptions manager for Pergamon Press, reflected that 'war-impelled research far outstripped the capacity of this genteel publishing industry. A new breed of publishers saw the commercial possibilities in a business that, they foresaw correctly, would set enviable standards of growth and profitability in the succeeding decades.'

Working under Maxwell during the 1960s, it was Cox's role to increase the sales of the publisher's journals. 'Since the circulation of the journals grew by 5–10 per cent each year during the 1960s, I could have expected to be popular with my employer,' he wrote. 'But quite often I was upbraided, not for failing to achieve targeted sales, but for exceeding the targets. Why had I set the targets so low?'

Pergamon was ahead of its time in many ways. In 1968 the publisher became the first to digitise its records, creating separate computer-based systems to store the addresses of subscribers and a record of all the journals they subscribed to. It had never been so easy to target institutions for their cash.

---

[45] More information on the history of Butterworths: Thornely J. *Butterworths: History of a publishing house.* By H. Kay Jones. *The Cambridge Law Journal.* 1981; 40(1): 182–183. DOI: https://doi.org/10.1017/S0008197300096598.

[46] http://openscience.ens.fr/ABOUT_OPEN_ACCESS/ARTICLES/2017_06_27_Guardian_on_Elsevier.pdf.

[47] https://onlinelibrary.wiley.com/doi/pdf/10.1087/095315102760319233.

Meanwhile, universities were rapidly expanding beyond their budgets, and by the 1980s a lack of core funding meant academic libraries, were struggling to keep up with the growth in publishing and rising costs involved. At the same time, much of Europe was facing severe economic downturn: rising oil prices among other global factors led to a significant peak in inflation, rendering existing budgets flat. This became widely known as the 'serials crisis'.[48] 'Rising prices coincided with falling budgets,' wrote Cox. 'The truth came out that academic journals had never been inexpensive, simply because they sell in very small quantities.'

Maxwell, meanwhile, remained determined to push for more journals, more sales, more subscriptions, '[accepting] for publication applied material that the learned societies did not consider as proper ... An STM journal selling 2,000 copies around the world is the equivalent of a trade book bestseller. Most journals sell only in the hundreds.'[49]

Academia had expanded beyond the reach of any 19th-century scholar's imagination – as too had the publishing industry surrounding it. Research by Microsoft suggests the number of scientific documents published between 1865 and 2005 increased by 0.8 per cent per month on average.

The subscription-based model of accessing journals offered several advantages to the academic consumer: for one thing, it made selection simpler for the librarian faced with a thousand choices of journal to purchase. The subscription model promised an established practice, with a solid peer review system taken care of by the publishing editor.

For the academic researcher, the subscription journals available through their libraries had also become a much-appreciated tool conducive to their own workload. They personally did not have to worry about the logistics of publishing the article, or the peer review that took place, nor did they have to cover the costs of the subscriptions – that was a problem for the librarian to sort out. Furthermore, it provided them with a single metric of quality. In many regards, why would they care about who had access to the papers they published, or who would actually read it? The academic researcher's job was to investigate their chosen subject and present the findings, end of.

Of course, this is a sweeping generalisation, and fortunately there were researchers even at the very beginning who did care about who could get access to their papers. Over the years their numbers would increase.

---

[48] Fyfe A, et al. *Untangling academic publishing: a history of the relationship between commercial interests, academic prestige and the circulation of research.* 2017. DOI: https://doi.org/10.5281/zenodo.546100.

[49] Cox B. The Pergamon phenomenon 1951–1991: Robert Maxwell and scientific publishing. *Learned Publishing.* 2002; *15*: 273–278. DOI: https://doi.org/10.1087/095315102760319233.

1.5 The internet and OA: the early pioneers

With the dawn of the 1990s came the invention that would change almost every aspect of human existence, not to mention scholarly communications: the World Wide Web.

Its creation provided a new promise of freedom for information, and a whole host of opportunities for OA advocates who wanted to disseminate scholarly findings more widely. But, as researchers from the University of Montreal point out in a report, *The Oligopoly of Academic Publishers in the Digital Era*,[50] the internet has also made things easier for those seeking to make a profit.

'The top commercial publishers have benefited from the digital era, as it led to a dramatic increase in the share of scientific literature they published. It has also led to a greater dependence by the scientific community on these publishers,' they conclude. Smaller, society publishers, meanwhile, 'did not have the means to adapt to the digital era and therefore were more likely to be acquired or have agreements with big commercial publishers for the publication of their journals' – therefore enabling the five big players to grow even further.

By the mid-1990s, commercial publishers' share of academic output had increased to 40 per cent in the US, while in the UK Elsevier accounted for around a fifth of all papers published around this time.[51]

Peter Suber was an emerging scholar at the time of the internet's birth, teaching philosophy at Earlham College in the US. 'I was in the first generation of academics who had to deal with that,' he recalls. 'I also taught computer science on the side, so, while the web was not a primary interest, I had a geeky side. When the internet did come along, I was fascinated by it. I wanted to play with it, and one way I did that was to translate some of my publications into HTML.'

Out of pure curiosity for code, Suber uploaded his work onto his college website, free of charge for fellow geeks to access, or anyone else who knew how. Looking back, he says, 'I really didn't have any expectation as to what it would do for my scholarly audience – but then I started to get serious correspondence with philosophers that I had never had while the works were in print. And some of these papers were more than 10 years old, so they had been out there in print long enough to attract whatever attention they were going to attract – and it wasn't very much.'

---

[50] More information in Larivière V, Haustein S, Mongeon P. The oligopoly of academic publishers in the digital era. PLoS ONE. 2015; *10*(6): e0127502. DOI: https://doi.org/10.1371/journal.pone.0127502.

[51] Tenopir C, King DW. Trends in scientific scholarly journal publishing in the U.S. *Journal of Scholarly Publishing*. 1997; *28*(3): 135–170. See also: Vickery J. The market for scientific, technical and medical journals: A statement by the Office of Fair Trading (OFT 396). *Interlending & Document Supply*. 2003; *31*(1): 61–64. Retrieved from https://econ.ucsb.edu/~tedb/Journals/oft396.pdf.

He continues, 'It was easy to assume in those days: "Oh well, that's because nobody cares about my topics". Or that they were not persuaded by my argument, or were too busy to read them. All those are still possible explanations, but there was also an access barrier, and putting these things online removed the access barrier. I wasn't the only person at that time doing the same thing and who noticed that when you removed that access barrier, suddenly you find people who really do care about your topics, your arguments, your work – who simply didn't know about it before or didn't have access to it before.'

It was an exciting discovery for Suber, particularly in the knowledge that other researchers were clearly having the same idea: that the web could function as a possible medium for scholarship, broadening horizons and opening up new room for discussion and long-distance collaboration. As a full-time university professor, he had neither the time nor the intention to go down the advocacy route – but it became apparent that nobody else was going to step up to talk about the possibilities of the web for scholarship in the way that he wished them to.

Suber began writing about the topic 'involuntarily', he says, 'because it was just too cool not to be writing about it'. He launched a newsletter to gather together the thoughts of like-minded individuals over email, and within two years, he had – somewhat begrudgingly – become 'the expert I had been waiting for'. Suber happened to have a sabbatical coming up, during which he had planned to finish some philosophy work. 'But as soon as it started I just cleared my desk and started to write about OA full time, all the time,' he says. 'Eventually I realised this was no short-term mission; I had to quit my job.'

Meanwhile, down in New Mexico, a physicist working at the Los Alamos National Laboratory was busy developing a similar means for fellow scientists to store and share their work. Paul Ginsparg's resulting eprint repository, arXiv .org, started in 1991 initially as a preprint service for physicists. He describes how his invention was intended as a 'quick and dirty' means of providing 'short-term access to electronic versions of preprints until the existing paper distribution system could catch up' – 'short-term' meaning that submissions would be kept for three months, during which he expected that their printed paper counterparts could be effectively disseminated in the non-virtual world.

'The original intent was to eliminate some of the inadvertent unfairness of the paper preprint distribution, where advance access to information was not uniformly available due to geography or institutional hierarchy,' he explains. What started as an insiders' club for physicists has since expanded across numerous disciplines, and to date the repository holds around 1.75 million total articles submitted by 364,000 users. Ginsparg expected to receive around 180,000 new submissions in 2020 alone.

According to Ginsparg, the original set-up of the archive was 'just the online version of what high energy physicists had been doing for decades with paper'. Within his community, there was therefore 'no scepticism' about the idea of sharing papers before they were rightfully owned by a journal. 'This was before the World Wide Web,' he explains, 'so most of the rest of the world didn't even know what it would mean to be online.'

There were some 'early concerns' from Ginsparg's own American Physical Society that uploading preprints in this way might undercut their subscription model, he recalls, 'but they soon realised it was no more threatening than the paper distribution had been, and officially endorsed its usage by members.' That said, 'once the web started picking up in the early to mid-90s there were some concerns from other fields ... I remember an editorial in the *New England Journal of Medicine*[52] not quite calling me a public health hazard but expressing concern about the public health consequences of dissemination of unrefereed materials "of uncertain provenance".'

The main thread of the argument against such large-scale archiving is similar to the one that still persists today: naysayers, mainly larger commercial publishers, argued that the public needed professionally curated academic journals with editors to serve as gatekeepers and authenticate findings. 'In retrospect there's certainly an argument for that, though the problem is not articles produced by academics,' says Ginsparg, noting some prominent recent exceptions to this statement.[53]

Heather Joseph, executive director of the Scholarly Publishing and Academic Resources Coalition (SPARC: https://sparcopen.org/open-access), remembers those early days of the internet – and the promise of opportunities it presented science – vividly. It was early on in her career, during the early 1990s, that she started working for a group of pioneering scientists at the American Astronomical Society (AAS). Peter Boyce, the executive director at the time had been a recipient of a National Science Foundation grant to create a prototype electronic journal, which would eventually become *the Electronic Astrophysical Journal of Letters*.

Joseph says, 'Peter Boyce, my boss, said – and I'll never forget this – that there was this really cool thing coming out of the pipe, this digital communication

---

[52] *The New England Journal of Medicine* is a weekly medical journal published by the Massachusetts Medical Society.

[53] e.g., a study into the effects of hydroxychloroquine use on Covid-19 patients: Gautret P, Lagier JC, Parola P, Hoang VT, Meddeb L, Mailhe M, Doudier B, Courjon J, Giordanengo V, Vieira VE, Tissot Dupont H, Honoré S, Colson P, Chabrière E, La Scola B, Rolain JM, Brouqui P, Raoult D. Hydroxychloroquine and azithromycin as a treatment of COVID-19: results of an open-label non-randomized clinical trial. *Int J Antimicrob Agents*. 2020 Jul; 56(1): 105949. DOI: https://doi.org/10.1016/j.ijantimicag.2020.105949. Retrieved from https://pubmed.ncbi.nlm.nih.gov/32205204. A statement from the *International Journal of Antimicrobial Agents* on 3 April 2020 said that the March 20 article 'does not meet the [International Society of Antimicrobial Chemotherapy's] expected standard, especially relating to the lack of better explanations of the inclusion criteria and the triage of patients to ensure patient safety.'

thing ... we were going to have email, and our scientists were already collecting their information digitally, talking to each other digitally. I was super lucky to have a job as a 25-year-old where my boss's sole desire was for us to look at the internet and say, "how do we use this great tool that scientists have created to communicate science better?" We very much felt this was the way it was going to go.'

Joseph subsequently left to take up a job at Elsevier – where she experienced a major culture shock. 'When I left the AAS, we'd just launched the electronic journal and so I literally thought Elsevier had hired me away from AAS to do more of the same for them,' she explains. 'I thought my job was going to be building more of this online communication, when actually I was managing spreadsheets to a profit margin ... I didn't even last a year before returning to non-profits.

'The greatest thing about the launch of our journal was that it came at the same time Paul Ginsparg launched arXiv, so there was this huge debate in the physics and astrophysics community in 1994: should we be doing preprints instead of journals? And our stance was, well, there's room for both.

'I used to go to labs where there would be these yellowed mimeograph papers on scientists' doors and they were called "yellow papers". You'd rip a copy of the yellow paper down, read your colleague's work, shove your comments on it and give it back under their door. And that's why Paul decided to take these yellow papers and make it digital. So it was in their culture to do that anyway.

'Having been raised in that community, I thought this was how all science operated. Different disciplines acted differently, but the basic principle was that this new technology was an enabler for scientists to do things with less friction, faster and more efficiently. I've always viewed OA as an enabling strategy – it's never been a punitive thing to hurt publishers. It's become such a contentious issue because there's so much money involved, but I literally always assumed in those early days that the scientific community would always be 100 per cent on board with it. And that didn't happen.'

Fast-forward to 1997, when Joseph was working for the American Society for Cell Biology, and Harold Varmus, the director of the US's National Institutes of Health (1993–99), spotted something of a discrepancy with the way public money was being spent. 'He said, "Hey, the NIH has all of this digital info now – data, preprints, articles – that are being generated out of our funded research. What I want to do is create a database to make everything freely available, openly available on day one",' says Joseph. 'We were about two miles from the NIH offices, and Harold happens to be a cell biologist, so my editor-in-chief at the time was open-minded enough to say: "It's an interesting idea. It's going to screw us over as publishers, but let's go talk to Harold and see what he's thinking."

'So I was in a really privileged position to be in a room where Harold Varmus and a whole bunch of publishers and scientists were hashing out the tension between – if we just dump all this stuff out in the open, is it really good for science? Can we do it all at once? Will there be confusion if there's peer-reviewed and non-peer-reviewed stuff?'

Varmus made a decision to start the digitisation process with peer-reviewed journal articles in the first instance – the result would eventually become *PubMed Central*, a free digital repository that archives OA scholarly articles that have been published already in biomedical and life sciences journals. Joseph became the editor of the first journal to commit all its content to the repository, and has worked tirelessly to campaign for OA publishing ever since.

The European campaign

A key influence in the OA movement at the dawn of the internet age, and still today, was played by the Max Planck Society (MPG), an independent non-governmental and non-profit association network of German research institutions. For several decades already it could be argued that the Society's activities had been driven by the key principles of transparency and fairness, but in 2003 the MPG cemented this mission statement in publishing 'The Berlin Declaration on Open Access to Knowledge in the Sciences and Humanities'.

The declaration, presented at a conference in Harnack House in Berlin, set out its member organisations' goals and global vision for implementing open access to scientific knowledge. The Berlin Open Access Conference has been organised by the MPG every year since then, bringing together scientists, academic organisations, funders and research policymakers from around the globe to discuss the transition from subscription model publishing to OA. The MPG even set up a dedicated team, OA2020, to support the project globally. It was launched at the 12th Berlin Open Access Conference (held in 2015) with the aim of assisting global research partners in sharing knowledge and experiences on how to realise the transition to full and immediate OA.

For many years the project was driven primarily by Professor Ulrich Poschl, director of the MPG Institute for Chemistry, and has since steadily grown to gather signatures from all over the world. Notably, in 2017, four University of California (UC) campuses joined the initiative, among them UC Berkeley and UC Davies. The OA2020 group can be credited with the introduction of now-common terminology such as 'transformative agreements' – also known as 'offsetting' or 'read and publish' deals between academic institutions and publishers, designed to shift the funds traditionally paid to publishers for paywalled journal subscriptions towards OA publishing. But much more on this in Parts Two and Three.

A new era for academic publishing

Just as these early adopters anticipated, the power of the internet as a tool for reaching more readers has spurred on the progress made towards full OA today, and its role should be celebrated. But, as Suber puts it, with the understanding that knowledge *can* be disseminated online brings an ultimate responsibility that it *should* be done. Rather than online access simply being an addendum to the existing system, or a bonus way of reading printed research papers, to choose not to make new information freely accessible to read online – particularly in a world where so much else is available to read online in its wake – is dangerous.

One famous example of this came out of the 2014 Ebola crisis. In an article for the *New York Times* ('Yes, We Were Warned about Ebola'[54]) a group of senior health researchers including the chief medical officer of Liberia wrote that the devastating spread of Ebola could have been prevented. In fact, the epidemic had been predicted as far back as 1982 – but the research was published in a subscription-only journal with limited readership. Not enough people had access to the information to learn about it or conduct the necessary further research to work towards preventing the problem.

At the time of writing, there is a much larger-scale outbreak in our midst. Since March 2020, the Covid-19 pandemic has triggered a rush by subscription publishers to make their Covid-related articles free to access, effectively admitting to the absurdity of their own business model. It begs the question of how many lives could have been saved if research findings such as these had been freely available from the start.

1.6 The Wellcome Trust and Gates Foundation pave the way for OA

By the turn of the new millennium, dissent among those wishing to move away from the traditional publishing system was unmistakably in the air, notably not only from researchers from within the system who felt exploited but also from policymakers and government ministers across the western hemisphere.

The charity funder Wellcome was well ahead of the curve in this respect, setting out its first OA policy in 2005. But, according to Robert Kiley, who joined Wellcome in 1996 and has been involved in its open access policies from the beginning, the OA directive was put in place at the organisation even earlier. 'Back in 1996, Wellcome was involved in supporting the sequencing of the human genome and specifically the Bermuda Principles, which was really the foundation of our OA principles,' he explains.

The Bermuda Principles were a set of rules drawn up by scientific leaders at a 1996 summit on the Caribbean island, requiring that all DNA sequence data should be released into the public domain within 24 hours of generation. These principles contradicted the existing tendency for scientists to make such information available only after publication in a journal. The Human Genome

---

[54] Dahn B, Mussah V, Nutt C. Yes, we were warned about Ebola. *New York Times*, 7 April 2015. Retrieved from https://www.nytimes.com/2015/04/08/opinion/yes-we-were-warned-about-ebola.html (accessed 13 March 2021).

Project, a multinational effort to map human DNA, generated vast quantities of data about the genetic make-up of humans and other organisms, which experts agreed should be shared more readily for the betterment of science.

As the largest funder of biomedical sciences, therefore, 'Wellcome had a responsibility to make sure that DNA material was made open at the time of publication,' says Kiley. But by 2003 the funder's policymakers 'were getting increasingly concerned' that there were other barriers preventing this from happening. 'I was in the library at this time – in those days we had a library advisory committee, populated by university librarians. And they were voicing their concerns that the subscription prices to journals were just rocketing completely out of proportion to inflation, and was there something like a funder like Wellcome could do? Because actually they were having to pay for research that we had funded.'

In true Wellcome style, Kiley and his colleagues decided to commission some economic studies into this predicament. The research provided evidence that the percentage increases of journal prices year on year had risen from an average of 5 per cent in 1990 to 25 per cent in 2000 across all journals.[55]

It was enough to fuel the funder to publish its very first OA policy, coming into effect in 2006. 'At that point, we had been working very closely with folks like David Lipman at the US National Center for Biotechnology Information (NCBI) and National Institutes of Health (NIH) funding body, and they had a public access policy at that time, but it wasn't a mandate, and it allowed NIH funded research to be embargoed for 12 months. Ours was the first policy to say: "if you take our money, you agree to these things", and one of the things was that research articles must be made OA.'

To some, the move seemed radical; to others, forceful. But to Kiley the rationale behind it was simple. 'Wellcome is a mission-driven organisation, and our mission is to improve human health. We spend a billion pounds each year and the best way of maximising the impact of that spend (and to get a return on investment), is to ensure that everyone can read and reuse the research we have funded. Why would we spend millions on a piece of research and then hide that piece of research behind a paywall?'

A year later, there was already clear evidence of the mandate's success when compared directly to the early efforts of the NIH. Reflecting on the two policies in a SPARC Open Access Newsletter, Peter Suber wrote, 'The Wellcome Trust has proved that funder mandates work and the NIH has proved that mere requests, encouragements, and exhortations do not work … There's no point in setting OA as a goal and then getting only 3.8 per cent compliance from grantees, which is what the NIH has been getting. Funding agencies that want

---

[55] SQW Limited. *Economic analysis of scientific research publishing: A report commissioned by the Wellcome Trust*. Wellcome Trust; 2003. Retrieved from https://wellcome.org/sites/default/files/wtd003182_0.pdf (accessed 13 March 2021).

OA enough to set it as a goal now have empirical evidence to show that only a mandate is likely to help them reach their goal.'⁵⁶

A study into author OA archiving published in May 2005 that also compared the two mandates concluded that 94 per cent of authors would comply with such an OA mandate if asked to by their funder. The NIH compliance rate could improve tenfold if it even managed to reach half that rate of compliance, the study's author noted.⁵⁷

In theory, all it would take for full OA compliance was for funders to put forward a simple but firm policy stating as such. Wellcome had set a precedent – and yet it would take many more years and further debates and declarations before others began to follow suit.

***

What the Wellcome Trust did for OA in Europe, the Bill and Melinda Gates Foundation did for the United States. In 2014 the foundation announced a robust open access policy to enable the unrestricted access and reuse of peer-reviewed research articles and their underlying data. Given its prestige – and budget of $4.6 billion per year spent on grants and resulting in some 2,000 papers – it was obvious that the move would give the drive for OA an enormous boost in the US and beyond.

In 2017, after a two-year grace period, the Gates Foundation's policy was implemented – and immediately led to clashes with a number subscription-based journals, including *Science* and *Nature*, whose representatives argued that OA policies stripped authors of the right to publish in their journals. Some decided to adapt their own business models and publishing policies to adhere to the new rules – such is the influence of the Gates Foundation. The *New England Journal of Medicine* (NEJM) was one of them.

The American Association for the Advancement of Science (AAAS), meanwhile, signed an agreement for a trial run, whereby the Gates Foundation paid the cost of OA publishing in *Science* and four other AAAS journals for recipients of their grants. The pilot came to an end in 2018 to the great satisfaction of Peter Suber, who, in writing about the pilot scheme in an issue of *Nature*, labelled it 'a prestige tax' that was 'unnecessary and undesirable'.⁵⁸ Imperial College London's Stephen Curry, another OA advocate, welcomed the Foundation's decision to end the deal. For him, and many others, for a key area of research such as global public health, there should be just one rule: immediate OA.

---

⁵⁶ Suber P. *Ten lessons from the funding agency open access policies*. Harvard DASH; 2006. Retrieved from https://dash.harvard.edu/bitstream/handle/1/4727444/suber_tenfunding.htm?sequence=1&isAllowed=y (accessed 13 March 2021).

⁵⁷ Swan A, Brown S. *Open access self-archiving: An author study*. 2005. http://cogprints.org/4385/1/jisc2.pdf.

⁵⁸ *Nature*. 2018; 559: 311–312.

Interestingly, the decision to end the scheme did not lead to a decline in quality applications to BMGF grants – on the contrary: the foundation remains one of the most prestigious and attractive funders to researchers around the globe.

A brief timeline of key events

2001

- The Scholarly Publishing and Academic Resources Coalition (SPARC) is established in Europe to promote open access.

2002

- The Budapest Open Access Initiative, a public statement outlining the principles of open access research, is announced following a meeting of advocates at the Open Society Institute conference in Hungary. This small gathering of individuals is recognised as one of the major defining events of the open access movement. On the event's tenth anniversary, the principles were reaffirmed by its founders with additional recommendations for achieving the goal of OA as 'default' within the following 10 years.
- Meanwhile in Latin America, Redalyc (Red de Revistas Científicas de América Latina y El Caribe, España y Portugal), a bibliographic database and a digital library of open access journals, is established by the Autonomous University of Mexico with partner higher education institutions.

2003

- On 11 April, the Howard Hughes Medical Institute held a meeting to discuss better access to scholarly literature. The group agreed on a definition of an open access journal as one which grants a 'free, irrevocable, worldwide, perpetual right of access to, and a license to copy, use, distribute, transmit, and display the work publicly and to make and distribute derivative works, in any digital medium for any responsible purpose, subject to proper attribution of authorship' and from which every article is 'deposited immediately upon initial publication in at least one online repository'. The statement is known as the Bethesda Statement on Open Access Publishing.
- On 22 October, another international statement regarding open access principles was made, this time by the Max Planck Society in Berlin (the Berlin Declaration on Open Access to Knowledge in the Sciences and Humanities). These three statements are now commonly referred to as the key defining events for the open access movement in its contemporary form.

2004

- Springer Nature launches its first hybrid-model journal.

2005

- The Directory of Open Access Repositories[59] begins publication.
- Wellcome makes history in becoming the first funding agency to set out a mandatory OA policy for publications – specifically that research articles supported in whole or in part by Wellcome funding grants had to be made open access as soon as possible, and in any event within six months of publication.

2007

- The European Research Council issues its first Scientific Council Guidelines for open access.

2011

- Sci-Hub, a website for sharing pirated research papers, is launched by Alexandra Elbakyan to great effect, and huge outrage from commercial publishers.

2012

- The Cost of Knowledge protest begins against high prices charged by Elsevier.
- In October, the Brussels Declaration is signed by policymakers agreeing to the principles that publicly funded research in Belgium should be open for access.
- At the annual meeting of the American Society for Cell Biology in San Francisco in December, stakeholders draw up the San Francisco Declaration on Research Assessment (DORA).

2013

- The UK's Higher Education Funding Council for England (HEFCE) – at this time the UK's main public funding body – proposes adopting a mandate that, in order to be eligible for submission to the UK's national university assessment programme (Research Excellence Framework), all peer-reviewed journal articles submitted after 2014 must be deposited in the author's institutional repository immediately upon acceptance for publication, regardless of whether the article is published in a subscription journal or in an open access journal.

(Continued)

---

[59] See more at https://v2.sherpa.ac.uk/opendoar.

> - Around the same time, John Holdren, director of the Office of Science and Technology Policy under the Obama administration, issues a memorandum directing United States' Federal Agencies with more than $100 million in annual R&D expenditures to develop plans within six months to make the published results of federally funded research freely available to the public within one year of publication.

1.7 The Finch Report: taking OA to a political level

In 2012, David Willetts, then the UK's government minister for universities and science, commissioned a report into the necessity and availability of research through open access means. The Finch Report[60] – named after its author, Dame Janet Finch – would mark a significant step in the UK's progress towards OA, as well as a change in attitude among those who were collaborating alongside it.

Following its publication, the government announced that all funding bodies would be required to share details of their publishing positions, and declare their intentions to move towards OA – effectively making publicly funded scientific research available for anyone to read. The move would 'likely see a major increase in the number of taxpayer-funded research papers', the announcement boldly declared, and all of this in the space of two years.

This would be made possible, the report explained, by shifting towards a 'gold' publishing model – a response that was widely welcomed. But to suggest its outcome offered clear direction and relief to OA campaigners would be misleading. One particular concern felt by researchers centred around where money would come from to fund such an endeavour. In their report, the Finch group estimated that the transition could cost UK higher education an extra £60 million each year – to which the government responded that it would have to think about it. With library budgets down and academic grants not as generous or easily secured as they once had been, could authors really be expected to fund the shift to OA themselves?

Two years on from the announcement, Willetts's team had hit a wall. Looking back now, Willetts admits he may have been 'overoptimistic' in his approach. 'But this was a different world, remember – a pre-Brexit world[61] – and,

---

[60] Finch J, et al. *Accessibility, sustainability, excellence: how to expand access to research publications*. Report of the Working Group on Expanding Access to Published Research Findings, RIN; 2012.

[61] It has occurred to me that there may well be someone reading this who is unfamiliar with Brexit. Effectively, in 2016, the UK held a referendum

without sounding arrogant, I believed in Britain's constructive role in the EU,' he reflects. 'There was a year when we had the chairmanship of the G7, and I was chairing a subgroup of that. We had a good position influencing science and research discussions in Brussels. So while I could see that you couldn't do it on your own, there was perhaps a window where the UK [could drive OA forward]. It seemed to me that we were on the cusp of something – that we could make this happen with quite a large amount of international coordination.'

Plenty of people now tell Willetts he was naive to expect such rapid change. The need for regulation of APCs, for example, was not included in the report. Without it, publishers could continue to raise fees at the expense of the public purse. These concerns were echoed by Ian Walmsley, pro vice-chancellor for Oxford University, who predicted that the gold model could lead the university's spending to increase by as much as 350 per cent overnight.[62]

At the same time, the Finch Report was significant in that it put OA firmly on the political agenda, and many of the challenges highlighted in it are indeed still being discussed today. 'Looking back, could we have done more? Who knows,' says Willetts. 'Maybe, could I have put it more on the agenda for a more explicit EU initiative? At that point, there were science ministers in the EU who were interested, but it wasn't really on their agenda at all – we were really starting from quite a low level of interest and sympathy. But could I have done more, faster, maybe? Well, yes, looking back, perhaps I could have done. And then the other thing was to be more explicit about the financial cost and trying to get a budget. But you know, I was an elected MP and a government minister still trying to win hearts.'

1.8 Brussels gets involved; the momentum picks up

Meanwhile, OA had also begun to appear higher up on the political agenda in Brussels. On 17 July 2012, the European Commission issued a formal recommendation on 'Access to and Preservation of Scientific Information', in which it

---

to determine whether or not its citizens wanted to stay within the European Union. The result was close, but 52 per cent voted in favour of leaving the union, to widespread shock and the disappointment of almost half the nation. An eye-watering amount of money was spent on campaigning and negotiations, and campaign leaders on both sides were accused of perpetuating false information in the process. It all led to a heated debate and anger from all sides. The UK formally left the EU in 2020.

[62] See also: Jump P. Finch's open-access cure may be 'worse than the disease. *Times Higher Education*. 28 June 2012. Retrieved from https://www.timeshighereducation.com/news/finchs-open-access-cure-may-be-worse-than-the-disease/420392.article?storycode=420392 (accessed 13 March 2021).

called upon the 28 Member States of the EU to 'define clear policies for the dissemination of and open access to scientific publications resulting from publicly funded research'. The recommendation even asked for 'concrete objectives and indicators' to measure individual national bodies' progress regarding implementation plans and the associated financial planning.

Since the Commission wanted to lead by example, its leaders decided to make OA publications mandatory under its multi-billion-euro research funding programme Horizon 2020 (active 2014–20). Beneficiaries of grants under the new programme were obligated to make resulting publications openly accessible through whichever platform desired, but no later than six months after publication. For this they were free to select a repository of their choice. In recognition of the additional challenges this might present for humanities and social sciences, these fields were given a deadline of 12 months after publication.

The new ruling was a major shift compared with the previous EU 7th Framework Programme (2007–13), which had defined OA merely as a pilot action in select areas, with obligation only on the side of the researcher to demonstrate 'best effort' in making their own publications OA. That the new mandate required concrete action plans from Member States should have, in theory, generated a more visible shift towards OA than previous recommendations and demonstrations of intent.

To support the scientific community with making their publications OA, the European Commission set up OpenAire – a Europe-wide platform composed of 28 national desks set up ready to provide advice on OA. A host of other initiatives with eccentric names such as e-SciDR and DRIVER II were also supported.

When research Commissioner Geoghean Quinn and European Commission vice president Neelie Kroes presented the recommendation at a press conference, the question of what this would mean for the big commercial publishers inevitably came up – to which Kroes replied in a no-nonsense style: 'They will just have to look for a new business model.'

To create awareness about the importance of OA publications under the new initiative, on 13 July 2012, Kroes organised an online conversation with Robbert Dijkgraaf, a well-known physicist. Leading the session, Kroes told of how she became an OA convert after meeting with a group of young innovators for whom sharing and collaborating was a normality and, in their view, the only way to boost creativity and progress. Dijkgraaf responded by telling the meeting that in the field of physics, sharing preprints was common practice and truly a global phenomenon.

Openness, access and sharing were very much at the heart of science and referred to practices in the 16th and 17th centuries. For Dijkgraaf, OA was therefore 'reinventing the past, but with modern technology'. He called for leadership from Europe on OA and expressed the hope that within five years there would be consensus that openness was the way forward, that many business models in scientific publishing would be OA and more open data and software would become available.

As it turned out, his ambitions were not entirely unrealistic. But monitoring the implementation of the European Commission's formal recommendation on OA and specifically the actions taken of the EU Member States to boost OA publications proved to be difficult. Collating the hard facts and figures required was a struggle, but what was collected confirmed one thing: that process was undeniably slow.

Working for the Commission as head of unit for science policy and foresight at the time, and later on the Open Science Unit, Jean-Claude Burgelman was responsible for leading some of the process. 'The problem was that the European Commission is still a relatively small power,' he explains. 'We only directly "control" 5 per cent of the funding of Europe, and thus what we issued in 2012 only applies for a small research portfolio, and on top of that what we started doing was very timid. It was a pilot – you could opt out of it, and a lot of exceptions were possible.'

But he does not view the recommendation as a failure by any stretch: 'OA has long been viewed as an exotic topic for people who wanted radical democracy in science. The argument I have always preferred is that OA is better for science – because you get more return, because you get more published, because people read faster because ideas circulate faster. Once the new recommendation for science had been made with that argument, it became mainstream – it became much more of a business case in terms of science efficiency, and that has led to progress.'

Open science and notably open access were the key topics for the Dutch presidency of the Council of the European Union in the field of research during the first half of 2016. 'We were very fortunate that the Dutch state secretary of science, Sander Dekker, was a strong advocate of OA and wanted the Council to reach some firm conclusions on it during the six months that he was chairing the meeting of Europe's 28 science ministers,' explains Robert-Jan Smits, who was at that time director-general of the Directorate-General for Research and Innovation at the European Commission.

To arrive at this, Smits proposed to Dekker that a conference of the Dutch presidency be organised in Amsterdam, bringing together stakeholders, funders and policymakers – all with the hope of achieving some kind of declaration calling for action on OA in Europe. The event, which took place on 4–5 April 2016, resulted in what is now known as the Amsterdam Call for Action on Open Science, which defined 'two important pan-European goals for 2020': full open access for all scientific publications and a fundamentally new approach towards optimal reuse of research data.

Dekker subsequently brought the call for action to the table of Europe's science ministers, who, on 27 May 2016, agreed unanimously to adopt the Council conclusions, reaffirming their commitment towards making open access to scientific publications the default option by 2020. Speaking in an interview after the event, Dekker stressed: 'The Action Plan calls on everyone, national authorities, the European Commission and all stakeholders. This cross-border collaboration is important as science and scientific publishing are international processes ... all parties must get to work.'[63]

'It was a real turning point,' says Burgelman. 'If the Dutch had not been so pushy, probably the Council would have not followed. So it is like everything in history: a mixture of pushing, determination and serendipity.' Smits also considered the Dutch presidency a huge success: 'Thanks to the excellent cooperation with Sander Dekker and his team, we got exactly what we wanted – robust Council conclusions on open access endorsed by the 28 EU science ministers.' The Dutch had a huge supporter in the Germans – in particular George Schutte, Dekker's German counterpart.

On 25 April 2018, the European Commission updated and replaced its 2012 recommendation with a new one, in which EU Member States were told that it was 'preferable' for publications resulting from publicly funded research to be made available 'at the time of publication' – therefore dropping embargo periods – that licensing should not unduly restrict text and data mining (TDM) and that intellectual property rights resulting from the research should remain with the author.

The major novelty of the new recommendation, however, was the section regarding open access to scientific data and the European Open Science Cloud (on which, more to come later in this book). As such, the recommendation took a more holistic approach towards access to the results of publicly funded research, the conclusion being that research should be 'as open as possible, as closed as is necessary'.

1.9 Slow progress: the move towards OA stagnates

The positive progress made towards open access over the past two decades is not something to be sniffed at: by July 2020, the number of open access journals listed in the Directory of Open Access Journals (DOAJ: https://doaj.org) sat at more than 15,000 across 133 countries. That's an impressive jump from a total of 9,500 in 2017 and 4,800 in 2009. But the figures only tell half a story – while new OA journals and repositories appear online almost by the day, they are by no means replacing the existing – and dominant – closed-access journals that existed before them.

Meanwhile, pressure placed on commercial publishers to transition their journals from subscription access to full OA has had limited success, with moves by some larger publishing houses to launch new OA titles or so-called

---

[63] See more (Dutch): https://www.neth-er.eu/onderzoek/dekker-039-we-will-realise-open-access-by-2020-039-.

'hybrid' titles, criticised as empty promises or a distraction from their other costly titles that continued to exist and exploit readers.

A heavy question remains over why – despite the growing support for OA, the key role played by funders such as the Wellcome Trust, and the robust conclusions of Europe's 28 science ministers – by 2018 open access had still not become the default option for newly published work. There were several reasons for this.

Reason 1: Big business, big financial interests and demanding shareholders

As mentioned earlier on, the academic publishing market is dominated by five big companies: Elsevier, Springer Nature, Wiley, Taylor & Francis and the ACS – all of whom depend heavily on subscription payments for their profit. It doesn't take a genius to realise, therefore, that paywalls continue to exist because the subscription access model cultivates huge profits for these companies, their shareholders and associates, and many more stakeholders besides.

Analysis by the European Universities Association (EUA) found that in 2017, the overall expenditure on academic publishing by 26 European countries came to €597 million.[64] As much as 75 per cent of that total (€451 million) was spent on subscriptions to journals published by the 'big five', despite those five publishers accounting for only 56 per cent of the total articles published. It's worth noting that this is a far from complete picture, however: only a handful of universities replied to the questionnaire given. But the EUA's analysis presented a good first indication of a troublesome landscape.

Recognising the undeniable dominance seen by these main players was what first motivated Jean-Claude Burgelman to embark on a career in OA policy. With his background in the political economy of communications and information technologies – 'how are new digital services developing, and so on' – Burgelman recognised in academic publishing something referred to in the media and telecommunications field as an 'abuse of the dominant position … So, once a digital actor becomes a leader, monopolisation is quasi-inevitable because of the advantage then already have. That is, based on the exclusive access they have to the digital resource: the data.

'It's why Facebook, Apple and Google are now dominant: once they are controlling X per cent of the market, it's almost impossible for a competitor to come up. That's exactly why I think OA is so important: it is to avoid that situation where one, two, or in this case five actors are controlling the output of a

---

[64] Stoy L, Morais R, Borrell-Damián L, *Decrypting the Big Deal Landscape: Follow-up of the 2019 EUA Big Deals Survey Report*, EUA report; October 2019. Retrieved from https://eua.eu/downloads/publications/2019%20big%20deals%20report.pdf (accessed 1 April 2020).

public research system. We should not allow that, mainly because it is not good for the quality of the competition.'

The existing narrative around open access and the clear animosity felt between some publishers and the research community makes it easy for newcomers to the OA debate to incorrectly assume the argument boils down to two sides – 'us vs them' – those who believe commercial publishers are bad and those who do not. It would be just as wrong to assume that all open access advocates are morally opposed to commercial publishing.

It is not that Burgelman objects to profit being made somewhere along the line – in fact, he freely admits he has no problem with paying for OA. Rather, his own advocacy is led by the argument that OA is best for furthering science. 'I don't mind the cost; I am not a communist. I don't mind if a company gets paid for a good service, on the condition that it is made immediately available.' Equally, he personally has 'no problem with Elsevier or anyone else making money. If you accept that we are living in a capitalist society, then I don't see the issue. I am not teaching at my university for free either!' What he does have a problem with is 'anyone making excessive money in a non-productive way. It's the monopoly position of their journals, with regards to controlling access to the service they provide, which is not acceptable.'

Neither does Peter Suber believe that the 'end game' is to eradicate paywalled journals altogether: 'We can have 100 per cent OA and I do think we ought to. But what we will not have is 0 per cent closed access – it's a slightly different thing,' he explains. In his view, 'OA is compatible with paywalled literature because the same work can exist in both a paywalled edition and an open edition.'

As a published author himself, for example, four of Suber's own books have both OA editions and paywalled, print editions. 'If selling one edition helps pay for the OA edition, then it's desirable,' he says. 'What that means is, the paywalled editions will continue to exist even in a world in which everything is open by default – and if that helps to pay for OA then I don't want to wish it away.'

Many OA advocates, Suber notes, 'especially in the early days, made undermining non-OA publishers the main goal, or a goal on a par with fostering OA. I always argued against that position.' In his own online overview of OA, he puts it this way, for example: 'The purpose of the campaign for OA is the constructive one of providing OA to a larger and larger body of literature, not the destructive one of putting non-OA journals or publishers out of business. The consequences may or may not overlap (this is contingent) but the purposes do not overlap.'[65]

The difficulty comes in achieving the right balance between commercial profit and action for the public good. Every academic publisher out there will

---

[65] Suber P. (2004). *Open access overview*. Retrieved from https://legacy.earlham.edu/~peters/fos/overview.htm (accessed 14 March 2021).

swear blind that they have good intentions, that they exist for a public good – even, to a greater or lesser degree, that they personally are fighting for OA. But billion-dollar corporations have big shareholders to soothe – and can afford to go to great lengths to protect their profit.

Since OA first came about in the internet age, Elsevier has invested a great deal of time and money into actively lobbying against it, in order to protect its business model.[66] It is something Heather Joseph, director of SPARC, has seen first hand. She knows the lobbyists well, in fact, since a major aspect of her work is counterarguing and myth-busting some of the claims they make.

'Elsevier's presence in the US lobby predates OA – they've been lobbying on things like tax issues for decades and decades. OA became another issue that threatened their finances for them to include in that work,' she explains. 'STM, the American Association of Publishers, individual companies like Elsevier have also had a presence in the lobby, but for Elsevier it's also applied on the state level. When we were arguing in the California State Legislature over a state-wide mandate for open access, Elsevier sent lobbyists to California to fight it.'

'When SPARC first hired me, in 2005, it was to launch a project that would help keep scholarly society journals running independently,' she says. 'It was in response to a big movement in the journal field that's been happening over decades, where independent publishers are increasingly becoming operated by or owned by the five big commercial players.

'When I first started out, the industry was much more diverse. There were a couple of dozen even smaller publishing outlets that were out there like Pergamon, Blackwell … but we have seen the larger players subsume them. The next trend was then for the large players to lock up contracts with either ownership or publishing rights for five to 10 years for scholarly societies. SPARC and the library community knew this was a really dangerous trend – we were on track to becoming a fully commercial operation, when really this is science for the community, that should be owned by the community.'

In 2004, Elsevier submitted evidence to the UK's House of Commons Science and Technology Select Committee to argue that OA posed a threat to scientific integrity and quality of research. A couple of years later, in 2007, the company led a PR campaign connecting OA to government censorship while lobbying the US Congress.

In his editorial writings, the late OA advocate John Tennant raised attention to the fact that, in the US, Elsevier supported 'a range of anti-open bills, including the Research Works Act, for which they made numerous financial contributions to members of the House of Representatives. All of this has stifled the

---

[66] Lobbying Disclosure Act, 1995. Retrieved from https://soprweb.senate.gov/index.cfm?event=getFilingDetails&filingID=835b4a27-ecc8-4543-82cc-4de778f4c2cb&filingTypeID=51 (accessed 13 March 2021).

growth of public access to knowledge and slowed the advance of Open Science, benefiting nobody except Elsevier.'[67]

Elsevier is not alone in its anti-OA campaigning, of course. In 2019, a proposal by the US federal science funder, the OSTP, to make federally funded research open upon publication (scrapping the existing 12-month grace period for publicly funded research) received a major backlash from several publishers – with an open letter published by the Association of American Publishers supported by 125 signatories. 'The commercial journals mounted this furious counter-attack,' recalls ASAP's Randy Sheckman. 'Even some of the academic publishers like the American Chemical Society went ballistic, and said this would be the end of American dominance in science. But the ACS makes hundreds of millions of dollars a year publishing its journals – and pays its editors handsomely through it – so go figure.'

Others are quick to point out that not all commercial publishers have the same outlook – indeed, the big five vary widely in their individual business models, even if they do all have a history of chasing a large profit. But the anger and resentment felt towards Elsevier in particular has tarnished others with the same brush, argues Stephen Inchcoombe, chief publishing officer for Springer Nature. 'We are basically assumed to be guilty unless we can prove our innocence,' he says. 'Although people think they know how much money Springer makes, they don't – because we are not a public company. They assume we make the same sorts of profits as other commercial publishers, yes, Elsevier … I can't prove it, I can't show the numbers because we are a private company, but we don't. But then people say, "well you would say that, wouldn't you", because we have a self-interest. And so it goes on.'

It is true that, as a private company, Springer is under no obligation to publish its figures. But its senior leadership team has made a number of failed attempts to float the company on the stock market in recent years – and so the publisher faces something of a personality crisis. There have been moments when it has been necessary for the company to show off its profitability to entice shareholders; on the other hand, its leadership must maintain the idea that the company is really not so wealthy at all if it is to keep the research community on side. As such, some figures have been shared – and taken down again – at semi-regular intervals. Analysis by the data analytic company Statista reports that, in 2019, Springer Nature generated a profit of €590 million, an increase on the previous year.[68]

---

[67] Tennant J. Elsevier are corrupting open science in Europe. *The Guardian*. 29 June 2018. Retrieved from https://www.theguardian.com/science/political-science/2018/jun/29/elsevier-are-corrupting-open-science-in-europe (accessed 13 March 2021).

[68] Watson A. *Revenue generated by Springer Nature from 2007 to 2019*. Statista; 2020. Retrieved from https://www.statista.com/statistics/272557/reveune-of-springer-science-and-business-media (accessed 13 March 2021).

'If the big commercial publishers would have really been committed to OA, the transition would already have occurred years ago,' maintains Robert-Jan Smits. 'For them, however, academic publishing through subscription journals is a cash cow to which they want to hold on as long as possible. The work they do on OA is just paying lip service to show that they are good guys.'

Pirates at sea: the Sci-Hub revolution

As the film and music industries have proved, wherever a paywall goes up, rebels will find a way to go around it. Sci-Hub was founded by Alexandra Elbakyan in 2011 to do just that. Then a graduate student in Kazakhstan, Elbakyan, like many, had grown frustrated at the high cost of accessing research papers. Using her skills as a scientist with a talent for programming, she set about creating her own platform of pirated PDF articles for fellow scholars to download illegally. Today, Sci-Hub is used extensively worldwide – in September 2019, it was reported that the website served around 400,000 requests every day. At the time of writing, the total number of articles available to download stands at around 80 million.

How Elbakyan managed this is not something she is willing to reveal, but the site is believed to be supported by several thousands of contributors who share PDFs downloaded through their own academic institution library subscriptions. Opinion is divided on Sci-Hub – be in no doubt, the website operates illegally in sharing files the owners do not have the rights to – but Elbakyan is regarded as a hero in many academic circles. The *New York Times* once compared her to the American whistle-blower Edward Snowden, and even Springer Nature's flagship journal *Nature* included her in its 2016 list of 'top ten people that mattered in science'.

Perhaps one of the most fascinating problems highlighted by Sci-Hub is the trouble academics face accessing articles even when they have access to a subscription. Analysis by *Science* magazine in 2016 (using server data provided by Elbakyan) found that, in many cases, the highest density of downloads took place in locations near universities that already had good journal access. But, if they had perfectly good subscription access, why would scholars use Sci-Hub instead? They could have been working off campus or had forgotten the required library logins and passwords. Some suggest the pirate website makes text-mining more

(Continued)

> straightforward. A survey accompanying the magazine's analysis suggested that, much of the time, using Sci-Hub was just easier.[69]
>
> Sci-Hub and Elbakyan were sued twice for copyright infringement in the US, in 2015 (by Elsevier) and 2017 (by the ACS), and lost both cases by default. In 2017, the court awarded Elsevier $15 million (US dollars) in damages for copyright infringement.
>
> Elbakyan is currently in hiding, but remains an active contributor to the OA debate. In the 2018 feature film *Paywall: The Movie*, Elbakyan remarks of her nemesis, Elsevier: 'I like their slogan "making uncommon knowledge common" very much, but as far as I can tell Elsevier has not mastered this job well. Sci-Hub is helping them to fulfil their mission.' In January 2021, Twitter suspended Sci-Hub's account, accusing the owner of violating the counterfeit policy of the social media platform.[70]

Hybrids: a halfway house

At the turn of the 21st century, commercial publishers were keenly aware of the pressure facing them to turn their attention to the growing OA movement. To this end, they invented a new model of publishing that incorporated a mix of open- and closed-access publishing options – the idea being that they could appear 'open' without jeopardising their huge profits. These platforms became known as 'hybrid' journals – the first of which was published by Springer Nature in 2004.

This new method was established in theory as a way of assisting publishers in transitioning their journals towards full OA without a sudden change to their business model or revenue. But, like all the models discussed so far, it's imperfect – and more recently the approach has been criticised by OA advocates as hindering the transition process itself. Several publishers have failed to make the switch to full OA even years after implementing a hybrid system, and many have been accused of 'double-dipping' – that is, charging authors APCs while at

---

[69] 'Whereas more than 50 per cent of respondents said a lack of journal access was the primary reason for turning to Sci-Hub, about 17 per cent picked simple convenience as their top motive and 23 per cent reported doing so mainly because they objected to the profits publishers make.' More here: Bohannon J. Who's downloading pirated papers? Everyone. *Science*. 28 April 2016, Available at https://www.sciencemag.org/news/2016/04/whos-downloading-pirated-papers-everyone (accessed 13 March 2021).

[70] https://torrentfreak.com/sci-hub-founder-criticises-sudden-twitter-ban-over-over-counterfeit-content-210108.

the same time implementing subscription fees – essentially taking money from the research community, and therefore the taxpayer, twice for the same work. In 2019, the average APC for a hybrid title cost $3,208 (£2,560).[71]

'Hybrid journals were presented by the commercial publishers as the ideal way to facilitate the transition to full and immediate OA,' says Robert-Jan Smits. 'However, when I then asked them when this transition would be completed, they were silent. The reason for this was clear: they saw hybrids as a way to continue the status quo.'

Then there is the issue of embargo periods – some publishers offer what could be seen as a compromise by opting to set a rule that the papers they publish must be kept behind a paywall for a period of time, usually six months or longer, before finally being released for free. Some like to refer to this as 'offsetting', the idea being that the embargo period with paywall helps to pay for the OA option later on. Others referred to the approach as 'delayed OA', and public funding bodies have been outspoken in their criticism for the way it delays access unnecessarily to the cost of the public purse. Some high-profile OA advocates argue that the hybrid model has legitimacy in certain instances, however, such as academic book publishing. 'What is the benefit of embargo periods for science and society? I see none at all,' says Robert-Jan.

Hybrids have their dedicated fans, but are increasingly disregarded by publishers and overseers of the academic publishing industry. The DOAJ, for example, does not take into consideration the existence of hybrid journals in its database. As the DOAJ's founder, Lars Bjørnshauge puts it, 'Hybrid journals are not open access; we have no interest in giving such journals a platform. Frankly, from the publishers' perspective the hybrid model only works because it allows them to get paid twice: once via subscriptions and then again via APCs.'

Reason 2: Obsession with 'impact factor'

For many of the people working within the academic sector, structural pressures – and, specifically, journal impact factor – have a lot to answer for.

The term 'impact factor' was coined back in the mid-1960s by the American librarian and linguist Eugene Garfield.[72] A prolific indexer of scientific work and patterns, Garfield wanted to develop a kind of bibliographic record for the number of times a scientific paper is referenced within other scientific papers – in a sense determining its usefulness or at least the level of interest attracted by

---

[71] More here: https://sustainingknowledgecommons.org/2019/11/26/apc-price-changes-2019-2018-by-journal-and-by-publisher/, https://www.timeshigher education.com/news/university-california-open-access-deal-springer-nature.

[72] http://www.garfield.library.upenn.edu/papers/multiple_meanings_impfactor.html.

it. His resulting citation index, which came to be known as journal impact factor, therefore offered a rough calculation of each individual paper's influence.

For publishers, meanwhile, the citation index presented a new commercial opportunity. By adopting impact factor as a way of ranking their products, they could begin to advertise the most heavily cited products as 'high-impact journals' and charge more, accordingly. As part of her ongoing research into scientific culture and bibliometrics, the scientific director of Leiden University's Centre for Science and Technology Studies, Sarah de Rijcke, seeks to determine why exactly it is that the academic community struggles to separate itself from journal impact factor. The answer, in short, is that the existence of indicators like it has created something of a paradox: 'It becomes increasingly hard for researchers to care about and value anything else but how their work scores in terms of performance metrics,' she explains. 'Especially in the life sciences, indicators are no longer one way among others of attributing worth, but the dominant way.'[73]

'What our research shows is that researchers (and evaluators) continue to use the JIF in assessment contexts – despite the technical shortcomings – for the complicated reason that the indicator is already so ingrained in different knowledge producing activities in different fields,' says de Rijcke. 'Our findings suggest that in calling for researchers and evaluators to "drop" the JIF, people are actually calling for quite fundamental transformations in how scientific knowledge is currently manufactured in certain fields. This transformation is the primary, but also a quite daunting task.'

It's a culture that irks ASAP director Randy Sheckman. 'Impact factor was never intended to be a measure of scholarship; it was intended to be used by librarians to decide which journals to subscribe to. But as journals saw it as a way to sell themselves, they adopted it in ways Garfield had not intended,' he says. 'There are some publishers that use the number probably with some justification, but publishers like Elsevier and Springer Nature use it for more avaricious reasons, primarily to sell magazines. Elsevier is the worst and they are unrepentant.'

In later life, even Garfield himself referred to his creation as 'like nuclear energy … a mixed blessing' – an analogy that, for many researchers, does not feel overdramatised. Seemingly overnight, impact factor had become an accepted measure of success, not only for journals but for scholars themselves.

'Scientists are vain, just like normal people,' says Sheckman. 'They like to see the publicity attracted from premier so-called high-impact journals.' Hardly surprising when publication in prestigious journals has come to be associated

---

[73] See paper: Exploring the epistemic impacts of academic performance indicators in the life sciences. *Research Evaluation.* 2017; 26(3): 157–168. Retrieved from https://academic.oup.com/rev/article-abstract/26/3/157/3933574?redirectedFrom=fulltext (accessed November 2020).

with job offers, promotions, further funding alongside a greater chance of getting more work published – and so the cycle continues.'

'Young scholars especially are between a rock and hard place, and I will argue until I'm blue in the face that we are being hijacked,' says Sheckman, who admits to being 'guilty of having published in these journals as I was coming up' in his early career as a scientist. He references the discovery of the biological clock, circadian rhythms, that went on to win the Nobel Prize in 2017 – the founder of that field, a prominent physicist called Seymour Benzer, had died by that time. Back in the 1970s, Benzer published a paper in the journal *PNAS* that was revolutionary and ultimately led to the Nobel Prize discovery.

'Impact factor and the way it's applied savours reports that are going to create an instant sensation. The calculation is based on a window of just two years' worth of citations in a journal, which is ludicrous,' says Sheckman. Benzer's paper on the biological clock, meanwhile, was cited just 10 times in the following 10 years after publication, 'not because it wasn't important, but because it was far ahead of its time'.

Suffice to say, not all important scientific discoveries will generate headlines, and not all headline science will go on to generate Nobel Prizes. But the dominance of impact factor in the academic world has several other consequences. For one thing, academics become trapped within a system whereby they are pressured to pursue 'top' journals for the sake of furthering their careers. The incentive therefore will always be to submit work to the longer-standing recognised commercial publishers – who more often than not deploy paywalls – and not to the newer, less 'impactful' open access platforms.

Interestingly, many researchers working in humanities subjects feel that impact factor occupies much less space in their fields. 'The problem with impact factor and the humanities is you're talking about much longer cycles of half-life for citation of articles, so you don't build that highly cited factor very quickly,' explains Martin Eve. It's for this reason he believes that humanities scholars in particular are 'very sceptical' of using citation metrics – and therefore impact factor – as a way of judging work. 'For instance, a history essay might not comprehensively cite everything else on the topic. It will selectively curate the things it cites. And also, I think there's a lot of feeling that citation needs to be contextualised in humanities … we cite things often because we want to criticise them and take issue with them, so, yes, that might be a measure of attention but it's not done with positivity.'

In his subject at least (English literature), Eve believes the hierarchy of journals is much more informal: 'I know which journals will do the most for my career and have the highest prestige – but I couldn't tell you what the impact factor of any of them is,' he says. He does acknowledge, however, that this statement suggests that a pressure to publish in 'good' journals will likely always exist – index or no index.

Sheckman believes that the tide is turning on impact factor in the sciences, too – in Europe and North America, at least: 'I do think that IF is diminishing in its lustre. There are some journals that still shamelessly advertise their IF, but I don't see it quite as much anymore. The problem is the rest of the world is catching up – metrics are really pathological in Asia,' he says.

In recent decades, the Chinese government in particular has introduced major incentives for researchers to perform well internationally. It comes as part of the country's push to redefine itself as a knowledge economy: China's strategy focuses heavily on science and engineering subjects, and the National Natural Science Foundation of China increased its budget from 80 million yuan (€10.22 million) at its founding in 1986 to 31.11 billion yuan (€3.97 billion) in 2019.[74] In 2018, China overtook the US for the first time to become the world's largest producer of scientific research papers, making up almost a fifth of the total global output, according to analysis by STM of the global publishing landscape.[75]

One way of ensuring its researchers are competing to the highest level, Chinese policymakers realised, was to offer financial rewards for publications in top journals – and one way of determining this easily, of course, is by using journal impact factor as a measure for success. According to one report by researchers at Nanjing University of Science and Technology, Wuhan University and McGill University, Chinese institutions will offer their scientists awards of around €185,000 in return for papers in *Nature* and *Science*.[76]

'I have seen even complicated mathematical formulas calculating the bonus as a function of the impact factor number,' says Curry, whose work has taken him to China often. 'They certainly have been criticised for that, but I think another way of looking at it is the Chinese are just really being very upfront about something that we have been doing in the West for decades ... We know that our own system financially rewards those who publish in good journals because if you are "recognised" by a "good journal" you get more funding, and if you get more funding you get promoted and paid more. The only difference in a way is that the Chinese are just a bit more upfront about it.'

---

[74] Nsfc.gov.cn. *About Us – NSFC at a Glance*. NSFC; 2016. Retrieved from http://www.nsfc.gov.cn/english/site_1/about/6.html (accessed 13 March 2021).

[75] An overview of scientific and scholarly publishing is published every three years by STM: Johnson R, Watkinson A, Research C, Mabe M. *The STM report: An overview of scientific and scholarly publishing celebrating the 50th anniversary of STM*. STM; 2018 Retrieved from https://www.stm-assoc.org/2018_10_04_STM_Report_2018.pdf (accessed 13 March 2021).

[76] Quan W, Chen B, Shu F. Publish or impoverish: An investigation of the monetary reward system of science in China (1999-2016), *Aslib Journal of Information Management*. 2017; 69(5): 486–502. DOI: https://doi.org/10.1108/AJIM-01-2017-0014. For open access version see: https://arxiv.org/ftp/arxiv/papers/1707/1707.01162.pdf (accessed 13 March 2021).

He continues, 'The other thing to remember is that they're playing a game that they didn't invent – you know, impact factor was invented by western society. So I think one wants to be careful about criticising China for that.'

Reason 3: Lip service to DORA

Linked to the financially competitive landscape set out by the commercial players is another clear sticking point in shifting publishing to OA: the reward culture within academia. At a meeting in San Francisco on 16 December 2012, a group of journal editors and learned society publishers met to discuss the problems presented by impact factor and the existing cycle of judgement. The outcome of that meeting was the publication of a formal statement known as the San Francisco Declaration on Research Assessment (DORA).

The declaration is essentially a list of recommendations set out in order for the sector to move away from the existing cycle of judgement – its primary statement being that stakeholders should 'not use journal-based metrics, such as journal impact factors, as a surrogate measure of the quality of individual research articles, to assess an individual scientist's contributions, or in hiring, promotion, or funding decisions.'

On paper, the meeting was a triumph: the resulting memo (published on 13 May 2013) was signed by more than 150 scientists and 75 scientific organisations, with signatories growing to reach 2,068 organisations and more than 16,500 individual parties to date. Today, DORA is a worldwide initiative, known and respected across all disciplines – but many remain critical as to the extent of its success.

Linguistics professor and OA advocate Johan Rooryck, for one, feels strongly that 'many universities have just paid lip service by signing DORA without actually implementing it in their evaluation forms and protocols for individual researchers. That has only been changing in the last year or so, with the University of Ghent and Utrecht leading the way,' he notes.

'DORA has the advantages and disadvantages of the way it is organised, right? It's a set of principles and recommendations and good practices that need to be adopted and implemented. And you either adopt them or you don't, but the disadvantage that I see now is that, as a university, you can simply sign off on it – and then do nothing. There is a big difference between saying you believe in these principles and concretely implementing it in the way in which we evaluate researchers in the university. And that latter thing has not been happening enough yet.'

Robert-Jan puts it more bluntly: 'It's shocking to see that the academic world has mostly paid lip service to DORA and that careers at universities still today are determined by one single metric: where you publish (which is not identical to what you publish) and not by the quality of your teaching, the science communication activities you are engaged in or your entrepreneurship skills.'

Stephen Curry took up the role of chairing DORA in 2017 and explains quite simply that: 'We don't enforce the principles, because we don't have the resources to do so.' At the same time, he feels positive that the declaration has had some impact in terms of cultural change. 'In around 2017 the organisation was sort of revitalised,' he explains. 'There were a group of us who were big supporters of DORA but a bit frustrated that it wasn't really getting the purchase within the academic community that we would like to see. The website was hard to find, and there wasn't really anybody banging the drum for it as such because they didn't have any staff – it was just a website run by a few volunteers who had a bit of spare time.'

The group was able to gather some funding from various supporters including Wellcome, which allowed for the employment of full-time staff as well as the resources to communicate better with the academic community about what was needed. Now, DORA has its own international advisory board with representatives from every continent, and the committee runs educational and analytical workshops at scientific meetings around the world. 'We ran a session in 2019 at the AAAS in Washington, for example, looking at the different techniques around research assessment – and the impact of bias in research assessment and how to address that,' says Curry. 'It's about bringing together lots of different stakeholders to talk about these issues but also figure out solutions.'

The renewed support offers some fresh hope that the declaration can contribute towards making a cultural change. At the same time, journal editors are incentivised to keep the reputation of their journal high – which many people have reason to believe impacts on the kinds of papers they choose to publish. 'These professional editors are absolutely given targets and financially incentivised to keep their impact factor high, so the publisher can continue to capitalise on it,' says Sheckman. 'That starts to change the kinds of things that you want to consider and publish. Research must grab headlines – it must sell magazines. Editors are 100 per cent complicit.'

Rooryck agrees that journal impact factor 'makes for a very conservative system. If you want to flip a journal [from toll-access to OA] you really need the approval of the publisher and the large indexing systems, because basically you have to start a new journal from scratch – which is unfair in lots of ways.'

It's clear the existing cycle of rewards and incentives cannot be broken without the willingness of the big commercial powers at play – Elsevier, Springer and Wiley – whose journals dominate the rankings. But to scrap journal impact factor would force temporary sacrifices on scholars, too, as well as impose new demands on them to develop an alternative evaluation system. Just as it takes time to shift the culture away from one system, time is also needed to build in a replacement framework of reward. It's a dilemma for PhD students and the supervisors who want them to succeed.

According to Rooryck, this is a major barrier to stopping more journal editorial boards from flipping their subscription journals over to full OA. 'Scholars are very stuck in their ways,' he says. 'They don't want to change the system. One of the greatest problems we have is that of "prestige". A journal acquires prestige over years and that prestige is currently anchored to the publisher. If you want to change that, the hurdles to overcome are enormous.'

'If a family buys a new car, it's still the same family. The family is not determined by the car. But that's how the entire reward system for journals works – the vehicle is more important than the people – editors, reviewers, authors – who drive and use the vehicle. Which is strange if you think about it. In my view, this means that scholars should own the journal, and hire publishers as publication service providers in the same way I pay a garage to maintain the family car.'

Jason Schmitt, a filmmaker and chair of Clarkson University's Department of Communication, Media and Design, is more direct: 'Academics are lazy, the tenure committee is lazy – they are running in 400 different directions, just as I am.' As someone who has been responsible for the hiring and promoting of colleagues, he can understand the appeal of a seemingly straightforward metric for success like journal impact factor: 'I don't have as much time to read as much as I say I do, so when someone gives me a proxy and a metric, I don't care if it's true and real, but if it's something that everyone agrees on – you know, that's a high-impact journal – that's an easy way to say, this person gets associate professor, and the more my day can progress.'

Marcel Swart, a chemistry research professor at the University of Girona, agrees that, if it weren't for impact factor, something similar would need to exist in its place. 'For all its problems, it's useful for understanding and evaluating people from other fields,' he explains. As a member of multiple academic boards and councils including the Quantum Bio-inorganic Chemistry Society, Swart is often responsible for hiring new fellows, for example. 'I know which journals are good in chemistry, but I don't know what is the best journal in nuclear physics. It could be that there is a journal I don't know about that's really respected in that community, and the impact factor is a reasonable indicator of that,' he says. 'Impact factor on its own doesn't say anything, but it can give you a picture, for example if a candidate is publishing in the top 25 per cent of respected journals or the bottom 5 per cent in that field.'

From *Glossa* to *Lingua*

As previously outlined, academic publishing means big business; anything that poses a threat to the heavily marketed, heavily profitable subscription journal industry is something that its publishers will fight against, something Rooryck knows about first hand.

In January 2012, the British mathematician Timothy Gowers posted a call on his blog to fellow scholars to boycott Elsevier and its journal

(Continued)

titles.[77] The reasons stated included the progressively high prices asked of libraries for individual journal subscriptions alongside the company's other alleged poor ethical practices. Elsevier disputed Gower's claims, but the post had already attracted a great deal of attention in the mathematics community and beyond.

Gowers's boycott, which would come to be known as the Cost of Knowledge protest, was not the first sign of divestment from Elsevier among the academic community: in 2006, the entire editorial board of Oxford University's Elsevier-published mathematics journal *Topology* had resigned in protest over the company's 'damaging' publishing policies. In 2008, the resigned board started up the same journal again – this time independently of Elsevier.

Then editor for the Elsevier journal *Lingua*, it was the boycott that got Johan Rooryck thinking about the principles of OA objectively for the first time. He explains, 'People started telling me: "Look, I no longer want to do reviews for an Elsevier journal, it's a principled stance because Elsevier is exploiting scholars". It made me wonder about the future – as a journal editor, you want to have the best peer reviewers because otherwise the quality of your papers diminishes. I started to think about alternatives.'

Resigned to the knowledge that Elsevier would not agree to take down *Lingua*'s paywall and transition it to become OA, Rooryck sought advice in 'flipping' the journal to OA himself. 'What I didn't want to do at the time was to pull out as an editor immediately, because I didn't think that contributed a solution,' he says. 'Of course you can resign as an editor, but then they will just find someone else and carry on regardless.'

It took another four years of planning, but finally an opportunity for financial support presented itself. With the backing of the journal's editorial board, Rooryck quit his Elsevier contract in 2015, resigning alongside his entire team to form a new journal under the name *Glossa* that adhered to open access principles.

Perhaps unsurprisingly, the publisher did not react warmly to the move. A very public back-and-forth ensued between Rooryck and the publisher, during which Rooryck says Elsevier's representatives 'tried to blacken my reputation … the reaction was not positive, shall we say.'

---

[77] Gowers T. *Elsevier — my part in its downfall.* Gowers's Weblog; 2012. Retrieved from https://gowers.wordpress.com/2012/01/21/elsevier-my-part-in-its-downfall/ (accessed 21 March 2021).

> As anticipated, Elsevier fully intended to keep *Lingua* going in its existing form, and the two parties came to an agreement that Rooryck would continue on in a temporary editor role for three months while a replacement for him was found. But, once Rooryck rejoined his team at *Glossa*, the dispute continued. '*Lingua* would contact reviewers and then reviewers would say, no, I'm supporting the new *Glossa*, and then they would get a letter saying, "Johan did this and that" and they shouldn't believe everything that was being said to them … It was very unpleasant.'
>
> 'What was even nastier was that they convinced the new editor to write these falsifying letters about me, so she'd been fed this nonsense … which I found really not good at all.' Finally, after writing a letter to ask Elsevier to cease and desist, the rumours stopped. But, for Rooryck, it's clear the scars still remain. 'I put all the correspondence on my website. That's all there is, judge for yourself – I have nothing to hide.'[78]
>
> Five years on, *Glossa* is thriving as an OA journal, and yet the sacrifices made to get there are not forgotten. 'We were only given an impact factor by Clarivate in July 2021, and have finally appeared in Google Scholar's top 20 h5-index for language and linguistics, despite the fact it's one of the biggest journals in the field,' says Rooryck. 'It is very odd that this entire community disappeared from the traditional industry standard radar for five years, while in actual fact it continued to function just like before. Luckily, this hasn't had an impact on our work since in our discipline an impact factor does not count for much.'

Reason 4: Resistance to change; reluctance to take action

While academics can't be blamed for the system they find themselves working in, their apparent lack of interest in changing – or, perhaps more accurately, lack of incentive to change – their own habits is the elephant in the room when it comes to the slow progress towards OA in past decades.

As Rooryck sees it, 'On the one hand, researchers are very progressive. Their role is to discover and share the newest insights – to challenge the world around them. But in terms of incentives and evaluation, they are extremely conservative.'

In many ways, it is understandable that researchers might feel wary of change when the risk is that change could come back to bite them. If a researcher knows

---

[78] Read the whole debacle on Rooryck's personal website: Rooryck J. *Lingua to Glossa*. Johan Rooryck; 2017. Retrieved from https://www.rooryck.org/lingua-to-glossa (accessed 13 March 2021).

their work is good enough to attract attention from the world's 'top' journals, why would they compromise by sending it to a less well known, less established journal for the sake of openness? But it makes for a negative cycle.

'This is why it's important that funders lead the way on OA,' says Rooryck. 'Because the people who are in charge at universities are the older generation – and the older generation wants the younger generation to be judged with exactly the same criteria as they were – there is no desire to move away from the existing system of rewards. Which is of course completely wrong, but it is the way it is.'

Younger researchers may equally fear the impact on their career if they are not seen as 'able' to publish in high-impact journals, 'but that is only because they have incorporated the old system', says Rooryck. 'I do think things are changing, but it will take at least another 10 years, because that older generation needs to retire for the newer generation to move into positions of power,' he adds. And this is assuming that upcoming generations do indeed recognise the need for change enough to prioritise OA in the first instance.

Bearing in mind that, depending on who you ask, rivalries and personal gripes will always play a role, there is also an unspoken understanding that certain subjects and disciplines are way behind when it comes to getting with the programme – that fear of sharing work outside the security of a respected journal still persists. 'I know there are some scientists who want to put their data under their pillow when they go to bed at night,' says Stan Gielen. 'But that's not the way you should do science.'

At the same time, when it comes to the issue of copyright – remember, the vast majority of academic authors are still agreeing to give away all copyright of their own work to the journals at the point of publication – one would hope the research community would be more demanding of change. It begs the question, why have academics put up with it for so long? 'Because of the power of the publisher,' says Gielen. 'Scientists want to have their papers published, and they will do anything the journal asks them to in order for the work to be accepted. Because it determines your career.'

What's depressing is the understanding that this is no new concept to get behind: academia had been pushing back against the problem of extortionate subscription fees, for example, long before the internet presented opportunities for digitisation. Martin Vetterli, president of École Polytechnique Fédérale de Lausanne in Switzerland and former president of the Swiss National Science Foundation's National Research Council, started out his academic career at Columbia University in the 1980s. 'When I was an assistant professor, just starting out, there was a library committee and I joined,' he recalls. 'Top of the agenda for discussion was a boycott of Elsevier by the US library association. And you know what? That was 1987. That's over 30 years ago and we haven't succeeded.'

A common comparison made by many is with the music industry: with the internet came the ability to upload and download songs from illegal streaming sites such as Pirate Bay and LimeWire. Sales of CDs went down and record companies were forced to address the issue head-on. Now, millions of music fans subscribe to online streaming services such as Spotify, for which they pay a monthly fee for unlimited downloads.

Using this analogy, Vetterli for one finds it 'hard to understand why' academia is possibly the last industry to evolve fully to the online market. 'After all, we are ok,' he says, 'a lot of people have tenured jobs, so it's not like musicians, whose lives have been destroyed by streaming. You download a song from your favourite artist and the artist gets something like 0.01 cent, right? It's a total rip off.

'In academia, I don't depend on selling my papers. It has been paid for with my salary. So it would be very easy for me to say, "ok, I'll run my own website and put my stuff up there". But the problem is the currency in academia is reputation, not money. The publishers have managed to corner that market by having journals under their control – they are the gatekeepers for promotion. That's where it's a scandal.'

The only solution, he believes, would be for 'all the university libraries at some point to hold tight and boycott the publishers. But you have to be ready to hold tight for a long time – and this nobody had had the guts to do. The reason is, if you do it for 24 months, your PhD students are in a very tight spot. So you cannot sacrifice a generation because of the mistakes of the previous generation. It's a paradox.'

1.10 Time for a radical intervention

By now, readers will have noticed a theme in that sector leaders and other academic thinkers have a fondness for signing agreements, recommendations and declarations. Almost every year since the first Budapest Agreement, the same groups of people had come together to seemingly pat each other on the back and remind each other of just how much they intended to work towards OA.

By 2018, the truth of the matter was that only 11 per cent of all scientific publications were fully OA. As with DORA and all the many statements and political declarations before it, it was becoming clear to policymakers that the recent Amsterdam Call for Action was not going to be enough to incite a change to the system on its own. Clearly, a major barrier persisted in the form of resistance by the large and powerful publishers, but there was also resistance coming from the research community itself.

'The biggest inhibitor to change in the academic system, therefore, had become the rigidity of the academic system,' reflects Robert-Jan. 'Due to the trap of journal impact factor, the academic community had become entangled in a cobweb it couldn't get out of. It wanted to – but, at the same time, the web had become very comfortable.'

Researchers had become very used to the simplicity of a system of rules led by prestige, even if they could not be blamed for the construct of that system.

Publishers had no real incentive to make a jump towards OA – to do so, in their eyes, was suicide.

Something had to change. Someone had to come up with a plan robust enough to flip the system on its head – even at the risk of causing a few casualties along the way.

Part Two

2.1 The open access envoy

Having served for over eight years as director-general for science and innovation at the European Commission, Robert-Jan Smits took up his new appointment as an adviser at the European Political Strategy Centre on 1 March 2018.

At that time, the EPSC was headed by Ann Mettler, and was well regarded as the think tank of Jean-Claude Juncker, then president of the European Commission – so Robert-Jan accepted the move. At the same time, he felt apprehensive. As a director-general he had overseen an EU budget of €10bn per year and a 2,000-strong staff body, and his new role was a significant shift away from that.

'I remember gazing out of the window of my new Avenue du Beaulieu office in Brussels,' he says, reflecting on that first morning in the job. 'It was early, and across the street I could see the lights switching on in an apartment block, families beginning to stir and prepare themselves for the day ahead. But my brain was already wired, waiting in anticipation for my first meeting with former boss.'

A mix of residential blocks and office buildings occupied by the European Commission, Brussels's Beaulieu district did not feel like a dynamic part of town. At that point in time there was no Starbucks or EXki – no cafes at all, in fact – which meant a place devoid of Commission staff exchanging the latest news. 'Who will receive what job, which colleagues have been fighting, what new policy initiatives are in the making … all the usual gossip. It was hard to believe this sleepy area of town was in fact home to departments such as the directorates-general of digitisation, cohesion funds and environmental policy,

---

How to cite this book chapter:
Smits, R-J. and Pells, R. 2022. *Plan S for Shock: Science. Shock. Solution. Speed.*
  Pp. 65–130. London: Ubiquity Press. DOI: https://doi.org/10.5334/bcq.c.
  License: CC-BY-NC

some of the most powerful cogs in the wheel of the European Commission,' says Robert-Jan. 'Beaulieu is just five short metro stops away from the Schuman business district, where the power centres of the EU can be found, but it feels like another world.'

In accordance with EU rules, directors-general can stay in post for a maximum of five years, or eight in exceptional circumstances. Robert-Jan's transfer was to be expected, therefore – and yet the announcement of his departure on 21 February felt abrupt, he recalls, 'taking everyone by surprise'.

The move had turned out to be part of a larger restructuring of European Commission services – a series of changes that would later become known as 'Selmayr-gate', after the appointment of Martin Selmayr, Juncker's former chief of staff, to the top post of secretary-general. The appointment led to widespread accusations of bent rules and lack of transparency within the Commission. 'It was a tense time that almost led to the downfall of the entire college system of European Commissioners,' says Robert-Jan.[79]

On this crisp March morning, Robert-Jan was due to meet with his former boss, Carlos Moedas, the European commissioner for science and innovation, to discuss his new assignment. Moedas was approaching the end of his mandate – leaving the Commission in just over a year's time – and he wanted to leave a legacy. 'In short, he wanted to see some kind of breakthrough on one of his top priorities, open access, before his time was up.'

Robert-Jan, too, had planned to return to his own home country of the Netherlands to pursue a career in academia, and had already sold his apartment in Uccle to buy a house by the sea in the north of Holland. 'In ordinary times, there would be ample time to prepare my departure from the Commission, apply for new jobs back home and make the move. But, with all the turmoil around Selmayr's appointment, things had been turned upside down,' he says. 'There was also no denying the attractiveness of Moedas's proposal. I had always been an advocate of OA, and, like him, felt disappointed by the lack of progress over all those years – despite the hundreds of conferences, manifestos and political statements being thrown about. It felt inevitable then, after some consultation at home, that I would accept the assignment and postpone the return home.

'This last year at the EPSC was supposed to be a kind of sabbatical, or "bureau de passage" to use Brussels-talk, but how naive I was: the following 12 months would turn out to be a non-stop rollercoaster of events.'

When Robert-Jan's former colleagues heard about his new assignment, they reacted with some scepticism. Not only had there been hardly any progress on OA by this point, but it was clear from the start that Robert-Jan would have no support staff of his own at the EPSC. Joining him in his new office were Cynthia

---

[79] More on this story here: Gotev G. *Parliament calls for Selmayr's resignation in landslide vote*. Euractive; 2018. Retrieved from https://www.euractiv.com/section/eu-elections-2019/news/parliament-massively-votes-for-selmayrs-resignation (accessed 14 March 2021).

> ### The exact assignment
>
> **Letter** signed by President Juncker:
>
> I have decided to create a new function of Senior Adviser for Open Access and Innovation in the EPSC and ask you to take on this role.
>
> Your mission will entail the following:
>
> - an analysis of the economic and societal opportunities and challenges of Open Access to publicly funded scientific publications
> - the preparation of an Open Access Roadmap, laying out where we stand on Open Access and what needs to be done until 2020
> - concrete policy recommendations for the Commission by 30 June 2019
>
> I would like you to present your roadmap, your recommendations and your report to me, Vice-President Ansip and Vice-President Katainen.

Bogaert, Robert-Jan's secretary, and Anne Mallaband, his assistant. For the rest, he was on his own: 'So each one of us would be multitasking – picking up visitors at reception, making coffee and photocopies – while at the same time developing a major plan to somehow boost OA.'

Really, for such a small satellite team, the scale of the plan and the responsibility that it entailed felt nothing short of crazy. But in the meeting room, Moedas talked a convincing game. 'He knew that, with my existing network of contacts, I was able to get things done. He flattered me, saying, "There is only one person who can accomplish this, and it's you." And to those words, how could I say no?'

2.2 Forming a plan

'I became obsessed. I started reading everything I could find on open access, driving my secretary, Cynthia, mad in the process, because I was still an old-fashioned paper man and printing enough articles to build new interior walls across the office,' says Robert-Jan. 'The photocopier was working extra hours and we had to steal printing paper from other floors.'

He also began the exciting task of getting in touch with experts on open access, primarily to seek out some facts and figures, but also because he wanted to hear what they really thought but never dared to say. 'I wanted to hear the story behind the story – because in that moment the narrative just did not make sense. Why had the open access movement not succeeded already, if it was widely regarded to be such a good thing? These campaigners had been pushing for 30 years already. What radical measure would it take to finally flip the publishing system in the right direction?'

One of the other pressing questions in Robert-Jan's mind was how to define himself in this new role ('it's not as if anyone has walked down this exact path before'). By chance, one of the first people who came to visit him in the new office was Richard Hudson, editor-in-chief of *Science Business*, a prestigious and widely read Brussels-based news platform focusing on European science and innovation. Rich was surprised by Robert-Jan's transfer and wanted to find out more about the new assignment.

'When I showed Rich the mandate letter from President Juncker, he said, "So you are a kind of envoy for open access?" After he left my office, I turned to Anne and Cynthia: "This is exactly what I am going to call myself from now on, the European Commission open access envoy. Sounds impressive, no?"'

As it turned out, finding people to talk to was not the hard part: everyone and their dog had an opinion to share when it came to how academic publishing should be handled. After meeting with *Science Business* magazine for the interview, Robert-Jan's appointment very quickly became public knowledge, and, before he knew it, people started reaching out to him: 'They'd heard some senior official had been appointed to work directly under Juncker on OA, and want to suss me out for themselves.'

Big commercial publishers were also anxious to meet with Robert-Jan in Brussels, and it didn't take a genius to realise it was because they were nervous – understandable, given the enormous commercial interests at stake. 'I deployed an open door policy, seeking all the views and input I possibly could,' says Robert-Jan.

One of the first groups of visitors to arrive, on 4 May 2018, was STM, the International Association of Scientific, Technical and Medical Publishers. 'They came as an army, having travelled over from London together with a whole delegation of representatives from Elsevier, Wiley, Taylor & Francis and Cambridge University Press. Led by Michael Mabe, the CEO of STM, the delegation had come, they said, to represent learned societies – for whom they publish small and very specialised subscription journals. Any naive hopes I may have had about collaboration were quickly extinguished. Relations were friendly on the surface, but the group's message was clear: they could not and would not willingly move towards full open access; to do so would be financial suicide.'

The debate between OA envoy and delegates went back and forth for some time, 'a game of business ping pong for 90 minutes', and Robert-Jan found the find the outcome of the meeting 'crushingly disappointing. They hadn't come to collaborate, or discuss a transition to full and immediate OA – they had come simply to throw their weight around.'

'It was frustrating,' says Robert-Jan, 'because up until that moment I'd thought, perhaps naively, that there would be a willingness to really work together – that even if they would not be that supportive of open access in principle, they would think constructively on how to make it work. But as they left I thought to myself, "this is not going to be as easy as I'd hoped".

A meeting with Wim van der Stelt, Springer Nature's head of strategic relations, went better, as Robert-Jan recalls: "'Hey, it's ok!' his body language seemed to try and say, "we're the good guys – we actually know what we're doing on open access already and you can leave it to us".

Here, a note on Robert-Jan's somewhat complicated relationship with Springer Nature: to be clear, the publishing company had done some good work on open access research, and the Nature Publishing Group had set up its first fully open access title, *Molecular Systems Biology*, way back in 2005 – progressive, for the time. By early 2020, the group would have come almost full circle, agreeing to open access terms and even posting the merits of full open access all across the Springer Nature website – a huge victory for the OA campaigners involved. But the road to get there would not be simple. Throughout the discussions and consultations leading up to that point, the Springer group would change its own narrative repeatedly, with relations remaining complex until Robert-Jan met with Daniel Ropers, then CEO, in 2019.

In the meeting room with Springer in early 2018, however, there was no clear sign any of that positive progress would happen. 'Springer's representatives were friendly towards me,' says Robert-Jan. 'They presented themselves as the original OA champions, making it clear they had already been sticking their neck out for open access – which is not, by definition, profitable for them.'

'On the one hand, you could see the argument clearly: they're a commercial company with a turnover that year of €576.4m. Their business model had clearly worked well for them so far – and they truly seemed to believe that subscription-based journals were what their consumers wanted. Why would they jeopardise that?

'And on the other hand … they're a commercial company with an annual revenue of €576.4m. Imagine! If anyone could afford to take a risk and lead a positive movement – and really act upon it – it was them.

'Springer's concluding message to me that day was: "yes, we think it's important and yes we have already invested in it – but we deserve recognition for this already,"' says Robert-Jan. Moreover, Springer wanted much more time to transition – something that would become a major sticking point in the months to come. '"More time?" I thought. "It's been decades already; how much more time do you need?"' The company's progress so far had been slow, painfully slow. Robert-Jan couldn't help but feel they were paying lip service, without any real anticipation of getting there.

And then there was Jasmin Lange, the chief publishing officer of Brill Publishing in the Netherlands. 'I meet a lot of people through my line of work,' says Robert-Jan, 'a lot of good people, and a lot of big egos as well. When meeting someone in business for the first time, I can't help but ask myself: would I lend them my wallet? With Jasmin, I feel instantly I could leave my wallet behind, pick it up a week later, and she would have kept it safe without even having looked inside. She is genuine, without pretension or political agenda, and she was clearly very worried about what my OA plan could mean for her organisation.'

Lange said that she wanted Brill to go the OA route, but could not help but see the stumbling blocks ahead. The publisher had some very specialist journals on its books – take, for instance, *Ancient Civilizations from Scythia to Siberia* – and authors who published there didn't always have access to grants. With that in mind, how on earth could this proposed OA system work? 'If we can't pay APCs, how should we do it?' she asked.

'In that moment I realised properly the avalanche that she and other smaller publishers saw coming. If the plan was not conducted with them in mind, it could wipe out businesses completely,' says Robert-Jan. 'I had always known there might be some collateral damage when it came to flipping publishers' business models – and a lot of OA supporters would argue that, if a business can't adjust to the demands of the modern market, perhaps they have no right to exist at all. But I realised in that moment that I was focusing perhaps too much on the large commercial groups – the ones who could survive it – taking that hit. Jasmin brought points to my attention that I hadn't yet considered fully, and I knew that a lot of careful thinking would be required to make this flip work without too many casualties.'

2.3 The impact on smaller publishers

The open access initiative that would come to be known as 'Plan S' was at that time yet to be named and unveiled fully – it was still a 'very vague idea', as Jasmin Lange recalls, with the key principles yet to be established. Lange caught wind of the plans very early on, however – as chief publishing officer for Brill and a member of the International Association of Scientific, Technical, and Medical Publishers (STM) public affairs committee at the time, Lange was and still is a prominent member of the publishing community, albeit in a very different circle to the big five commercial publishers. She admits she had immediate concerns, and she knew was not alone.

'My perception was that of a humanities publisher, and I knew from pretty early on that everybody in my community was concerned about the mandate that was being planned,' she explains. 'We are a small- to medium-sized publisher with about 170 employees. We don't have a big PR department or any lobbying or legal department, even, just a legal adviser working for us three days a week. Basically, we don't have that infrastructure the big publishers do.'

Brill already had some OA projects under way, and Lange makes clear that she had always aimed to transition the publishing company towards full OA eventually – but that progression had so far relied on hybrid-model publishing, which Robert-Jan had made clear he had no time for in his plans to mandate full and immediate OA.

'It was immediately going to be difficult if we could not publish with hybrid journals – other full OA journals do not work in the humanities sector, we don't have the APCs that are already established to cover costs in the sciences,' says Lange. 'All I could think was, "how will we do this?" I also noticed that my concerns were fundamentally different to those of the big publishers, because they already had this APC model very well established. Yes, it might hinder and restrict some of their planning, but for us it really meant this plan is not possible at a very fundamental level.'

Lange met with Robert-Jan in Brussels, full of anticipation. She had 'never spoken to any representatives of the ERC or European Commission before,' but she was surprised to find the meeting less intimidating than she had imagined. 'Robert-Jan was really very open from the very beginning to speak to me and make an appointment – it was great that we were treated with the same level of importance as the representatives of the bigger publishers,' she says.

'I tried to explain how our community works – that book publishing is significantly more important for us than journal publishing, and that we operate on much lower profit margins. I explained that we have a different way of funding articles and that the hybrid model is a nice means of publishing OA for us – also there are not many other alternatives in terms of models that are proving to work for the humanities and social sciences.'

Lange's expert understanding of the smaller-scale publishing world together with her calm and collected attitude made a lasting impression on Robert-Jan, and Lange remembers being equally impressed by his willingness to be open and listen to her concerns. At the same time, she admits she was 'shocked' by Robert-Jan's impatience. 'It was logical because he was at the very beginning of shaping the plan, but there were fundamental misunderstandings,' she recalls. 'And I thought, if these misunderstandings are not corrected, we have a problem.'

'What do you think we need to do?' Lange asked Robert-Jan.

'Well, flip everything to OA,' came the reply.

'You think we should switch our entire body of 300 journals over to OA right away?'

'Yes!'

'So I said, ok; we might as well put all my employees in a bus and we'll just drive into a wall,' she laughs. It was not a matter of inflexibility or unwillingness to change the business model – it was not even that Lange's group were intimidated by the scale of the mission, she says. The problem came down to the simple fact of cost. While the large commercial publishers tend to sell the majority of their journal content through package 'deals' negotiated through library consortia, smaller publishers like Brill tend to approach institutions one-on-one and have smaller, more personalised subscription agreements for individual journals. 'These are not expensive – between something like €150 and €400,' Lange explains. 'So we are not talking about big profit here.'

Brill also has long-standing relationships with around 200 individual libraries that pay a small fee of around €100–150 for Brill to publish their own institutional journals. This makes the financial situation more complex: 'If we wanted to switch that we would need all the other libraries to agree to put their funding into OA publishing instead of paying for the subscriptions.'

The publisher's own experimentation into open access had also left them with little financial evidence that full OA could be possible – even if the ethical intentions stood firm. 'All our subscription journals are hybrid,' Lange explains, meaning Brill's contributors have the choice to publish OA if they want to. And yet, by 2018, the percentage who had opted for the OA route could be counted on one hand. 'At this time we had hardly any revenue coming from APCs,' she says. 'There might be one or two OA articles published per year, and you can't publish a whole journal OA on that basis.'

A lot of the OA articles that were published in Brill journals came from university humanities professors, who were writing and publishing standalone articles – not as part of the kind of big research projects more common in the sciences, where often there is money set aside for publication costs. 'At the time Plan S was coming to be, we calculated the percentage and it was really only 5–6 per cent of our own publications. So based on that you can't really run a business,' says Lange.

From Lange's point of view, therefore, hybrids offered a sustainable solution, no question. But the Plan S narrative so far had been very much consumed by the bad behaviour of the Elseviers of the world. As Lange puts it, 'I felt this resistance to hybrids coming from the discontent with big publishers and the way they had handled publishing in the past where there was probably serial double-dipping going on' – a very different situation to the tight spot smaller publishers and society publishers like Brill found themselves in.

The fight over hybrids would continue for months yet. It was clear Robert-Jan had a responsibility to reduce the negative impact Lange's community would face from a radical shift – but he had no easy answer in that moment as to how.

2.4 Warning bells

There were other positive meetings in those early days, which kept Robert-Jan's spirits high. Noticeably different was the meeting he had with Frontiers, an OA publisher based in Switzerland, the representatives from which were – no surprises here – very supportive of the plans. 'The only thing they raised objection to was my plan to impose a cap on APCs,' recalls Robert-Jan. 'They tried to convince me to stop the idea, but I wouldn't. At least, that was my intention.'

Frontiers turned out to be the only company willing to provide Robert-Jan with detailed answers to questions he asked of all the publishers he met with: what was the real cost of publishing an article? How much does it cost to conduct the peer review, formatting, graphs and tables, and so on? In the following week, Frontiers sent over a detailed cost breakdown. The fact that none of the other publishers wanted to provide this made Robert-Jan wonder what lay behind their resistance. It confirmed, however, what many had told him already: that the science publishing market was far from transparent.

One of the interactions he had most been afraid of during the process was with the representatives of Europe's libraries. In the past, academic libraries, had been resistant to change – these are institutions that often come with hundreds of years' worth of history, after all – and let's not forget that, in keeping with the traditional publishing model, all the money for subscriptions is handled by libraries. If you're a chief librarian, therefore, you could be in charge of hundreds of thousands, maybe millions of euros. 'These people rub shoulders with the big commercial players, they go to nice lunches with them ... I had assumed that this community would be against Plan S,' says Robert-Jan.

But when he met with a leading German and a leading Swedish librarian representing LIBER, the Association of European Research Libraries, Robert-Jan realised he was pleasantly mistaken. 'Rather, their response to my proposals was: "What can we do to help?" The librarians explained to me that their member libraries, at least in the northern European countries, had very much moved on from this old-school narrative and were shifting their focus towards becoming knowledge information providers and data management services. In fact, they told me, this whole subscriptions thing was more a hassle than something they still saw as prestige. But they were also open in telling me that some parts of Europe are further behind – there, some work still needs to be done to get libraries fully on board with OA.'

Among the most interesting people Robert-Jan met with in Brussels were Saskia de Vries and Johan Rooryck. Both knew of Elsevier's practices 'well enough to have become vocal champions of OA', as Rooryck puts it. Rooryck's own experiences mean he knew exactly what it takes – and what it costs – to flip a journal from a subscription model to OA, and it was for these reasons that Robert-Jan was excited to meet with him. But, during a further meeting at the Apple Tree Hotel in Amsterdam, he and de Vries gave a warning about what he was getting into.

'Johan said to me, "You're taking on a €15bn market; just be aware that some people will be upset, very upset", says Robert-Jan, soberly. Rooryck then told Robert-Jan the full story of how, when he left Elsevier to set up *Glossa*, Elsevier badmouthed him to the community. To hear it, the story almost sounded like a joke – stupid playground bullying – but the situation became serious, even if it never made it to court. Rooryck still keeps a public record of all his interactions with Elsevier on his personal website, should the dispute ever require the evidence.[80] 'When Saskia and Johan said their goodbyes to me that day, their parting words were to "be careful", says Robert-Jan. 'And, while I'm no conspiracy theorist, I had enough common sense to realise what I was up against: very powerful commercial players who were apparently prepared to do whatever it took to stop their shareholder value going down.'

---

[80] More on this in Part One, 'Slow progress: the move towards OA stagnates'.

'The situation with Elsevier at this time was actually quite a bizarre one – there is for instance a history of tension between the company and the Dutch Ministry of Education and Science,' Robert-Jan explains. 'Three years previously, in 2015, I'd been invited in my role as director-general at the European Commission to a high-level workshop at the Royal Dutch Academy of Sciences in Amsterdam to discuss OA, and how we could go about transitioning European stakeholders towards it in the coming years. When I entered the room that day, I was surprised to see Rem Haange, then the CEO of Springer Nature, at the table – but not Ron Mobed, his counterpart at Elsevier.'

Robert-Jan had met Mobed before through his work with the European Commission, and so was surprised to see he was not taking part in the meeting. 'Elsevier had made it clear they had different politics to us – open access was not high on their agenda. But relations between Ron, Elsevier and the Dutch science minister were at this point so bad that Ron, it turned out, had not even been invited to the meeting – and the ministry made no secret about that.

'I called him afterwards to tell him, saying: "You know, you don't want to be in this position. I don't understand how it's possible for the relationship to have turned so sour." He reacted by telling me he was "very surprised" by it all, claiming that Elsevier had excellent relations with the Dutch government, which was clearly not the case.'

'Ron's an experienced player, always calm in his approach,' Robert-Jan adds. 'When I asked him about Elsevier's OA plans at a dedicated meeting one year later, he said that Elsevier was just a service provider, and that as long as scientists want to publish in Elsevier's journals and were allowed to publish in their journals, Elsevier would provide the service.'

'"Fair enough," I replied. So we were on the same wavelength. I started to say, "and if they are no longer allowed to publish in your journals…" – but before I could complete my sentence, Ron said with a smile, "Then we will have to change our business model. But…" the smile continued, and although he never finished his sentence, I knew what he wanted to say. In my mind, I could hear him say it: "You will never succeed. We are big, and furthermore the scientific community is on our side and will never accept this."'

Digging a little deeper, it became clear once more that Elsevier had already set about changing its strategy to focus more on data-related services. This is why the company had acquired Mendeley. Robert-Jan got the impression that Mobed saw China and India as growth markets for the publishing side of the business, countries that he apparently felt were unlikely to ever sign up to open access.

'It was a confident statement – too confident – and no doubt he had quite a shock later that year when China did in fact pledge its support,' says Robert-Jan.

On basis of what Ron had told me, it didn't take a lot of time to decide what needed to be done. 'If we really want OA to become a reality, we just have to make it obligatory, I thought: no more friendly requests, but rules and implications. Just suppose that all Europe's funding agencies would turn around and say, "If you get a research grant from any of us, you can only publish OA." Now that would be a game changer.'

When Robert-Jan presented the resulting plan to his trusted former colleague at the European Commission, Jean-Claude Burgelman, Burgelman smiled and said, 'Very daring. This would do the job, but it will lead to an open war with the publishers and perhaps even with parts of the science community.' Burgelman had another idea: he wanted to bring the monopoly position of the five big commercial publishers to the attention of Europe's competition authorities, challenging them on the grounds that they were distorting the market and hence violating Europe's competition policy.

'It was an interesting concept, but knowing the Directorate-General for Competition Policy and some of the complex cases they have dealt with, I knew it would have taken forever,' says Robert-Jan. 'Certainly with the battery of lawyers and lobbyists the publishers would be able to mobilise thanks to their deep pockets. No, I wanted to stick to my idea.'

And so, Plan S was born. It was a simple plan: funding agencies could sign up to the principles, and any researcher who receives a grant from one of them must only publish in an OA journal under a CC BY licence. To avoid the APCs getting out of hand, Robert-Jan included a clause in his drafted plans that the publication fees should be capped at €2,000.

'After all these people came to visit me, I realised what I must do. But I needed to be able to sell the plan well in order to gain allies,' he says. 'To make the plan work – to make OA obligatory – I knew I would need to get the funding agencies on my side. And so then came the real work: finding funders that were truly courageous enough to support me in adopting Plan S.'

2.5 Gaining allies

In those early days, Robert-Jan faced something of a conundrum: in order to gain the support of funding bodies, he had to build a strong base of support to present to them as evidence this was a stable plan. Nobody wanted to be first, so where to begin? He knew he would need to visit the funding agencies directly, starting with his home country, the Netherlands.

'I'd known Robert-Jan from our meetings with the European Commission in the past, and so I knew he was coming to me with a persuasive idea,' recalls Stan Gielen, leader of the Dutch Research Council (NWO). Gielen was one of the first funding body leaders to meet to discuss Plan S, and Robert-Jan held secret hopes that the NWO would be easy to convince given that the organisation had already implemented its own OA mandate some 10 years previously.

At the same time, the mandate had not exactly gone to plan, receiving serious backlash from scientists in the Netherlands. It was understandable, therefore, that Gielen might react sceptically, or feel wary of any new policy that appeared to simply repeat the same tired mantra.

'When we made it our policy that all the results to come out of projects funded by the NWO should be published OA, we had a lot of resistance,' Gielen explains. 'Because science is such an international activity and many of our top researchers publish with other scientists worldwide, the criticism was that, if NWO placed this restriction on them, that would make collaboration much harder because colleagues from the other countries didn't have this same requirement. So there was a lot of pushback and actually we never monitored whether our grant holders really published OA – neither publicised it nor sanctioned it.'

To sign up to Plan S, therefore, would signify a 'big change' – a pledge to be tougher on non-compliance. But it was a change Gielen was only prepared to make on the condition that others would follow from across Europe. 'Clearly if the Netherlands were to make a statement enforcing open access on our own, it would have no impact,' he says. 'To put it another way: if I was the CEO of Elsevier, why should I change my business model just because the Netherlands enforced Plan S? Actually, you have to serve the scientific community, and at that point, if you looked solely at the public statements, or lack thereof from national funders, it seemed that most of the world wanted subscription journals. So the only reason for publishers to change would be if a large community, a large number of powerful countries, told the publishers they had to change – that prospect was exciting as it could have a real impact.'

At the risk of appearing cowardly in the NWO's hesitation to sign up, Gielen was clear: 'There was no way that we as a small country funder would be powerful enough to create a tipping point for change. The only way to do so was to make a community of funders, to make it powerful enough to make a statement. So that's why I think I knew Plan S was going to be very important. I felt and still feel very strongly that counteracting this cannot be done by the Dutch on their own but has to be done by the international scene.'

The NWO therefore gave their conditional signature, and other agencies Robert-Jan visited would soon tell him the same. The message was consistent: only when there was a coalition in place would funders feel comfortable in joining in. Here, Science Europe, a membership association of 36 major research funders and research organisations from across the continent, proved to be an important ally.

As Science Europe's president Marc Schiltz remembers it, he and Robert-Jan bonded immediately over their shared vision for positive disruption. 'Did Plan S come at the right time? Actually it was overdue,' he says. As it happens, Schiltz remains one of the main constants in the science policy world. A founding member of Science Europe, he has been integral to the group since its beginnings in 2011, around the same time he took up leadership of the Luxembourg Research Fund. While many others involved in the makings of Plan S have since moved on or into different roles, Schiltz remains at the helm of Science Europe today.

'The Plan S principles Robert-Jan showed me reflected a lot of what we had published in our first statement as Science Europe in 2013,' he says. 'But, by that time, I had the unfortunate sense that there were very split, diverging views between countries and organisations on how to implement these ideas.' Clashes over the details of implementation – research organisation leaders who favoured green over gold publishing routes and vice versa – had caused the rifts to widen during Schiltz's time. 'For that reason, I felt the progress was not substantial. I'm not saying there was none at all, but I was very much coming to the conclusion that it was simply not good enough, that we weren't really united. I had also hoped for a bold change and so it made sense for us and Robert-Jan to work together.'

2.6 The European tour

Robert-Jan met with Schiltz in April 2018, soon after his appointment as Science Europe president, to present him with the plan. 'He said to me, "I love it, but I have no time to deal with it myself,"' Robert-Jan recalls. 'It was clear that, if I wanted to get the thing done, he would support me, but that I would have to do most of the work.'

That Schiltz also wanted to get something done on OA was in no doubt – Science Europe is a powerful organisation, representing all the budgets of all the European countries' funding agencies, equating to around €19bn a year – 'and yet he freely admitted to me the organisation had not been able to deliver on projects at a European level,' says Robert-Jan. 'It's a strange thing. I've always said that, if they would have put 1 per cent of their own budgets into a common pot, they would have created the European Research Council themselves 20 years ago already. But a combination of bureaucratic rules about pooling funds across borders, a very small common budget for the Brussels office and perhaps a lack of leadership, means that they are not a strong player at European level.'

It was refreshing, therefore, to hear that Schiltz was personally in favour of an OA mandate. 'There he was, a new leader, wanting to achieve something to prove that not only does having this organisation make sense at a European level but that he will deliver as a new president,' says Robert-Jan. 'All the same, I had hoped for a bit more, shall we say, proactive support at the beginning, beyond just words of encouragement. Given the track record of Science Europe in the past, I could have expected it. His blessing was, however, a boost of confidence to really get this plan tied down with signatures and hard statements of support from other European funders.'

And so a tour of Europe began, and with it a real insight into the individual characteristics and politics of each country's approach to its science budget. So far, Robert-Jan knew the Dutch were on board, but only on the condition of there being a critical mass of supporters; next on the list was Austria, the national funding body of which was led by Clement Tockner, who immediately agreed to sign up. It was a quick 'yes' from the Swiss, too. Much later on, they would withdraw, however, coming as a huge disappointment to Robert-Jan and to all those involved in Plan S.

Germany, meanwhile, remained ambiguous. 'They were not giving much away – neither outwardly for nor against the plan,' says Robert-Jan. Norway's research council, led by the charismatic John-Arne Røttingen, signed up straight away, and yet 'the Swedes, who are normally quite courageous people, were harder to convince. The Swedish funding agency leader was preoccupied by his fear of getting into a fight with his fellow scientists, and so was very prudent when we met, protesting constantly: "Yes, but… Yes, but…"'

Robert-Jan's schedule soon became hectic, taking him to two or three countries each week to meet with old and new allies, seeking support from university and sector representatives as well as those in charge of the purse strings. He began to receive invitations to meet with funders and policymakers further afield, too, in India, China and Japan – word was clearly spreading. 'Regrettably, I just didn't have the time,' he says. 'A trip like that would easily take a week out of my schedule if I really wanted to get something serious done, and I couldn't afford to spend that long out of the office. I felt like a circus performer spinning plates – if I dropped one of them, they could all come crashing to the floor.'

Besides, there was a lot to keep track of closer to home: 'Spain was very difficult to navigate on account of a recent change in government,' he recalls. 'As for Italy, the question was who to talk to. I was lucky with France, since Alain Beretz – whom I had known for many years in his capacity as president of Strasbourg University and president of the League of European Research Universities (LERU) – joined the French Ministry of Science and Innovation in 2016 as its director-general. I didn't need many words to convince him, since he was already a keen supporter of OA, and when he heard about my plans he signed his organisation up immediately.'

The UK, meanwhile, was a special case. With Brexit on the horizon, UK funders were facing a very turbulent time, with much of the political narrative around science consisting of promises from ministers that the academic community would not lose out on account of Britain's departure from the EU. Researchers themselves were not so confident.

'So it seemed like the perfect moment to secure support from the UK on this: ministers would surely be hungry for an opportunity to demonstrate their commitment to European science collaborations going forward and have something tangible to show to put the research community at ease.'

With so much on their plates to deal with at home, the UK's public funding overseers were somewhat difficult to pin down. But the day that Robert-Jan finally did manage to get hold of Mark Walport, then CEO of UK Research and Innovation (UKRI), he was at the Dutch seaside. 'It was June and the weather was beautiful, and so I had escaped to the coast – the same coast I had expected to be living near by now, let's not forget … Mark was a tough nut to crack, and on the phone to him I said: "Mark, even if Brexit happens, and even if you can't participate anymore in Horizon 2020 or the ERC, let's always stand shoulder to shoulder on science policy issues. I think that's important especially now that we show the science community that we are allies."

'But Mark went on and on, talking about the challenges involved, the practicalities. I kept persisting. Meanwhile, the ice cream I have bought starts to drip, first over my hand, then over my shirt and shoes.'

Two days later, Mark called Robert-Jan again to tell him that UKRI was on board. 'It was a huge relief,' says Robert-Jan. 'Now and each time I pass that spot on the beach in the future I will think back to that call, the melting ice-creams, the blazing sunshine, the big sales pitch won.'

As far as the UK's national funding body leaders were concerned, the reasons for supporting Robert-Jan's new initiative were obvious in that they had already pledged their support years previously, through the Amsterdam Call for Action on Open Science. A coalition of supporters for Plan S was, according to UKRI executive chair David Sweeney, 'the natural next step.'

'It was clear when Robert-Jan initiated the discussions on Plan S, his line was that we were failing to implement what the ministers had agreed across the EU,' he recalls. 'And obviously what they had agreed was what we [in the UK] had previously got to through our Finch Report discussions, and we could see that we too were failing to achieve what we had intended: full and immediate open access by 2020.

'The fact is the amount of material published OA was stalling and the cost of publishing was increasing. It required an initiative and I think that what Plan S did was provide that broad initiative,' he says. 'Really what we were faced with was a call to implement together something that we had already signed up to. So there was never anything in principle to disagree with.'

While Robert-Jan's determination to rule out hybrid-model publishing routes had triggered alarm bells among smaller publishers like Brill, it was this principle that further convinced Sweeney and colleagues of the plan. 'Hybrids had been the response of publishers to the OA call and we had long felt that it wasn't working,' says Sweeney, 'so that was influential.'

Sweeney himself had in fact spoken out against hybrids at the Academic Publishing in Europe conference in Berlin earlier that year – to a mixed reception – with no knowledge of what Robert-Jan was planning. 'I told that conference that hybrids had become an obstacle to OA rather than a route to it because of the perception, rightly or wrongly, that publishers were charging twice for the same service. I said, "I know that you do not consider that you are charging twice for the same service, but if the perception is that a supplier of services is doing something, then the supplier of services must respond to that customer perception, because this is what will drive customer behaviour."'

In short, it did not matter whether or not the publishers were knowingly charging twice – the fact that people believed they were was enough for it to be damaging. Relations between larger publishing groups and the academic community had noticeably soured by this time, and Sweeney says his comments reflected conversations held between UK funders and universities, who clearly felt that not enough was being done by publishers themselves to support the push towards OA. The 'regular endorsements from government ministers to push for openness' meant this building narrative against hybrids 'wasn't viewed as particularly controversial in the UK,' he says.

All this led to inevitable accusations that UKRI and Sweeney himself were acting 'against' the commercial industries, but he notes that there was 'criticisms from all sides'. To an extent, it was inevitable for any middleman; he believes, for example, that 'the whole point of Plan S really was to attempt to provide a route for all parties in the publishing industry to take part in the push towards OA'. But not all OA advocates felt, or indeed feel, that all parties in the publishing industry deserve a place in it given the exploitation felt by libraries.

'There is a cost to publishing and I understand those who take an ideological view that there shouldn't be profit margins on it, but that's simply not our line,' says Sweeney. He does believe that Plan S should play a part in minimising excessive costs, but universities are not blameless in that equation, he says: 'Those who pay the piper call the tune. Currently, the vast majority of the costs of publishing are met by universities or research organisations. If they truly can't afford it, then they've got to stop paying. If you want to implement a lower-cost solution, the only way to do it is to stop funding the system ... so that's not an issue for funders issuing mandates; that's an issue for those who spend the money.'

2.7 Support arrives from the universities

On 18–19 May 2018, members of LERU met at the University of Edinburgh for the biannual rectors' assembly. Top of the agenda was open access, and Robert-Jan had been invited to give a presentation on his intentions for Plan S, making this an important opportunity to get the rectors of some of the most prestigious and influential research universities in Europe on side.

The appetite for change among LERU leaders was ripe: back in 2016, Kurt Deketelaere, secretary-general for the association, issued a public statement decreeing that 'Christmas [was] over' for commercial publishers exploiting university budgets through subscriptions. The statement urged that 'research funding should go to research, not to publishers' and called for other research community members to join LERU in asking for future procurement activities across Europe to seek out solutions to the issue – namely, a new model to offset costs for APCs.[81]

The campaign was relatively successful, collecting some 10,000 signatures from university and research community stakeholders. 'That was at the time of the Dutch presidency of the EU, which helped,' Deketelaere reflects. 'It was

---

[81] Leuven. *Christmas is over. Research funding should go to research, not to publishers!* League of European Research Universities. LERU office; 2015. Retrieved from https://www.leru.org/files/LERU-Statement-Moving-Forwards-on-Open-Access2.pdf (accessed 14 March 2021).

all going very well, but then at the end of the day, even with all that pressure on publishers, the result had not been satisfactory. Publishers were not adapting.'

One of the main issues as he saw it was: 'No rector is going to oblige her or his own staff members to stop publishing in specific outlets, to stop being part of journal editorial boards, to stop doing reviews and things like that. So, although universities know that they pay too much for subscriptions, there is also the issue of: "can we to a certain extent impose on our own staff how they have to publish?" It's a fundamental problem which has really been abused for many years by the publishers themselves.'

With this in mind, could Plan S make a difference? The answer, in Deketelaere's eyes, was yes: providing it was the funders who took responsibility for the change. 'If your top researchers have easy access to all those top publications and somebody else is paying the APC or the subscription for those reviews, those individual researchers don't care at the end of the day if there is no open access to publications.

'So this has led to a situation where – and I said this to the group of rectors – in fact, we have been focusing on the wrong enemy for many years. It is clear that as long as companies like Elsevier see that you are going to pay, that you are even going to pay more than what you have in the past because you have a certain reluctance to go against your own staff – then it is a lost battle to continue to focus on the publishers, asking them to change.'

Not only did asking the funding agencies to lead the way on an OA initiative put the power of the public purse in charge; it placed power back into the hands of the universities, too, he explains. If the rules were put in place by the funders, university leaders would suddenly have the freedom to tell the publishers they could no longer live with embargoes or paywalls – not through any fault of their own but because it was out of their hands. 'That's why at a certain point in time [LERU] decided, we have had it. We don't lobby against the publishers anymore, we don't speak to them anymore, we are not going to engage with any nasty tweets online from this group … the only way there is going to be a change in approach by universities and their staff is if we focus on the funders of the research,' says Deketelaere.

He agrees with David Sweeney on the issue of cost: he believes this was in fact the main incentive for the university leaders under LERU to agree to sign up. 'In the first case this is a financial issue because huge amounts of money are going to the publications that we buy – be it print or online – and it's clear that this financial bill has only been increasing over the past few years.' It is true that institutions play a part in that – to paraphrase Sweeney, if universities do not agree with the system, they should stop paying for it. But Deketelaere points out that, 'very often, the price of subscriptions is imposed on universities through national agreements – deals that are favourable only for really specialised research-intensive universities.' The less specialised institutions, therefore, risk paying more than is necessary for their own researchers' needs, and the issue of overpricing continues indefinitely.

While Robert-Jan was happy with the support expressed by the LERU university representatives during their meeting in Edinburgh, he realised at the same time there was still work to be done. This became clear to him when, after watching the rectors applaud Plan S, he asked the audience who there was on the editorial board of a subscription journal. With some embarrassment, a few of them raised their hands. Walking the walk was clearly more difficult, it appeared – but Robert-Jan felt lucky to have the genuine and continuous support of Deketelaere, who would continue to push for this change on behalf of his members going forward.

2.8 Gaining support from the younger generation of researchers

For Plan S to really take hold, Robert-Jan knew he would need the support of early career researchers – for it was they who would become the future leaders, experts and policy advisers of the research community. More than this, it was crucial that Plan S be implemented in a way that did not threaten these junior researchers' career opportunities, and so he sought advice from some of the community's leading representatives.

Gareth O'Neill is a doctoral candidate in linguistics at Leiden University and has represented researchers in the Netherlands and across Europe for many years. In 2018, he held the title of president of Eurodoc, the European Council of Doctoral Candidates and Junior Researchers. At that time, the association was working closely with the European Commission already across several topics in relation to furthering and supporting researchers at the beginning of their careers – specifically, open science, career assessment, and mental health.

'We'd been engaging with the commission as we do as a stakeholder in many different ways, from consultations, through meetings, groups, you name it, even months before Plan S was realised,' he explains. 'I remember discussing with Robert-Jan how open access could work for early career researchers – I gave him the Eurodoc opinion and my own personal opinions as well – that early career researchers want open science, but they haven't a clue how.'

To give an example: when a Eurodoc working group ran a survey of 1,277 researchers across Europe to gather their opinions on open science, many respondents 'didn't really know what it was'. Three out of four researchers surveyed said they were yet to participate in any open access practices, and there appeared to be some confusion over individual institution guidelines around openness.[82]

---

[82] A Europa working group (the Steering Group on Human Resources and Mobility Working Group on 'Education & Skills') conducted a survey between March and May 2017 to assess researcher awareness around open access practices. A total of 1,277 answers were received by researchers across Europe, of which nearly 50 per cent were doctoral candidates.

'It was clear that researchers supported open access though, even if they didn't know much about it, so that was crucial,' says O'Neill. The group also stressed strongly to Robert-Jan that there needed to be more education and awareness surrounding OA – the Plan S network had a responsibility to manage that continued communication with the early career community. Once again, the impact factor dilemma came up: 'We said that if anything is to change, it has to take the rewards and incentive system into account.'

In O'Neill's experience, researchers are 'almost always positive. It's only when you get into the details that they get worried. They don't want to do it, and it's because they don't know how, and they don't know what it means.'

Through his involvement with Eurodoc, O'Neill frequently receives emails from PhD candidates and junior researchers in response to the association's careers advice articles, or asking for advice more directly. 'Most PhD candidates come in, they're working with the professor on a project, and the professor says: "This is where we're going to publish, and this is why",' he explains. 'Then the researcher emails us to say: "I love open access, but I asked my professor if we could do it, and he said no. So I can't do it this time". And the reasoning is simple: "He says that if I publish in a shitty open access journal it's predatory publishing, or it's going to ruin my career; we need to publish in *Nature* to be a success".'

Once again, the thorny paradox of impact factor was rearing its ugly head in the OA debate. It made potential compliance with Plan S among the Eurodoc generation difficult, but not impossible. The heart of the matter, O'Neill believes – and a change that really could start to offer some solutions to the problem – was that the world needed more open access journals to start with.

'This was my criticism of Plan S,' he says. 'I told Robert-Jan: if you want us to do this, you need to make sure that you have a threshold of journals we can all publish in. Otherwise, what's the point?'

He gives an example of a typical interaction: 'So, I want to publish an article, I go online, I go on the directory of open access journals, I search my particular field, put in the Plan S criteria, because that's what I want to do. And say I want diamond journals, because I prefer not to pay an APC – I don't want to waste taxpayer money if I don't need to. What happens is, I end up with three journals that I consider to be ok. Two are not indexed, and only one or two of them I recognise the names of. I send a message to two of them asking them to

---

The remaining 50 per cent were distributed across career stages, from the postdoctoral to the very senior research career levels. It found 'a majority of researchers are unaware of the concept of Open Science'. Link to more (written by the Working Group on Education and Skills under Open Science): *Providing researchers with the skills and competencies they need to practise open science*. Open Science Skills Working Group Report; 2017. Retrieved from https://ec.europa.eu/research/openscience/pdf/os_skills_wgreport_final.pdf#view=fit&pagemode=none (accessed 14 March 2021).

confirm their copyright policy, and in all likelihood I don't get a response. Can you please confirm your CC policy? And I don't get a response.'

The same exercise can be performed taking into account gold access journals – but the prices are high, and again, depending on the subject field, the titles are relatively few: 'Then once I've made it into one of those few, where do I go next? I'm kind of stuck.'

O'Neill was not the only one to feel stressed by the issue. 'When I heard about Plan S, my first reaction was: this is very bad,' says Marcel Swart, then chair of the Young Academy of Europe (https://yacadeuro.org). Once again, it was the apparent restrictions placed on authors that sounded internal warning bells – and Swart indulged his fears by reading some more into the potential scale of the issue. 'The most concerning thing was the ban on hybrid journals at that time – it was because of that that I started to look into the journal citation reports and the journal impact factor rankings that come from them. Looking at the top 550 or so most important chemistry journals, by the Plan S rules, only 4 per cent of the OA journals were compliant. The rest were hybrid journals. So, if you restrict your chemists to publish only in that 4 per cent of journals, it's surely not good.'

The issue was not limited to chemistry journals – further investigations into nine other major disciplines by Swart found the average percentage of OA journals made up between just 4 and 7 per cent of the total in each field. When Swart showed this to Robert-Jan he was shocked, responding, 'But if you really believe in OA, why don't you then not just start your own journal or platform?'

Swart's concerns were taken into account in the drafting of the Plan S key principles. Plan S members agreed to conduct a gap analysis of OA platforms in order to identify the specific subject fields and disciplines without plentiful publishing options for full and immediate OA articles. Supporting guidance on implementation of the rules also noted that members 'will collectively establish incentives for establishing open access journals/platforms or flipping existing journals to open access, in particular where there are gaps and needs.'

2.9 Compromises, compromises

By May 2018, the plan was taking shape, but it was clear that there would have to be some tweaks and adjustments, the issue of APCs becoming one of the biggest compromises for Robert-Jan. One of the very first people the OA envoy went to for an opinion on the Plan S principles was his long-time colleague Jean-Claude Burgelman. 'I remember it well,' Burgelman says. 'I was walking down the street about to go into my office and Robert-Jan phoned me and he simply said, "I'm getting enough funders on board. We're going to make OA mandatory." And I replied, "Go for it!" He was my former director-general, after all...'

As head of unit for open science at the European Commission, Burgelman had been witness to the efforts made by the commission back in 2012 to make OA mandatory within the research framework programme Horizon 2020. The

Commission had issued recommendations to EU Member States at the time, but the rules were advisory only, relying on trust and goodwill, and so had inevitably produced mixed results.

'Researchers get motivated by two things: recognition by their peers (citations) and grants,' says Burgelman. 'Money because they need it, and citations because they indicate the impact of their work and are vital for career progression. So they will follow the money.' Reflecting on the previous attempts made to mandate OA, he knows now that 'if you wait until spontaneously something changes, you will wait a long time. So I was fully supportive of the Plan S proposals, of trying to mobilise the funders to make mandatory OA a precondition for funding. And if funders and universities would also support the efforts their scientists made to go fully open access – well, then we would see no problem at all in making it the default.

'Robert-Jan showed me the key principles he had planned, and I offered some small corrections … he took it all on board apart from one thing, and that's the price capping.'

Robert-Jan remained determined to introduce a limit on APCs of €2,000 – after all, the spiralling cost of publishing OA in this way was becoming a common criticism against the movement by sceptics. 'I was completely against that,' says Burgelman, 'because it's arbitrary in the end. Who are we, bureaucrats and funders, to say the fair price is €2,000? My view was, let's not get into the pricing aspect because we are not equipped to say anything sensible about it, and because the funders pay for it anyway. Rather, concentrate on the mandatory aspect, and if need be go for a pricing structure solution via an economic regulatory mechanism, like for example a telecommunication price regulatory board. Not via a science policy regulatory mechanism.'

He continues, 'Pricing is not a science issue, it's an economy issue. Of course the two are related and it has an effect, but as a science policymaker you have no instruments to determine prices.' Furthermore, Burgelman was concerned that banning journals from charging above a certain level risked excluding the most popular titles from the plan. Scientists would not stand for this – as previously demonstrated, impact factor and prestige would not disappear overnight.

The idea behind Robert-Jan's price cap was that, in the first year of Plan S implementation, it would help stabilise the market and avoid an explosion in the price of APCs once OA became mandatory. In the end, however, democracy prevailed – a vote was eventually cast and the cap rejected, on account of too many members of the Plan S Coalition being against its enforcement. It was an outcome Robert-Jan regrets to this day.

2.10 The Coalition is born

By June 2018, Plan S had itself 11 national funding agencies on board: the Austrian Science Fund (FWF), the French National Research Agency (ANR), Science Foundation Ireland, Italy's National Institute for Nuclear Physics

Coalition S agreement and key principles

"After 1 January 2020[83] scientific publications on the results from research funded by public grants provided by national and European research councils and funding bodies, must be published in compliant Open Access Journals on compliant Open Access Platforms."

In addition:

- Authors retain copyright of their publication with no restrictions. All publications must be published under an open licence, preferably the Creative Commons Attribution Licence CC BY. In all cases, the licence applied should fulfill the requirements defined by the Berlin Declaration;
- The Funders will ensure jointly the establishment of robust criteria and requirements for the services that compliant high quality Open Access journals and Open Access platforms must provide;
- In cases such high quality Open Access journals or platforms do not yet exist, the Funders will, in a coordinated way, provide incentives to establish and support them when appropriate; support will also be provided for Open Access infrastructures where necessary;
- Where applicable, Open Access publication fees are covered by the Funders or universities, not by individual researchers; it is acknowledged that all scientists should be able to publish their work Open Access even if their institutions have limited means;
- When Open Access publications fees are applied, their funding is standardised and capped (across Europe);
- The Funders will ask universities, research organisations, and libraries to align their policies and strategies, notably to ensure transparency;
- The above principles shall apply to all types of scholarly publications, but it is understood that the timeline to achieve Open Access for monographs and book chapters may be longer than 1 January 2020;
- The importance of open archives and repositories for hosting research outputs is acknowledged because of their long-term archiving function and their potential for editorial innovation;
- The 'hybrid' model of publishing is not compliant with the above principles;
- The Funders will monitor compliance and sanction non-compliance;

---

[83] For funders agreeing after January 2020 to implement Plan S in their policies, the start date will be one year from that agreement.

(INFN), the Luxembourg National Research Fund (FNR), the Dutch Research Council (NWO), the Research Council of Norway, Poland's National Science Centre (NCN), the Slovenian Research Agency (ARRS), the Swedish Research Council (FORMAS) and UK Research and Innovation (UKRI), plus the European Research Council and the European Commission.

Collectively, the national members were in charge of allocating almost €8bn in research grants annually, alongside the European Commission with its Horizon 2020 research programme of a further €10bn per year. To welcome the new signatories and seal the deal with food, wine and cheer, Marc Schiltz hosted a dinner in Brussels to celebrate. It was at that dinner table that the 10 key principles of Plan S were decided upon.

By this point in time, it is worth noting that the principles were already becoming watered down somewhat from Robert-Jan's designs. He had initially just two demands: that publicly funded research should be made full and immediately open access, and that the authors should retain the copyright, specifically making the work CC BY-licensed. But every funder had their own particular wishes, and with every new signatory came new principles and conditions.

The German funders, for example, were very much pushing for a leeway on monographs and books, in part to give social science researchers (whose work more typically comprises long-form texts written over a longer period) more time to comply. After the meetings in France, the coalition had agreed to take on board the possibility of green OA, accepting that posting in repositories was already a positive part of the French research culture, among others.

Blissfully unaware of the problems to come with Germany, for Robert-Jan the dinner party was a clear success. From that point on, Schiltz took full ownership of the coalition, becoming very vocal in his support because he could see the outcome of the open access envoy's hard work. It was Stephan Kuster, the secretary general of Science Europe, who had the idea of naming the group, prompting Schiltz to suggest to Robert-Jan, 'Let's create a coalition and call it Coalition S.'

2.11 The first setbacks

Meanwhile, trouble was brewing among the German funding agencies. An investigation into the publishing habits of established researchers in July that year revealed more than 5,000 German scientists had published their work in at least one predatory journal, internet platform, or conference.[84]

---

[84] Offord C. German scientists frequently publish in predatory journals. *The Scientist*. 2018. Retrieved from https://www.the-scientist.com/news-opinion/german-scientists-frequently-publish-in-predatory-journals-64518 (accessed 14 March 2021).

The story had become so big that on 19 July 2018 it appeared on German primetime news, as well as almost all the German newspapers. It caused a row in the German academic scene and numerous universities and research centres began to issue statements condemning publications through these pseudoscientific platforms that did not uphold high standards of quality control and peer review. For the German science minister, Anja Karliczek, this was reason enough to call for further investigation into academic publishing practices.

Some newspapers saw the cause of the scandal as symptomatic of the enormous pressure placed on scientists to publish. Others made an unfortunate connection to the rise of open access journals. Robert-Jan recalls that some of the leading OA voices did not believe for a second that the date the scandal hit the press was a coincidence – just as Plan S was due to be announced.

There had also been a recent history of controversy around OA mandates in the country, which no doubt played on the German agencies' minds. In December 2015, the University of Konstanz in southern Germany implemented its own OA rule: its researchers were informed that all academic texts financed with at least 50 per cent public money must be made available for free through the university's own publication server, KOPS, within one year after publication in a journal. The embargo period given may seem common practice now, and indeed was not unusual in some countries even at the time. But a group of 17 university researchers filed a lawsuit against the university on the grounds that the new rules violated their basic right to academic freedom.[85]

The German funding agency leader, Peter Strohschneider, expressed his concern about the court case, where scientists had allegedly been forced by the university to publish OA. 'He felt very nervous to sign up to Plan S for these reasons,' Smits reflects. 'Ultimately, while I have some sympathy ... I felt he could have told us in the moment that he was not joining. I think when he attended the dinner he already knew he was not going to be signing up. His main goals of attending the dinner might have been to get a derogation for monographs and books, the main outlet for the [social sciences and humanities] community.'

Not long after the dinner, German representatives respectfully declined to continue as a part of the Coalition, a sad loss for all involved. But, when Switzerland began to get cold feet too, it came as a surprise additional blow. 'The main reason they gave was that they had just recently issued a new OA policy and that they could not enact a new one just one month later,' says Robert-Jan. 'It was a genuine response and they also promised to sign up a little bit later, when the time was right. I totally bought it, particularly considering I had enjoyed such constructive meetings with Matthias Egger, the president of the Swiss National Research Council in both Bern and over breakfast in Brussels.

---

[85] www.uni-konstanz.de. *Open Access regulations put to the legal test*. University of Konstanz; n.d. Retrieved from https://www.uni-konstanz.de/en/university/news-and-media/current-announcements/news-in-detail/Open-Access-Satzung-auf-juristischem-Pruefstand-7786 (accessed 14 March 2021).

Furthermore, Egger's deputy, Angelika Kalt, had attended the celebration dinner in Brussels and had at that occasion not given any indication that the Swiss would step out.'

According to Tobias Philipp, scientific officer for the SNSF's strategy division, the reluctance on the foundation's part came down to scientific autonomy. Like Germany, Swiss funding agencies place great emphasis on author choice – and the strict limitations implied for researchers ultimately proved too much for SNSF decision makers.

'We simply do not feel comfortable in prescribing to our researchers where to publish,' he explains. 'It's not our place to restrict their freedom in deciding where their output fits best or which kind of journal might have the best impact for their own specific community and the audience they target.'

Whether or not it was sheer coincidence that Switzerland had backed out soon after their German neighbours, it is difficult to say. But, to this day, Switzerland is yet to sign up to Plan S in all its forms.

A closer look into the Swiss OA example

As Robert-Jan had suspected, the fact that the SNSF had put its own OA policy in place a few years earlier also had an impact on the foundation's decision to separate from the Coalition. Since 2008, the SNSF had asked its researchers to publish any resulting articles on an OA repository at the very least in a 'secondary way' – i.e. a preprint on an institution's own repository or similar would fit the bill. In 2014, the funder tightened this advice into a strict requirement, asking that grantees make their articles available through a green OA route within six months of publication in a journal.

'We have always worked with the attitude that our most important decision body consists of the researchers themselves, so in 2017 the members of our national research council came together to decide on a revision of the OA policy, and the outcome included some key instruments for us which have proven very successful,' Tobias Philipp explains. The decision body moved to detach the funding required for open access publishing – money for APCs, processing charges and so on – from the main grants awarded. As a result, a separate, specific fund independent of the research grant now operates to handle publishing costs. 'On the one hand, we made it far easier for researchers to pay for OA,' says Philipp, but he notes: 'We explicitly excluded hybrids in this.'

The firm stance against hybrids makes the Swiss incentive stand out from many other European OA initiatives. But, like so many previous poli-

(Continued)

cies, compliance with the scheme is not policed or monitored fully, and so the true extent of its success is unknown. Philipp admits that there is nothing overtly stopping SNSF grantees from funding publication of their work in hybrid journals through other means: 'Since these costs are illegible within grants, our grantees don't really have to argue for what they spent the money on. If we wanted to monitor it, we would have to dig deep into the financial reports of each project. But this would take a lot of manual work to find out what they are using this money for.'

Preliminary analysis by SNSF did provide some insight, however: since 2018, around 20 per cent of work funded by the foundation has appeared in hybrid journals, 'so the grantees obviously find other sources to pay the fees or pay for publication themselves,' says Philipp. At the same time, he sees the policy as successful: 55 per cent of grantees have published in OA in one form or another. A further 20 per cent is marked down as 'unknown' – meaning the rate of OA publication could be higher. The 20 per cent figure refers to cases where the authors themselves declare the work as published OA but the SNSF is not able to automatically verify it. This can happen for a number of reasons: sometimes it is an issue of metadata – the paper has no clear digital object identifier (DOI) and so is not recorded automatically – or the grantee may publish with a very small and largely unknown publisher, again making their outputs difficult to trace using automation.

'Three years ago, the unverified work made up 30 per cent of all publications funded, but the category is getting ever smaller with increasing awareness on the researcher side, increasing engagement on OA with the publishers, and metadata getting better and better,' says Philipp. 'What we worry about today is the 25 per cent that are verifiably closed, and that comes down to legacy practices. People are used to publishing in a specific journal and it's really hard to convince them to publish elsewhere more openly.'

Predatory journals: not such an endangered species

A challenge persists in darkening OA's name in the form of predatory journals. These websites – set up with profit in mind – exploit the existence of APCs by targeting researchers, often through the medium of poorly spelled spam emails, to lure them into submitting their work for publication. Crucially, these publishing platforms, sometimes referred to as 'pseudo-journals', claim to conduct peer review but do not – and charge the author for their services anyway.

Here is an example that landed in the inbox of one of our interviewees:

> Dear Dr.,
>
> Hope you are doing well.
>
> I will be thankful if you could concern on my request.
>
> I am pleased to inform you that Sociology International Journal is planning to release Inaugural Issue by the first week of July and we need your quality articles to accomplish this issue. In fact I am afraid as I am having hardly few days in my hand to release the issue. Hence I have chosen some illustrious people like you to support us for release the upcoming issue. So will you please help us by submitting Research/Mini-Review/Case Report for publication towards SIJ.
>
> Your prompt submission sustains us a lot and impacts my ranking in end of this month.
>
> Hope you understand my concern and your kind attention in this regard highly esteemed.
>
> Await your hopeful submission.
>
> Best Regards,

Such emails are effectively luring academics into a scam. The sender wants content – anything will do – and will charge a small but not insignificant fee for the privilege of having that academic's work published on their (unofficial, poor-quality) website. It is a system sadly made possible by the advent of the internet, and, unlike a printed subscription journal, the scale of a predatory website's content knows no end.

In his 2017 paper 'Who Is Actually Harmed by Predatory Publishers?',[86] Martin Eve argues the point that academic publishing cannot be split neatly into two categories of 'predatory vs reputable' – indeed, there are many examples of peer review conducted by 'reputable' journals gone

(Continued)

---

[86] Eve M, Priego E. Who is actually harmed by predatory publishers? *Triple C: Journal for a Global Sustainable Information Society*. 2017; *15*(2): 755–770. Retrieved from https://eprints.bbk.ac.uk/id/eprint/19356/1/867-3743-1-PB.pdf (accessed 13 March 2021); alternative link: https://www.triple-c.at/index.php/tripleC/article/view/867.

wrong. 'Peer review is very bad at predictively spotting excellent work, even when conducted by researchers within their own subfields,' he adds, giving the examples of Nobel Prize-winning work that was initially rejected by journals on account of the peer reviewers' comments.

Eve makes these points and more in order to fight back against the narrative adopted by many commercial publishers that predatory journals offer some kind of 'proof' that OA is a bad and dangerous thing. Rather, he points out, this argument deflects from the real issue at hand: the cultural pressures lying deep-seated within academia that make for a system worth exploiting by scammers. 'The actual site of questioning that we need to focus on is the space of research evaluation,' he concludes. 'When we have become so dependent upon proxies for evaluation as a gatekeeping tool that we are willing, in the name of saving labour time, to exclude the possibility of good work appearing outside of known venues, there is something very wrong with our system of verification.'

The perceived threat of predatory journals is often brought up by OA sceptics (usually publishers) as a reason to be fearful of opening up the publishing community beyond their elite expertise. After all, the argument that quality cannot be maintained in a sea of expanding quantity is persistent. But Paul Ginsparg, founder of arXiv, does not personally believe that predatory journals are nearly so much of a threat as some voices would make them out to be. Predatory journals, he says, 'don't play a role' in the open access debate, 'because they're not read by experts – actually it's not clear they're read by anyone'. In fact, he argues that 'few legit researchers would regard predatory journals as an issue since they're just not encountered – never referred to by the mainstream literature'.

'The only complaint is when researchers discover they've been involuntarily added to a masthead as editor,' he notes – referring to a known trick used by scammers to take names from respected institutions in an attempt to lure unsuspecting, inexperienced researchers to pay for publishing in the 'journal'. From an academic employment perspective, he adds that 'if we have to evaluate a job applicant with publications in journals we've never heard of, we just toss the CV.'

The DOAJ's Lars Bjørnshauge says that the culture around impact factor is also a major driver for predatory publishers. 'It's no coincidence – if you look at the "*Universal Journal of Science*" and crappy publishers' flash fake impact factors to cheat researchers into publishing in their journals. If researchers in certain countries can get away with paying very low APCs to the predatory publishers – €200 or the equivalent, sometimes – it pays off for them to get a certain paper on their CV, because their employers don't read the stuff; they are just counting the beans.'

According to Helena Asamoah-Hassan, executive director of the African Library and Information Associations and Institutions group (AfLIA), predatory journals pose a real problem for researchers in the developing world. She believes that not only do such websites target researchers from poorer countries (whom they believe might be more desperate for a chance to get published in an 'international' journal) but the very existence of predatory journals does damage to the OA movement in Africa overall, because it gives out a confusing message about the quality of online journals. 'First and foremost, some of the researchers don't understand what the whole concept is about,' she says. 'Some of them think that OA equals low-quality publishing – that OA papers might not go through the same recourse as the other ones do – because how could they?'

A bigger issue, she adds, is that 'the authorities sometimes think this too. So they will not want researchers to use OA in case it damages their reputation. And that is down to the old preconceptions that we have – they see printed journals and they see "high impact" and big names. If it's OA, they say where are you coming from? Are you sure the quality is good? Especially with the speed with which the articles come out. And sometimes they have a point, because people set up predatory online journals in Africa.

'Because of that, many of them don't want to accept researchers for promotion when they have published their work through OA only. They say the quality is poor. They think the process is too easy, too good to be true. That it's not a rigorous reviewing process – but of course that is not true.'

Through her work at AfLIA, Asamoah-Hassan and colleagues are working hard to challenge the misconceptions around quality and OA publishing in Africa through workshops and guidance papers. 'My message to research leaders is to follow the OA journals indexed by the DOAJ. If it is not there, there must be a question mark about that journal. Don't be taken in by these emails from predatory publishers, we tell them, and the message is helping.'

Assessing a journal's level of quality is more difficult than assessing on face value whether or not a journal is genuine, however. It is an easy mistake to lump predatory journals together with the other low-quality

(Continued)

> journals rejected from the DOAJ's approved database, but not all of them have bad intentions, Bjørnshauge notes; some are just small and inexperienced.
>
> 'There are some countries where it is almost a requirement from the government that more or less each department at the university should have its own journal ... So then we have journals where the whole editorial board is made up of the colleagues next door and they all cite each other in this little echo chamber that's not a guarantee of quality. But there are a lot of people out there with good intentions and a really big chunk of our work is actually to help those journals when they produce an application,' he explains. 'We can help them by telling them what's missing. We are good at sniffing out the bad guys, but we are also good at trying to assist the smaller journals in countries like India or Indonesia to try to adapt to what we call best publishing practice, to be transparent and so forth.'
>
> It's a huge amount of work and a big educational effort, but Bjørnshauge is 'absolutely sure' that in measuring and assessing the world's journals in this way, quality improves overall. It is also a way of ensuring that the movement towards full OA is spreads further: 'I hope this will help to make scholarly communications a global thing, not just a western/European and North American project,' he says. 'We are really trying to be inclusive and encouraging diversity in the publishing landscape.'

2.12 Putting the Science Europe face on; Plan S makes its first headlines

It was important to Robert-Jan for Science Europe to face the public and do some of the talking. As a European Commission employee, he did not want to give the impression that this was Brussels taking control or that it was a top-down approach to controlling research. The UK, for one, would almost certainly react badly if that were the case, given the very split politics of the country and sensitivities felt around the Brexit vote.

Presenting Science Europe as the leader on Plan S was therefore an obvious and deliberate choice. It was also a way on the Coalition's part of testing their commitment – luckily, they stepped up to the plate.

The following weeks were taken up with preparing Q&As, the Coalition readying itself for the big launch. By this point Robert-Jan felt confident – he had the backing of 11 powerful agencies with a collective annual spend on research of around €7.6b25n.[87] He knew those signatories sitting around the dinner table in Brussels were behind him, but the group still needed more members. Charities would begin to play an important role here, and Robert-Jan sought signatures from the Wellcome Trust, and began to talk to others.

In early July, the Coalition received a shock when Plan S got an unexpected preview at LIBER's annual conference in Lille, France. Stemming back from Robert-Jan's successful early conversations with the librarians' association, the brewing initiative had piqued the interest of Frédérique Vidal, the French minister of higher education, research and innovation. Vidal had been in touch with Robert-Jan beforehand, asking if she could announce Plan S at the conference, pledging her support for it. This came from the French media and communications side, who wanted to create a decent press headline for the event. But Robert-Jan responded that to pledge support would be premature, given there had been no formal announcement yet.

Vidal made her announcement regardless, and in doing so became the first politician to openly speak out in favour of Plan S. The Coalition subsequently became inundated with requests for information: what was this Plan S, and where and how could people find out more? The interest sparked was not unwelcome, and would help to build anticipation for another conference, due to be held in Toulouse later that month, where Robert-Jan was scheduled to speak.

September 2018: The launch

On 12 July, the Coalition was due to go live with Plan S at EuroScience Open Forum (ESOF) 2018 – a big European science fair, held that summer in Toulouse, France. Some 4,000 scientists, journalists and science policymakers would be in attendance from more than 80 different countries, making it the ideal place to present the plan. A press conference had been scheduled, and Robert-Jan would subsequently outline the initiative in a workshop dedicated to open science. For the organisers of ESOF, this was excellent news for the fact it would surely attract further attention to the event and no doubt generate some news headlines along the way.

These plans were torn to pieces, however, in the weeks prior to ESOF – when a row emerged at the European Research Council. Although the ERC Science Council had committed itself to support OA and welcome Plan S – and had subsequently mandated ERC president Jean-Pierre Bourguignon to take this position in conferences and meetings – it was becoming increasingly clear that Bourguignon was not wholeheartedly behind the initiative.

---

[87] www.coalition-s.org. *cOAlition S: Making open access a reality by 2020.* Plan S; n.d. Retrieved from https://www.coalition-s.org/coalition-s-launch (accessed 14 March 2021).

'When, at ESOF, a meeting was held to discuss Plan S with representatives of Science Europe, Commissioner Moedas and myself, Bourguignon went into great detail about how his field of specialisation, mathematics, was dealing with scientific publications and how his fellow mathematicians were sharing preprints,' says Robert-Jan. 'I could see quite clearly that the two UKRI representatives present were getting irritated, and at one particular moment lost patience, saying, "This is not about mathematics – we're discussing a strategic issue…" That Moedas appeared to take a neutral stand on the matter didn't help; at the end of the meeting he mentioned to the Science Europe representatives and myself that we had to convince Bourguignon – I had to bite my tongue.'

These mounting tensions made it clear that Robert-Jan would not be able to deliver the strategy in the way he had intended on 12 July, 'and so we decided last minute to call the whole thing off and cancel the press conference,' he says. At the open science workshop, the room was packed out – everyone expecting Robert-Jan to present Plan S. 'But I took a deep breath and told the audience I was going to disappoint them, that I was not there yet with my plans.'

That evening, at a reception organised by Science Europe on a boat on the atmospheric Canal du Midi, journalists pressed him to try and find out what was really going on. 'They knew something was up – had there been a change of heart? Had the pressure from big publishers to scrap the plan caused me to lose my confidence? The party was thriving, an abundance of excellent French wine flowing … still I managed to keep my mouth shut. I gave the excuse that I was about to get an additional large and influential funding agency to sign up to Plan S and preferred to wait for this before announcing any details. They bought it, thank God – just imagine the backlash if they had known the truth.'

With hindsight, Robert-Jan believes it was in fact a good thing he did not manage to present Plan S at ESOF after all. 'Given the holiday period, it's possible not a single journal would have picked the story up, and so neither would the science community, who were all eager to go on vacation.' He realised he had some homework to do, however, and got in touch with the Science Council's vice presidents.

'They were clearly surprised when I told them what happened, and promised to take this up with their president I travelled to Amsterdam to meet with Martin Stokhof, the ERC vice president responsible for open access – he supported Plan S and would take action, he told me – strong words.'

It would take the whole month of August before relations were smoothed out. Bourguignon did, however, contact his fellow French compatriots, with whom I had to spend hours on the phone to convince them to stick with the initiative, and promise that there will be a stronger recognition of green OA publishing models within the outlined plan,' Robert-Jan recalls.

The big reveal finally came on 4 September 2018, and the moment could not have been better. The details of Plan S were published in a press statement online, and, within minutes, Twitter was screaming. Within hours, Plan S had garnered 70,000 tweets; by the next day, 120,000 – far more than European Commission

President Juncker would receive for his State of the Union address a week later. 'My inbox exploded as reactions came in from all over the world: India, Brazil, Japan and South Africa ... and my phone rang non-stop with journalists pressing for interviews,' says Robert-Jan. I had to be selective and go for what I felt were the leading scientific journals and industry magazines: *Times Higher Education*, *Nature*, *Science Magazine*, *Science Business* and *Research Europe*.'

As promised, Robert-Jan's Coalition S associates and supporters also came through in publishing their own statements of intent and support to coincide with the announcement. 'Plan S represents an important move in the debate over how to achieve full Open Access', read a statement from Kurt Deketelaere, secretary-general of LERU. 'The move to full Open Access was stalling, and this plan is a major step forward in the right direction.'

'The statement is timely and welcome,' added Paul Ayris, Chair of the LERU INFO community. 'It is potentially a game changer in the move to full and immediate Open Access.'

'Their words meant the world to me,' says Robert-Jan.

To his big surprise, the mainstream media also picked up on the story: the UK's *Financial Times* ran a news piece that, very helpfully for both its audience and the Plan S initiative, outlined the economic benefits of making research open. *The Economist* did the same. A myriad of opinion pieces also began to appear: one powerful column published by *The Guardian* detailed the writer George Monbiot's own experience with cancer, and how he, like so many others, could not afford access to the scientific reports that would impact his health and life chances directly. 'Those who take on the global industry that traps research behind paywalls are heroes, not thieves,' he concluded.

Robert-Jan says, 'The media also wanted to know what the mysterious "S" could stand for – "no, not Smits", I told them, "but S for science, speed, solution and shock." I was delighted to find that, while the news reportage was largely fair and balanced in its outlook, the overall response to Plan S was hugely positive. What helped was that I had asked organisations and individual influencers in favour of Plan S to issue statements of support on the day we went public. Almost all of them delivered.'

From here, Robert-Jan began to receive invitations to present Plan S at various events and to different audiences. The demand was exciting and a little overwhelming, and so for this purpose he put together a standard set of slides that could be adapted slightly for each occasion. 'I also decided to back up my slides with some strong supporting statements, which I would repeat constantly in the hope that the message sank in.'

As of autumn 2018, the global market of scientific publishing was valued at USD15bn and was dominated by no more than five multinationals. Some of their journals made profits in the range of 30–40 per cent – figures that Amazon, Microsoft, Google and Walmart could only dream of. 'There is enough money in the system; it's just in the wrong place,' Robert-Jan's slides told each and every recipient. 'These statements became my battle mantra,' he says.

Bullet points from Robert Jan's presentation

- 'The role of the public purse is to fund top notch research and subsequently make sure that the results of this are disseminated as widely as possible and without delay.'
- 'The role of the public purse is not to let publishers make a big profit off the back of the taxpayer so that they can pay their executives high salaries and do "nice things" for science.'
- 'The public purse is paying three times: for the research itself, for the salaries of the professors who peer review articles for free, and for the academic libraries, to pay for the subscriptions.'
- 'We have created for ourselves a cobweb, which we all want to get out of, but fail to succeed.'
- 'The biggest inhibitor of change in the academic system is the academic system itself.'
- 'We need to get rid of the systemic obsession with the Journal Impact Factor.'
- 'Where you publish has become more important than what you publish.'
- 'As long as researchers are rewarded for where they publish instead of what they publish, OA will not get off the ground.'
- 'Even in the so-called most prestigious, high impact journals, a significant number of articles are never cited – not even by the author themselves (27 per cent of articles in the natural sciences and 32 per cent in social sciences, research by the University of Montreal suggests).'[88]
- 'The commercial publishers are not the enemy. On the contrary. I call upon them to go for a Big Flip to complete the transition to full and immediate access for once and for all.'

'We need to bring common sense into the system,' Robert-Jan urged these new audiences. 'If I go out onto the street and ask someone, "What is the role of the professors here at this university?" they will say, "To teach." And if I then ask, "What should these professors be rewarded for?" the answer I will get is: "For how they teach." And if I then tell them that they are rewarded for the number of articles they write in journals which are so expensive that hardly anyone can afford to pay for this, they will ask: "Why is my taxpayer money funding this?"'

---

[88] Source: https://arxiv.org/ftp/arxiv/papers/0809/0809.5250.pdf. Source found /cited from LSE blog: https://blogs.lse.ac.uk/impactofsocialsciences/2014/04/23/academic-papers-citation-rates-remler.

His challenge was also to stay in the news, whatever it took – to make sure that journalists kept writing about Plan S and that the debate kept going. For this to happen, he needed to come up with new developments – new signatories to the plan, statements of support by key players, new details about its implementation.

'It was great news, then, that we were able to welcome the twelfth member of the Coalition just a few days after the official launch,' he says. On 9 September 2018, FORTE, a Swedish research council for health, working life and welfare, became the second Swedish funder to sign up to Plan S. Later that month, the Academy of Finland (AKA) would announce its support for Plan S and its intention to join the Coalition, bringing the number of confirmed funders to 13. 'All the same, I knew I would need all the help I could get to keep building the public interest that was growing around open access, and the scandal that was going on within academic publishing,' says Robert-Jan.

By this time, a proposal for a new European research funding programme, Horizon Europe, had been prepared, and Robert-Jan was keen to discuss how the provisions of Plan S were going to be laid out within its plans for implementation. 'I used the summer to reconnect with my former Research and Innovation director-general colleagues at the European Commission. Two members of the legal unit came to see me at my office in Beaulieu and together we drafted the articles to be inserted in the model grant agreement.'

Robert-Jan had hoped that the European Commission would formally sign up to Plan S and join the Coalition, but realised the legal and institutional implications of this would be complex. 'It would require a special decision by the College of European Commissioners mandating Commissioner Moedas to go for it,' he explains. 'Moedas realised that this would expose him and could cause political damage. Plan S is controversial and there are powerful lobbies out there wanting it to fail. Yet, it was Moedas who had asked me to come up with a robust proposal in the first place.'

For these reasons, it wasn't possible for the European Commission to sign up to Coalition S as a member in and of itself. The statement Moedas gave on 4 September 2018 was, however, a clear signal of his support for Plan S.

2.13 To the movies

By sheer coincidence, around the same time Robert-Jan was preparing the Plan S launch, a documentary filmmaker in the US was embarking on his own personal crusade against the exploitation by commercial publishers. Jason Schmitt released (the suitably dramatically titled) *Paywall: The Business of Scholarship*[89] on 5 September, the day after Plan S first hit the headlines. And it really was by sheer chance, Schmitt reflects.

---

[89] *Paywall: The Business of Scholarship*. 2018. Retrieved from https://paywallthemovie.com (accessed 13 March 2021).

'What first got me interested in this debate was how everyone in academia and especially the western academics are so focused on helping underrepresented communities – and yet, by sticking to this outdated publishing system, they are so complicit in my mind in excluding those very populations we are trying to empower. It's a whole conundrum that some don't even know exists.'

As both journalist and academic, Schmitt had a unique vantage point in that he could see the system for what it was with both insider's and outsider's perspective. In making a film and effectively dramatising the subject of academic publishing, it was Schmitt's hope that he might draw attention to these injustices from a wider audience, but also from the academics themselves more effectively. As he sees it, it was understandable to some extent in that 'the bulk of academics don't have time to pursue this. They have their own specialities that they are interested in, rather than global knowledge for the global populace – they are just these innocent bystanders.' And yet, 'I do these talks about *Paywall* all over the place and who comes along? It's deans, it's provosts, it's librarians but you know who doesn't come? It's the faculty.'

Schmitt secured a $40,000 grant – a very small budget, really, for making a film – and, with the help of his students, set about travelling some 50,000 miles to gather views from some of the most hacked-off voices in and outside academia. The resulting film is a fierce critique of the commercial publishing industry; Elsevier – whose representatives declined to take part in the documentary – comes across particularly badly.

'When I did this I had no idea Plan S was in the works – I didn't know Robert-Jan, and it was really one of the funniest coincidences of my life,' says Schmitt. Within 15 days of the Plan S and *Paywall* launches, the stock price of Elsevier had dipped by 15 per cent.

Robert-Jan and Schmitt met on 9 October 2018 in Rotterdam during the premiere of *Paywall* in the Netherlands. After the movie was shown, there was a lively debate with the audience, most of whom were either working or studying at Erasmus University in Rotterdam. The issue of open access to data came up and was addressed by Pearl Dykstra, professor of empirical sociology at the university. She said that the time had come that the academic community stopped its 'data hugging' and that the culture of 'these are my data and no one can use them' had to end – a poignant message that stayed with Robert-Jan and that would ripen in discussions further down the line.

After the event, both Robert-Jan and Schmitt were congratulated by the president of Erasmus University for their bold mission. But, once she had left, one of the researchers mentioned that the institution had just inaugurated a new research centre that had been given a KPI (key performance indicator) or ultimatum: its researchers must collectively get five articles published in the most prestigious subscription journals within the centre's first years. It was, once again, a confirmation of what Robert-Jan already knew and kept on repeating: that the biggest inhibitor to change inside the academic system is the academic system itself.

Meanwhile, the world awaited the reaction from publishers – and react they did. Interestingly, Elsevier was the first to speak out. In a hurried phone interview with Dutch newspaper *De Volkskrant*, former Elsevier spokesperson Tom Reller told a reporter, 'If you think information shouldn't cost anything, go to Wikipedia' – a quote that would circle around social media seemingly for eternity, or at least long after Reller's eventual departure from the company in 2019. 'Above all, it was a silly statement which did not help to improve Elsevier's reputation,' Robert-Jan reflects. Other publishers followed in issuing their own statements, which were in most cases a bit more diplomatic.

Springer Nature followed with a quip that the plan 'potentially undermine[d] the whole research publishing system' – and that the removal of hybrid and subscription publishing options for researchers in Europe failed to take into account a 'global view'. The AAAS, which publishes the journal *Science*, maintained that Plan S would 'disrupt scholarly communications'. They weren't entirely wrong: disrupting the system was always Robert-Jan's intention. But they also argued that implementing stringent rules would 'be a disservice to researchers, and impinge academic freedom'. This was a more difficult argument for Robert-Jan to accept. 'A disservice? I knew in my head and in my heart that removing paywalls would actually be a service – not only to researchers but to benefit public health and education across the world. How could they deny cancer sufferers the right to learn more about their own fate?' Robert-Jan would continue to debate these questions and more over the following weeks, starting at one of the first meetings since the Plan S launch at the 10th Conference on Open Access Scholarly Publishing (COASP) on 17-19 September 2018 in Vienna.

COASP is held by the Open Access Scholarly Publishing Association, a membership organisation of scholar-led and professionally published books and journals. The group has a clear mission: 'To encourage and enable open access as the predominant model of communication for scholarly outputs.'

'The room was packed when I gave my talk about Plan S, and the discussion that followed was lively – with clear statements on issues such as the role of diamond and platinum publishing, the cap on APCs, the transparency on the costs of publishing, the role of hybrid journals in the transition phase, the derogation for monographs and books, the green model. It was a good warm-up for the many more events I would be participating in during the months to come,' says Robert-Jan.

Meanwhile, credit rating agencies started calling Robert-Jan from the London stock market. 'Working as part of such a small office team meant I was often the one to pick up the phone, and was therefore easy for everyone to get hold of – good and bad,' he recalls. 'The first person I spoke to wanted to know what my expectations were with regards to Elsevier's business model. Oblivious, I started to engage in his questions – but then stopped myself, asking him why he was so interested. As soon as I realised he was a stock market analyst, I put the phone down and sent a message round to the Coalition to warn them that vultures were circling. "We can't talk to any of them," I told them, "because we don't want to win the game in this way. That would be cheap."'

2.14 October 2018: the US road trip

With so much positive activity and discussion taking place around Plan S, Coalition leaders didn't want to drop the ball. It had always been part of Robert-Jan's plan to expand the initiative to other continents, and dropping hints to the international press, he knew, helped to make his intentions known to those he was targeting. On a global level, the US has also been seen as closest to Europe in its social and scientific values. Combined, the two continents produce at least two thirds of the world's academic papers – getting US counterparts on board with Plan S, therefore, would almost certainly flip the wider publishing system. It made sense to aim high and start lobbying across the pond.

With the help of his former colleague Mary Kavanagh, minister-counselor for research and innovation at the European Union's US delegation, Robert-Jan and David Sweeney took a whistle-stop tour around Washington, DC, joined in part by Jean-David Malo (now director of the European Innovation Council task force) and Marc Schiltz. News of Plan S had already caused something of a stir among US funders and OA advocates, and, helped by Kavanagh's extensive list of contacts, the group found it easy to arrange meetings with some of the biggest names in science and research.

Visiting the capital opened a lot of doors for the Coalition; according to Kavanagh, the trip was successful for a number of reasons, the main one being that 'Robert-Jan had a very clear message, and he had an audience that at that time was very interested to hear what Europe was doing'. But the timing of the mission was also very good, she explains. 'The National Academies had just published its report, *Open Science by Design*,[90] and, although it hadn't yet been announced, it became clear during the visit that the administration was thinking about what it was going to do on OA going forward: whether they needed to do something explicitly policy-led, whether there could be a policy-led change.'

OA policy in the US is government-led in accordance with the Holdren memorandum,[91] published in 2013 by John Holdren, who was then director of the Office of Science and Technology Policy, and science adviser to the president under the Obama administration. According to that publication, which is still the overall governing document at the time of writing, researchers publishing

---

[90] National Academies of Sciences, Engineering, and Medicine. *Open science by design: Realizing a vision for 21st century research*. Washington, DC: The National Academies Press; 2018. DOI: https://doi.org/10.17226/25116.

[91] The White House. *Expanding public access to the results of federally funded research*. The White House; 2013 Retrieved from https://obamawhitehouse.archives.gov/blog/2013/02/22/expanding-public-access-results-federally-funded-research (accessed 14 March 2021).

work funded with public money are allowed up to one year before providing OA to their publication. 'They didn't say it outright but it did seem at that time that they were thinking of reviewing the Holdren memo of 2013,' says Kavanagh.

First up was a meeting with those at the very top: the US government's Office of Science and Technology Policy (OSTP). Its new director Kelvin Droegemeier was yet to be brought in at this point, but the office of Michael Kratsios, the acting head, was located right in the White House complex itself – exciting and nerve-wracking, to say the least.

Kratsios was young and exceedingly bright (he has since been promoted to chief technology officer of the US and acting chief of research and engineering at the US Department of Defense, which has the largest budget for research on the planet) and had a lot of detailed and interesting questions for the Plan S representatives. One of his big questions – and this would become a theme throughout the course of the next few days' meetings – was why exactly hybrids were not a suitable answer to making publications open. With hindsight, this level of interest from the US side was to be expected. After all, hybrid publishing had become the default option for most publicly funded research since the Holdren memo's publication.

Regrettably, hybrid publishing was one aspect the two sides of the meeting failed to agree on. Asides from this obvious sticking point, Kratsios was noticeably impressed that funders in Europe were taking control of the publishing system to push it towards OA. But, for their US counterparts, it would not be a simple case of signing on the dotted line; not only is the US federal funding system a lot larger, richer and more influential, and therefore its decisions more impactful on the research community, but it is more disjointed than European national funding systems.

In Europe, the majority of public funding for research comes from national government bodies. Meanwhile each Member State of the EU contributes a percentage towards broader European funding programmes such as Horizon 2020. In the US it could be considered the opposite; while some research funding is distributed locally from the relevant state, the vast majority of public funding is distributed through the federal funding agencies.

Each US agency is more or less independent in terms of what they can do: once they receive their allocated funding by Congress, they can approach distribution how they like, and can have different approaches to certain issues. What made the Holdren memo so important, therefore, was that it impacted across all agencies. To complicate matters further, US universities also run to a very different system to that of Europe. But more on that later.

Next on the Plan S team's calendar was a meeting with the director of the National Institutes of Health, Francis Collins – again, a very exciting and encouraging step, given that Collins is one of the busiest and most sought-after people in the global science world.

'The first thing Francis Collins said when he came in was that Plan S was music to his ears – and that, if it was up to him, he would sign up to it right away,' Robert-Jan recalls. 'He said everyone who is not publishing a science journal recognises that OA is the future. But, there again, scientific societies are addicted to their income.'

Another major barrier to the US signing up to Plan S was the very active publishing lobby in Washington, DC.[92] Collins assured the group that the NIH was very sympathetic to the 10 principles of Plan S – made clear by the fact he was personally familiar with every word of the mandate as it stood, reciting the details back to the group with ease. What would be ideal, he suggested, is if there could be a cross-agency approach to navigate such rules.

'He said he would raise it at the next meeting of the science funding agencies,' says Robert-Jan, 'but then we never heard after whether anything happened, so obviously nothing came of it. I guess, like everybody, he had to choose which battles to fight, notably because it was becoming increasingly clear that science was not high on President Trump's agenda, to say the least.'

The meeting with France Córdova, director of the NSF, was less forthright but nevertheless interesting, because she was able to reveal to the Plan S group that the NSF were at the time looking for a financial model for OA. What they wanted to avoid, Córdova explained, was having to pay APCs as well as subscriptions – not just as a result of hybrid-model journals but because of the complicated nature of science funding in the US.[93]

Robert-Jan's visit to the Bill and Melinda Gates Foundation reconfirmed the commitment of this impressive funder of science towards OA. The meeting was straightforward, the spokespeople agreeing that they would sign up to Plan S in good time. Just three weeks later, they would deliver on the promise, becoming the first US member of the Coalition.

Heather Joseph, executive director at SPARC, was similarly engaged, congratulating Plan S as 'an enormously important signal' that the organisation would support them in. The group also met with representatives from the University of California: already a strong supporter of OA, as seen by their leadership in this field and subsequent actions to stand up against the larger commercial publishers. The meeting with the Association of American Universities concluded that it was important that US Funding agencies align their policies in order to succeed in reaching full OA.

Another coincidence in the timing of the European team's trip was that they arrived in the US immediately after the publication of the aforementioned

---

[92] soprweb.senate.gov. *LD-2 disclosure form*. US Senate; n.d. Retrieved from https://soprweb.senate.gov/index.cfm?event=getFilingDetails&filingID=835b4a27-ecc8-4543-82cc-4de778f4c2cb&filingTypeID=51 (accessed 14 March 2021).

[93] While Europe's Horizon 2020 funding grants include fixed overheads of 25 per cent, in the US each institution negotiates its own overheads. Overheads can include all sorts of things including library subscriptions, and so overheads in the US can range in proportionate percentage of a grant.

National Academy Report, *Open Science by Design*. In Boston, Kavanagh and Robert-Jan met with Alexa McCrea, co-chair of the committee that produced the report. 'She said Plan S completely resonated with her and the work they did,' says Kavanagh. McRae also confirmed to them that she believed the OSTP was working on a revision of the Holdren memorandum.

While in Boston, Robert-Jan met with Peter Suber at Harvard University's Widner Library. Long regarded as one of the intellectual founding fathers of OA, Suber was able to advise Robert-Jan generously on the next steps for Plan S: the development of its implementation.

Later, in a meeting at MIT, representatives from the university's library and publishing arm said Plan S would be very helpful in getting OA mainstream. At the time they were already publishing a number of OA journals, but they understood the hybrid model hadn't delivered – that it was too much of a great deal for publishers. They were not able to sign their allegiance to the Coalition, but made clear a plan was under way to move the institution towards full and immediate OA.

There were some tough meetings in the States, too, predominantly with publishing representatives. Other than the fear of loss of revenue for the publishers and the scientific societies, the main theme of the US parties' concerns was the possible loss of peer review rigour that full OA might introduce, as well as a fear that high APCs might lock out some researchers from publishing where they desired. 'OA in the US had splintered conversation,' says Robert-Jan, 'because there are many players and each is coming at it from a slightly different place with different reasons. And it's not just the difference between the publishers and the institutions; it's the difference between the bigger institutions and the smaller and less well-off institutions regarding the publishing costs, for example.'

A meeting with Wiley's publishing house came equipped with a room full of representatives ready to make their case. They wanted to be at the forefront of OA, and it was the publisher's intention to work with Plan S, but the company wanted more of a managed transition that would take three to five years. Their concerns were that they had different requests on OA coming from different countries, and they feared that long-standing relations with the learned societies they published journals for might be damaged. At the same time, organisation leaders said they recognised the need to exit some of these relationships with learned societies. 'Interestingly, they also said if all the funders were lined up they would be able to flip to OA – but the funders weren't lined up. So they couldn't flip easily,' says Robert-Jan.

The tensest meeting of the trip took place with Rush Holt, then CEO of the American Association for the Advancement of Science (AAAS). 'It was a bizarre lunch,' says Robert-Jan. 'Rush clearly didn't like OA, and everything to do with Plan S, because his whole business model was built on subscriptions. He became very emotional about it.' At the time, AAAS members were outspoken in their strong concerns about Plan S – a major concern being that a mandate would jeopardise their flagship journal and magazine, *Science*, which would be a huge loss to the scientific community. Publishers such as themselves brought added value to the science community, Holt's team stressed – not only in the academic papers published but also in the news and analysis published in *Science* and disseminated at conferences and elsewhere. 'Of course we knew what *Science* did was extremely valuable, and we assured them of that,' says Robert-Jan. 'But they would have to find another business model nonetheless, perhaps separating the magazine out from the other journals.'

All in all, the trip was hugely positive for the Plan S team. Relations were strengthened; commitments to full OA were made clear. But the US funders' sentiments fell just short of the commitment that Robert-Jan had hoped for. 'If only the NIH would have jumped fully on board, announcing a fully OA mandate for all its funded work, I am sure everyone else would have followed,' Robert-Jan reflects, 'but it didn't work out that way.' In any case, the fact that Robert-Jan and colleagues were able to meet the key science policy leaders in the capital showed that OA was indeed hot and high up on the US agenda.

At the time of writing, federal funders are yet to fully require full open access as per Plan S – but those tuned in to the US publishing system remain optimistic that a new memorandum to move public agencies towards immediate OA is in the works. For one thing, the former OSTP head, Kelvin Droegemeier – whom Kratsios was interim for – once worked as an OA adviser to SPARC, but during the Trump administration there was no change in policy. A major breakthrough would come in September 2020, when the US-based charity funder the Howard Hughes Medical Institute agreed to sign up to Plan S in full. But more on that in Part Three.

2.15 You win some, you lose some

After riding high on the success of the US trip, the Coalition's confidence took a knock a month later. The fifth of November 2018 was a day of two halves: first, a celebration – both the Wellcome Trust and Gates Foundation released a joint statement to confirm their allegiance to Plan S.

Robert-Jan had met with the Wellcome Trust's OA team in July at their London headquarters – he was aware that they were reviewing their own OA policy, and so this seemed like the right moment to explore their willingness to sign up to Plan S. 'We compared the main principles of our OA policies and discovered that these were very much aligned. Yet it did require some adjustments and, ultimately, a decision,' he recalls. Furthermore, the Wellcome Trust wanted to bring in their trusted partner the Gates Foundation. 'I couldn't wish for more,' says Robert-Jan. 'I had already received moral support from the Gates Foundation when Plan S was presented and had put in a request to them to sign up. Getting the two largest funders of biomedical research on board with a combined annual budget of $5.5bn was just a dream turned reality.'

For Wellcome, the announcement was timed in parallel with new details published updating its own open access policy, which came into effect as scheduled on 1 January 2020.

In accordance with the new rules, all published articles that come about through financial support by the charity funder must be made freely available at the time of publication. Embargoes will no longer be permitted, and neither will publication in hybrid titles be supported – a move that Wellcome director Jeremy Farrar stated was 'a fundamental part of Wellcome's mission to improve health for all'.[94]

The Gates Foundation said it too would update its own OA policy to become even closer in line with the Plan S principles over the following 12 months. 'We believe that free, immediate and unrestricted access to research is essential to accelerating innovation, helping to reduce global inequality and empowering the world's poorest to transform their own lives,' said Trevor Mundel, president of global health at the foundation at the time – marking a significant statement of support for the Coalition. Two months on from the Plan S initiative's official launch, the announcements also provided a welcome news update, keeping the project's momentum going in the world's media. 'It was a great day for European and global science,' says Robert-Jan.

But there was a second Plan S news story brewing in the trade press that same day: an open letter with 800 signatories, mostly chemists, had been published denouncing the proposals as a measure 'too far' and 'too risky for science'.[95] The letter, led by Lynn Kamerlin, a biochemistry professor at Uppsala University in Sweden, argued four main points – the first being that hybrid journals played a justifiable role in the academic publishing system. 'Effectively Plan S would block access to exactly those journals that work with a valuable and rigorous peer-review system of high quality,' it stated.

The second point made in the letter was that Plan S risked excluding a large proportion of the world's researchers. It felt unlikely that funders outside Europe would sign up, the group argued – the fact that even some European countries including Belgium and Spain had declined to take part was surely a bad omen. Without mass participation, the Coalition risked 'splitting the global scientific community into two separate systems,' they said, which would in turn

---

[94] Wellcome. *Wellcome and the Bill & Melinda Gates Foundation join the Open Access Coalition*. Wellcome; n.d. Retrieved from https://wellcome.org/press-release/wellcome-and-bill-melinda-gates-foundation-join-open-access-coalition (accessed 14 March 2021).

[95] Plan S Open Letter. *Reaction of researchers to Plan S: Too far, too risky*. Plan S; n.d. Retrieved from https://sites.google.com/view/plansopenletter/open-letter (accessed 14 March 2021).

have 'a strong negative effect on collaborations between the Coalition S countries and the rest of the world, because joint publications in the highest quality selective journals ... won't be possible anymore'.

An apparent focus on the gold open access model for compliance also presented a problem, in Kamerlin's view: with researchers having to pay high APCs for each publication, 'the total costs of scholarly dissemination will likely rise instead of reduce under Plan S'. Finally, the initiative 'ignored the existence of large differences between different research fields' – Kamerlin's own field of chemistry suffering a much larger negative effect than others, she argued – and all of these points taken together meant that Plan S, in the signatories' eyes, presented 'a serious violation of academic freedom'.

The letter came as a surprise to Robert-Jan, to say the least. Why didn't Kamerlin's party reach out to Coalition members first to discuss their concerns? 'I knew Lynn from the time we worked together to prepare the Bratislava Declaration on Young Researchers – she could have contacted me to discuss all this, but choose a full-frontal attack,' he says. But it wasn't just this that upset him – he also felt that much of the content of the open letter was simply not correct. 'The petition said that Plan S is all about gold OA – well, it is not. The Plan S proposals were not talking about any one particular model of OA publishing at this time – there was no mention of gold, green, diamond or platinum.'

Reflecting back on that time, Kamerlin explains how she felt the open letter was necessary, 'to show that there are in fact very diverse opinions among researchers, and many researchers from across the world and all walks of academia – and many from industry and non-profits too – that have serious concerns'. The open letter was 'mainly to raise awareness, both for scientists, but also to get researchers' voices heard'. She was aware of the message put out there by Robert-Jan – that his door was always open to welcome discussion – but felt the project was exclusive nonetheless; that the door was not necessarily open to criticisms so bold as hers. 'I did, however, subsequently reach out to individual funders as part of Coalition S, as well as all major Swedish funders, and had constructive discussion with several of these funders,' she notes.

A breakdown of the common criticisms to Plan S

The hybrid debate strikes again

Kamerlin is clear that her resistance to Plan S is not borne out of a resistance to open access – she considers herself an OA advocate and publishes in OA platforms. 'The resistance is being told where we can publish,' she explains. That the initial 10 principles of Plan S exclude hybrid publishing as an approved model presented, in Kamerlin's eyes, more problems than it pledged to solve. 'In chemistry, for example, our society journals all have open access routes and often that's done through hybrid. I actually am a fan of the hybrid model if the journal does "offsetting", where they essentially adjust subscription costs taking into account the percentage that's available through open access. Because the thing is that, in a hybrid scheme, anyone can publish – even if you have no grant funding, and you basically scrape together a small pot of money and to do a cool project, you don't have the additional problem of finding several thousand euros to also pay someone an APC,' she says. 'Because, ultimately, if you can't publish the research, no one will be able to read it. If you at least publish it behind a paywall, it's there – and someone can email you for a copy.'

For chemists, the hybrid debate is where 'a lot of the resistance to Plan S came from', Kamerlin explains, 'because, ultimately, we're being told we can't publish in *JACS* [the Journal of the American Chemical Society] and *Angewandte Chemie*. But we can publish in for-profit, pure open access journals. People like to claim that all societies do is organise conferences, but this is actually not true. If you look at the list of activities, they're engaging in advocacy in promoting chemistry, education grants to underprivileged communities … You're not paying your subscription so the chemists can go to fancy conferences; there's a huge ecosystem of what the society does.'

It was around this time that learned and society publishers were also becoming more vocal about feeling threatened by the changes proposed under Plan S. Speaking to *Times Higher Education* magazine in October, Peter Richardson, then the interim joint chief executive of the UK's Association of Learned and Professional Society Publishers, warned that many of these smaller publishers relied on income from subscription-based journals just to survive. He even stressed that some societies could 'disappear altogether' if their concerns were not heeded.[96]

'If Plan S results in article processing charges being capped, that would have a marked effect on those organisations,' he explained. 'It's important that the conversation about implementation isn't dominated by the larger commercial publishers.' The short time frame given for Plan S compliance was also a sticking point, said Richardson, suggesting that it would not be possible for existing society publishers to make a complete switch to OA before the proposed deadline of January 2020. 'I think what we would hope for is a transition period to be put in place to give [us] more time to adjust.'

Publishing its own document in response to Plan S,[97] the British Society later seconded these concerns on account of the fact that, in the humanities and the social sciences, 'nearly all reputable journals are hybrid'. The organisation said,

---

[96] Pells R. Plan S 'could prove fatal' for learned societies. *Times Higher Education*. 2018. Retrieved from https://www.timeshighereducation.com/news/plan-s-could-prove-fatal-learned-societies (accessed 14 March 2021).

[97] *Science Europe's Plan S: making it work for all researchers A commentary by the British Academy*. The British Academy; 2018. Retrieved from https://www.thebritishacademy.ac.uk/documents/965/British_Academy_paper_on_Science_Europe_Plan_S.pdf (accessed 14 March 2021).

'We cannot accept that attempting to abolish them all would contribute positively to the successful dissemination of scientific research, nor do we believe that preventing researchers from publishing in the journals which they believe to be the most appropriate is an ethically sustainable position.'[98]

Following consultation with representatives from some of the learned societies as well as early career researcher groups, the Coalition agreed to soften its stance on hybrids. By this time, Wellcome had also come into play, and had confirmed that its own practical approach to hybrid publishing would be neither to forbid it nor to agree to pay for it through Wellcome grants. Despite persistent concerns that the larger commercial publishers might take advantage, it was agreed that greater support for smaller community publishers took priority, and on 27 November 2018 Plan S coordinators confirmed that a three-year transition period on the use of hybrid journals would be implemented. Researchers working with public funding grants would therefore be permitted to publish in hybrid journals, providing that the journals were part of a 'transformative agreements' by the publisher, and that any APCs paid for hybrid publishing were justified in some form through a subscription rebate.[99]

The move may have been inevitable to some degree – hybrids continue to be one of the more evocative and divisive issues in the publishing world – but notably, at the time of writing, the acceptance of hybrids has failed to get US federal funders on board. Many others have expressed their disappointment that the Coalition is not taking a harder stance on a method that has been so widely condemned for showing a lack of demonstrable progress towards full OA.

APCs and the quality debate

A key concern for Kamerlin, as stated in the letter and still today, continues to be the cost issue, and specifically APCs – which she believes are 'an unfair burden' on the researcher. She is a staunch defender of the prestige of journals and the value that an experienced editor can bring; these two factors are intrinsically linked, and ultimately damage the researcher's freedom of choice to publish where they like, she argues. 'People ignore that hierarchy has already been cemented in the OA world as well as the subscription journal world. So, yes, there are high-quality OA journals, but unfortunately they have high APCs because peer review is expensive,' she explains. 'It's not cheap to run an online publication – there are service costs and electricity costs and so on. A lot of the

---

[98] Pells R. Plan S: three-year transition period for hybrid journals. *Times Higher Education*. 2018 Retrieved from https://www.timeshighereducation.com/news/plan-s-three-year-transition-period-hybrid-journals (accessed 14 March 2021).

[99] Coalition S. *Principles and implementation | Plan S*. Coalition S; 2018. Retrieved from https://www.coalition-s.org/addendum-to-the-coalition-s-guidance-on-the-implementation-of-plan-s/principles-and-implementation.

people who try to make publishing in journals sound like it's just a case of putting some PDF online. They completely ignore the cost of data storage backup, maintenance … there is still a big price tag. And what the OA model does is it pushes that cost onto the author.'

APCs also present a problem for researchers in the Global South, who typically have much smaller budgets to work with than their northern counterparts. As a snapshot example, one study conducted by the African Education Research Database suggests just 10 per cent of educational research studies by scholars in Africa receive any funding at all. Researchers typically fund their work using their own salaries, which are also small by comparison.[100]

Helena Asamoah-Hassan, director of AfLIA, explains that this financial gap makes it just about impossible for most scholars in Africa to contribute to a higher-tier journal without some kind of subsidy. 'Most of them are not able to access research funding at all, so they do the research on their own, often in their own private time. When it comes to publishing the work in a journal, they are then faced with having to pay X amount on top of that – a number which makes sense for a richer country, maybe, but which becomes a problem for Africans, because the salaries are so low when compared to those in the Global North.'

The danger of spiralling costs was precisely the reason why Robert-Jan was determined to implement a cap on APCs from the very beginning – but he was up against many economic minds who argued the impracticality of this and, as mentioned previously, when the matter was put to a vote the Coalition voted against a cap.

However, in December 2018, the Plan S Coalition confirmed it would devise a plan to ensure that researchers from low- and middle-income countries do not become priced out of publishing – or from taking part in collaborations with researchers from the Global North. Official Plan S implementation guidance stipulated that 'automatic article processing charge waivers for authors from low-income countries and discounts for authors from middle-income countries must be provided by the journal or platform' in order for the work to be Plan S-compliant.[101]

For Kamerlin, meanwhile, APCs present additional ethical dilemmas that go beyond straightforward economics. 'If you think about other forms of publishing, in creative literature, for example, if you pay to publish your work this is considered vanity publishing – and usually people are much more suspicious of this kind of stuff, where the authors pay to publish, right?

---

[100] African Education Research Database, Asare S, Mitchell R, Rose P. How accessible are journal articles on education written by sub-Saharan African-based researchers? *Development and Change*. 2021; 52(3): 661–669. Retrieved from https://onlinelibrary.wiley.com/doi/full/10.1111/dech.12639.

[101] Guidance on the Implementation of Plan S. *Making full and immediate open access a reality*. Coalition S; n.d. Retrieved from https://www.coalition-s.org/wp-content/uploads/2020/09/271118_cOAlitionS_Guidance_annotated.pdf (accessed 14 March 2021).

'Say you were going to buy a novel, an author you don't know anything about; you just want something to read on the train. You see two books next to each other: one from a reputable publishing house and one a pay-to-publish book. You'd probably pay to pick up the one from the reputable publisher.'

Kamerlin makes the case that traditional publishers contribute a lot to science in terms of quality control, checking for fraud and so on. That Plan S threatens to disrupt these commercial publishers' business models, therefore, could have a damaging effect on the quality of research: 'The role of the publishing side is very diminished in a lot of the discussion around OA,' she says. 'The thing is, I support the whole spectrum of the ecosystem and I'm pro-open science. But you don't have to throw publishers under the bus to be pro-open science ... I believe the discussion around Plan S has very much removed the value of quality control and gatekeeping.'

Lack of global awareness/coordination

Kamerlin insists that, despite the best intentions of those involved, the project will always remain a European privilege, thus making international collaborations more complicated. She is also outspoken in her belief that 'unfortunately ... most researchers have never heard about Plan S, especially outside Europe', her evidence based on her own experiences within the chemistry field. When the ACS announced its new gold OA journal, *JACS Au* – the gold sister journal to the flagship *JACS* – in 2020, 'people did not realise the role of Plan S in triggering the existence of *JACS Au*, and there was big outcry on Twitter in the chemistry community about it,' she says. 'Many people, including highly influential chemists from the US, for example, realised what Plan S was for the first time and that started a whole Plan S discussion that was similar to when we first wrote the open letter.'

'I don't fault Coalition S, who have really been giving out a lot of information on this,' she adds. 'The main issue is lack of researcher engagement with science policy issues, and I really don't know how to address that, although I try my best with advocacy and raising awareness.'

The published letter was circulated relatively widely, receiving a total of 1,791 signatures to date. But, as Kamerlin herself suggests with the ACS journal example, the letter failed to reach even major players in her own field – proof if ever there was some of just how difficult it continues to be to coordinate information across research borders.

Then there is the matter of subject-specific wants and needs. It's true that Plan S sits less comfortably among researchers from certain fields than others. Chemistry is an interesting example: unlike biology, for instance, its publishing hierarchy is dominated by society journals and in particular those run by the American Chemical Society. Chemists are also traditionally less used to publishing their work in preprint servers before publication – perhaps on account of the perception that discoveries in chemistry move faster than most, with studies often run by very large teams with arguably a lot to lose if a finding happens to be 'scooped' by rivals.

Historically this has been led by the publishers, too, who want to be able to unveil new research in their own journals as an exclusive selling point. But the differences in attitudes towards publishing, and trends of where to publish what with whom, also come down to the specific culture of each subject field – and, as discussed in this book already, culture is a different notion to shift.

An attack on academic freedom?

As a fellow chemist, Marcel Swart says he agrees with Kamerlin that different subjects face different publishing challenges, and that Plan S should be open to the idea of implementing variations on different rules for different disciplines – an idea his group put forward as a suggestion to the Coalition during an early career researcher consultation session in October 2018.

'I think this is fair,' he says. 'In chemistry it's really different from social sciences, from archaeology, from medicine. Some parts of physics for example, they don't care about Plan S because they are used to publishing preprints – it's part of the culture in physics that most people are looking at the preprint server and not the journals.'

Swart also agreed with some of Kamerlin's concerns regarding the proposed restrictions on hybrid journals – his own feelings on which had led him to conduct the quick analysis of pure OA journal abundance (or lack thereof). He disagreed with the way her group's critique was conducted, however. 'The way the letter was handled … they were really pushing it on a personal level, attacking people who were in favour of Plan S, and this I didn't like,' he says. The notion that Plan S would impinge on academic freedom, even in some way be harmful to science, he believes to be 'most incorrect. The rest of the details of Plan S were good for research – the call for transparency on costs, in terms of what the publisher does with the APCs, and of course the copyright retention, I really like.'

One of the biggest causes for disagreement around Plan S and other policies that impact on research life, Swart believes, is a common 'confusion over what things mean. OA means different things for different people – gold OA to chemists is an alarm bell because to them it means paying money, but, in general, gold OA just means immediate OA. It can be paying the APCs or it can be for free,' he says.

As a trained biophysicist and signed member of the Coalition, the NWO's Stan Gielen agrees that 'it is completely false to say we are limiting researchers' academic freedom' through OA mandates. 'That's not fair,' he argues. 'I'm not telling them what they should do – I'm not saying you should or should not publish in *Science*, I'm just telling you that you have to publish OA.'

As an example, Gielen explains how, in the Netherlands, NWO grantees have for decades been required to write a summary describing the results of their funded projects once their grants near expiry – a common practice among public funding agencies in many countries in Europe. 'Is that a limitation of their freedom? I don't think so. It's not perceived that way, even though they have to do it to receive the final payment. We expect them to publish their results in high-quality, international journals,' he continues. 'Is that limiting their academic freedom? I don't think so.'

In Gielen's view, 'it makes sense that the government who spends public money puts some guidelines on how the recipients of that money should behave'. But still, today, a proportion of researchers will continue to argue that Plan S restricts academic freedom for the simple fact that it prevents them from publishing in any journal in the world. And Gielen says he receives emails every week – from chemists, more often than not – arguing this point. 'If I give an answer to one of them, they ask someone else to send me a new email,' he says. 'I have a standard reply now that says, if you can come up with a new argument, or a new vision of how what we are doing is wrong, or if you have a question about our policy, I am willing to have a meeting with you – but I will not respond anymore to the same questions time and time again. We have answered them often enough.'

For Robert-Jan, the accusation that Plan S presented a serious violation of academic freedom was 'below the belt … since Plan S calls for the widest dissemination of scientific output and wants to avoid a situation whereby researchers hand over their copyright to publishers – and as such are hampered in their academic freedom.'

Furthermore, scientists could still publish in subscription journals – there was no law to stop them there – just not using grants provided by the members of Coalition S. They could do it at their own costs. But what Robert-Jan found most shocking from the open letter was the statement that Plan S would have a negative effect on global science cooperation, the assumption being that joint publications in subscription journals were no longer possible. 'I had always been under the impression that scientists worked together to extend the frontiers of knowledge and find solutions for the grand societal challenges,' he says. 'If scientists now say that they will no longer work together because they cannot publish behind paywalls, this presents a very poor image of science and the science community – and might call for the need for a more profound debate on the role of science in our society.'

That the open letter originated from the chemists – and notably was signed by chemists – illustrated to him that the fallout was very much coming from one particular sector that was vocal about its dislike of Plan S. 'It led to a big debate inside the science community, as well,' Robert-Jan adds. 'I remember reading a blog post from a physicist saying, "Why can't chemists do as the physicists do?" It was just too bad that the open letter did nothing else but complain, with no attempt to provide solutions to accelerate the transition to full and immediate OA. As such it was a lost opportunity.'

See you in court

The ripples brought upon the academic publishing system were not only caused by Plan S. Court cases were being filed that threw the legality and legitimacy of the publishing system into question, on the grounds of lack of transparency and market distortion. The targets were the big commercial publishers.

Back in 2016, a group of prominent OA advocates led by Martin Eve filed a complaint to the UK Competition and Markets Authority against the Elsevier RELX Group for 'anti-competitive practices' and 'abuse of dominant market positions'. The claim, filed by Eve with Jon Tennant (Imperial College London) and Stuart Lawson (Birkbeck, University of London), asserted that, since Elsevier held a dominant market position, it was able to enforce non-disclosure agreements upon its customers – libraries and higher education institutions – in order to keep its pricing policy secret.

This series of events had resulted in profit margins above 40 per cent, which in itself was seen as proof of a substantial market disfunction. Two years later, on 30 October 2018, the EUA, representing 800 European universities, sent a letter to Margrethe Vestager, the commissioner responsible for Europe's competition policy, because the association was 'deeply concerned about the lack of transparency and competition in the scholarly publishing business sector in Europe'. The EUA outlined three key reasons for its concern: the dominant position of a few large publishing houses (RELX Group, Springer Nature, Wiley-Blackwell, SAGE, Taylor & Francis), the use of strict confidentiality clauses in contracts leading to lack of pricing, and a clear asymmetry in negotiation power between publishers and their customers.

The EUA letter asked DG Competition to 'undertake an analysis of the competition policies which allow the scholarly publishing sector to be concentrated in a handful of powerful large publishing companies'.

On 28 November 2018, Michael Eisen, a geneticist at the University of California, Berkeley, and well-known advocate of OA publishing, published a counter open letter in support of the principles of Plan S. This letter, published through his own website, proved as popular as Kamerlin's, gathering some 1,400 signatures of support within its first week.[102] While the letter did not directly

---

[102] Van Noorden R. Researchers sign petition backing plans to end paywalls. *Nature*. 4 December 2018. https://www.nature.com/articles/d41586-018-07632-2 (accessed 13 March 2021).

name Plan S, Eisen quoted the initiative's key policies, urging fellow stakeholders to 'welcome efforts on the part of public and private research funders to require that publications based on work they fund be made immediately freely and openly available without restrictions on access or use'.

Posting about the petition on Twitter, Eisen referenced the damaging divide witnessed in the research community which had been brought to light by Kamerlin's own letter. 'The only way to achieve universal open access to the scientific literature is for research funders to require it of their grantees. They're finally doing it, but are taking a LOT of flak,' he wrote. Inevitably with Twitter, a fiery debate opened up once again – as it would do time and time again over the months to come.

It was clear that researchers, and not just publishers and investors, remained divided in their opinions on the implementation of a mandate like Plan S. But, in the words of Robert-Jan, the important thing was that the stone had already been thrown in the pond – and the ripples were turning into waves.

2.16 Towards a Plan S implementation guidance

By mid-November in 2018, the Coalition was ready to publish its draft guidance on the implementation of Plan S – the proposed details of the new rules that every stakeholder had been waiting for. In the weeks since the launch, Coalition members had been reading with interest the variety of comments made about and reactions put out there to Plan S.

The 10 principles as they stood had been drafted with input from representatives of the publishing sector, early career researcher groups, charity groups, and of course the individual funding agencies themselves. But it was important to Science Europe and to Robert-Jan that the guidance also be informed by those outside their immediate sphere – and that every stakeholder around the globe could have the opportunity to give their feedback if desired.

On 26 November, the draft implementation guidance document was declared open for public consultation, with a formal presentation of it given in London the day after. Together with Robert-Jan and the UKRI's David Sweeney, John-Arne Røttingen, chief executive of the Research Council of Norway and co-chair of the Coalition S implementation task force, outlined the three main roads established for Plan S compliance:

- Publication in open access journals or platforms;
- Deposit of versions of record (VoR) or author accepted manuscript (AAM) in open access repositories without embargo;
- Publication in 'hybrid' journals only under transformative agreements.

Interested parties were given until 1 February 2019 to submit their feedback (later extended to 8 February to account for high demand). Contributions would be taken into account to draw up the final approved guidance document, due to be published later that year.

Around this time, consultation was also taking place for Horizon Europe, the ambitious €100 billion European research and innovation funding programme set to succeed Horizon 2020.[103]

The proposal for Horizon Europe was made as part of the EU's long-term budget planning beyond 2020 (the multiannual financial framework) and it was important, therefore, that the rules of participation document for Horizon Europe integrated the rules set by Plan S for public research funding.

Coalition S agreement and key principles

With effect from 2021,[104] all scholarly publications on the results from research funded by public or private grants provided by national, regional and international research councils and funding bodies, must be published in Open Access Journals, on Open Access Platforms, or made immediately available through Open Access Repositories without embargo.

In addition:

- Authors or their institutions retain copyright to their publications. All publications must be published under an open license, preferably the Creative Commons Attribution license (CC BY), in order to fulfil the requirements defined by the Berlin Declaration;
- The Funders will develop robust criteria and requirements for the services that high-quality Open Access journals, Open Access platforms, and Open Access repositories must provide;
- In cases where high-quality Open Access journals or platforms do not yet exist, the Funders will, in a coordinated way, provide incentives to establish and support them when appropriate; support will also be provided for Open Access infrastructures where necessary;

(Continued)

---

[103] European Commission. *The Commission's proposal for Horizon Europe*. European Commission; n.d. Retrieved from https://ec.europa.eu/info/horizon-europe/commissions-proposal-horizon-europe_en (accessed 14 March 2021).

[104] For funders agreeing after January 2020 to implement Plan S in their policies, the start date will be one year from that agreement.

- Where applicable, Open Access publication fees are covered by the Funders or research institutions, not by individual researchers; it is acknowledged that all researchers should be able to publish their work Open Access;
- The Funders support the diversity of business models for Open Access journals and platforms. When Open Access publication fees are applied, they must be commensurate with the publication services delivered and the structure of such fees must be transparent to inform the market and funders potential standardisation and capping of payments of fees;
- The Funders encourage governments, universities, research organisations, libraries, academies, and learned societies to align their strategies, policies, and practices, notably to ensure transparency;
- The above principles shall apply to all types of scholarly publications, but it is understood that the timeline to achieve Open Access for monographs and book chapters will be longer and requires a separate and due process;
- The Funders do not support the 'hybrid' model of publishing. However, as a transitional pathway towards full Open Access within a clearly defined timeframe, and only as part of transformative arrangements, Funders may contribute to financially supporting such arrangements;
- The Funders will monitor compliance and sanction non-compliant beneficiaries/grantees;
- The Funders commit that when assessing research outputs during funding decisions they will value the intrinsic merit of the work and not consider the publication channel, its impact factor (or other journal metrics), or the publisher.

2.17 Berlin 2018: a radical intervention

One of the most amazing moments for Plan S came in December 2018, during a meeting organised by Gerard Meijer at the Max Planck Institute in Berlin. The research network had organised the sessions as part of its OA2020 initiative, and academic stakeholders from every continent were in attendance.

As an institute director and keen open science advocate, Meijer had been involved in the OA movement since the early 2000s. But it was in 2012, when he was approached to become president of his alma mater, Radboud University in the Netherlands, that he realised he had 'a responsibility towards the researchers at the university to take this more seriously'.

'It was around that time that the Dutch state secretary of science and education had said in parliament that he wanted all scientific publications in the country to be made OA by 2024, with a 10 per cent increase each year,' Meijer recalls. 'Well, the Netherlands is relatively small – there are only 13 universities, and the presidents meet on a monthly basis. So in one of the next meetings after this I said to my colleagues, "If OA is put on the agenda like this, we can no longer leave the publishing negotiations over to the heads of our libraries."

'It was clear that, if we really wanted to reach 100 per cent OA – and we wanted to make this happen with the publishers on board – we needed to negotiate that into any new contracts with them. And it was clear that the university leaders also had to be involved.

'When I said this to my colleagues, they replied, "If you think this is the right thing, then why don't you do it?"'

Together with Koen Becking, the president of Tilburg University, Meijer began to set up meetings with Wiley, Springer and Elsevier, where they were able to negotiate the costs of their subscription deals more directly. When Meijer's term as president of the university ended in 2017, he returned to Germany – where he was asked by the president of the Max Planck Society to speak on behalf of the network for its nationwide negotiation team, DEAL.

'Very early on, in one of the first meetings we had with Elsevier, I realised that on the opposite side of the table there were exactly the same people as I had seen in the Netherlands,' says Meijer. 'Whereas, on the academic side of the table, they were all novices. It suddenly hit me: this is a truly bizarre situation. We only have a few of these larger publisher representatives in the world. They are highly experienced and professional in their negotiating. And it's always the same team that goes to different countries – they know exactly what deals are being made in each country.

'Meanwhile, the other side of the negotiation table is vulnerable. They have less practice and understanding of business. They are made to sign NDAs normally, so do not tell anybody about what is in the agreement, which is a crazy thing. It is not a fair exchange.'

This was in early 2018, around the same time Robert-Jan started in his role as open access envoy. Meijer decided to write to him. 'I told him the situation, I said what we are going to do is we are going to organise a meeting in Berlin where we invite several negotiation teams from the Netherlands, from Austria, from the UK, and just see what experiences people have had with publishing contracts.' That preliminary meeting took place in early May – and was so productive in clearing the air around publishing deals that Meijer decided to do the same thing again ahead of the annual OA2020 conference in Berlin in December – but bigger.

'It was a closed meeting – a safe space,' says Meijer. 'This time we asked representatives of something like 20 negotiation teams worldwide including China, Japan and South Africa to openly discuss how much they actually paid for their subscription deals, and what their experience was like with the different publishers. That was an eye-opener.'

That stakeholders were openly discussing money for the first time was radical – NDAs had kept the lid on contracts tightly shut for many decades. But, once details were out in the open, participants very quickly realised the extent to which they had been duped by these large commercial companies.

'Different countries were paying completely different amounts for exactly the same product,' says Meijer. Even worse was the realisation that the wealthiest countries were not necessarily paying the most, either: 'We learned what the libraries in South Africa paid for access to Elsevier journals, for example – it was more than the average cost paid by universities in Germany. Which was a scandal.'

The message, it seemed, was finally out: keeping contracts secret helped nobody but the billion-dollar publishers. 'It's not as if the prices were completely unknown,' says Meijer. 'Some people in the UK, for instance, had called upon the Freedom of Information Act years previously, so some information was out there.' But it was outdated, and nothing like on this scale.

Naturally, the publishers who had set those contracts and NDAs reacted badly. 'Elsevier certainly didn't like what we had done, and even said it was not allowed. So my reaction all the way was: "Just sue me, then."' And did they ever try to sue? 'No.'

Meijer may have made some enemies, but he has no regrets: 'If I tell this to politicians – that there was absolutely no transparency where millions of dollars' or euros' worth of university money was spent – they cannot believe it. I cannot believe it. So I think the publishers realise very well that it was a strange situation. They would always tell us that one reason to have the NDAs in place was because the deals that they would make with us were always much better than they make with any other country. But they tell that to everyone. Once this became common knowledge, it was clear the publishers had no leg to stand on.'

China shocks the world at OA2020 in Berlin

The 14th Berlin Open Access Conference, held on 3–4 December 2018, would be remembered as a key moment in the OA movement – and not just by the 200-odd participants representing 37 countries. This was the event where policymakers, funders, librarians and researchers from around the globe made it clear that they were united in their cause to make OA a reality – and that they wanted this to happen fast. The title of the conference was 'Aligning Strategies to Enable Open Access', and Robert-Jan had been invited to give a keynote speech on Plan S.

The conference was preceded by a closed session with some of the key policymakers, at which, to the surprise of everyone, the Chinese representatives read out a formal statement saying that China would move to the OA model of publishing. The statement made explicit reference to Plan S; Robert-Jan could not believe what he was hearing, but the very fact the Chinese delegation was reading out this formal statement indicated to the audience that this was serious stuff and not just the whim of a few individuals in Europe; this statement had been approved by those at the very top in China and the conference attendees were the first to know.

Gerard Meijer and the team of OA2020 had organised the conference cleverly, Robert-Jan felt. After he had given his presentation, one by one the CEOs of Elsevier, Springer Nature and Wiley were given the floor to state how they would contribute to accelerate the transition to OA. After this they were faced with statements from a panel of representatives from different continents issuing one collective and clear message: OA was happening, and they were going to enforce it.

These representatives were sitting next to each other on the podium, shoulder to shoulder to underline their united stand. It was clear the CEOs had not seen this coming. It was the second wake-up call for the big publishing houses after Plan S was announced: a global coalition was being created, composed of powerful players. That China was part of this was the biggest shock of all. It was clear after the Berlin conference that things would never be the same.

Upon its conclusion, the conference issued a statement that underlined the commitment of its participants to the key principles of OA and mentioned Plan S specifically, pledging 'a shift to full open access within a few years'. The publishers were called upon 'to work with all members of the global research community to effect complete and immediate open access'.

Transforming the narrative

Another key focus of the Berlin meeting was the opportunity for change posed by 'transformative agreements', and it became clear from the statements given at OA2020 that stakeholders from across the world felt ready to adopt such agreements in their OA strategies.

Transformative agreements are effectively contracts negotiated between institutions (libraries and national and regional consortia) and publishers that should aid the transition to OA rather than tie up more money into subscription journals – the idea being that publishers agree a fair price for their subscriptions in return for their commitment to making more content OA, based on the number of articles the contracted institution publishes each year. The agreement replaces the old lump-sum payments of subscriptions with fees based on the number of articles read and published by the institution. This has also come to be known as a 'publish and read' model agreement.

The ESAC (Efficiency and Standards for [Open Access] Article Charges) initiative offers a clearer explanation: 'The transformative mechanism of these agreements is grounded in the evidence-based understanding that, globally, the amount of money currently paid in journal subscriptions, which amounts to an average cost of €3,800 per article, is amply sufficient to sustain open access publishing of the global scholarly article output.'

Transformative agreements also tend to require that copyright is retained by the author and not transferred to the publisher – as in keeping with Plan S. We will delve a bit further into this in Part Three.

2.18 Celebrating rebels

At the start of 2019, Elsevier saw the entire editorial board of its prestigious *Journal of Informetrics* resign and begin a competing OA publication, titled *Quantitative Science Studies*. The reason for this bold move, the board of editors said, was that their position working under the existing Elsevier publication model was no longer tenable; they wanted to embrace open publishing practices.

The board wrote in an open resignation letter: 'Because our position on ownership, open access, and open citations is fundamentally irreconcilable with the position of Elsevier, we consider it is no longer in the interest of our community to continue working together with Elsevier as members of the JOI editorial board.' Giving the company's formal response, Elsevier representatives said that they deeply regretted the board's decision to resign and would search for members to draw up a new editorial board.

Elsevier's reaction – to simply replace the rebels with more compliant worker bees – was a cynical one. At the time, Robert-Jan called the resignation of the editorial board 'great news for the open access movement', expressing hopes that the example would 'inspire many more to follow suit'.

While the *JoI*'s board resignation appeared to be at least in part inspired by the movement being created by Plan S, editorial boards had resigned before. Indeed, something similar had happened in 2015 with Elsevier's well-known linguistics journal *Lingua* (as outlined in Part One). Similarly, in 2013, editorial board members of the *Journal of Library Administration*, owned by Taylor & Francis, decided to quit on account of the fact that their researchers had to either wait 18 months to see their articles being made OA or pay almost $3,000 for full and immediate OA. Furthermore, there was no Creative Commons licence deployed, they noted.

Editorial rebellions are not limited to Elsevier and Taylor & Francis: in September 2018, Wiley saw the majority of its *Diversity and Distributions* journal editorial board resign over an issue of APC pricing, after the company decided to transfer the journal from subscription to OA.

Notably, in Germany, many scientists resigned from their editorial boards of Elsevier subscription journals in 2017. This can largely be explained by the breakdown of negotiations between that publishing house and the aforementioned Project DEAL, a consortium of German universities, research institutions and libraries. Project DEAL was a game changer in that it meant the end of hundreds of libraries and universities in Germany each negotiating individually with the big commercial publishers, and the start of a coordinated, nationwide negotiation aimed at reaching 'publish and read' deals.

When the negotiations between Elsevier Elsevier and Project DEAL collapsed, some 200 DEAL member organisations retaliated by refusing to renew their subscriptions to Elsevier's journals. Elsevier responded by cutting the organisations off from its online access to journal content for several weeks, before eventually restoring access to allow 'good faith discussions to carry on'. Some remain sceptical over this supposed olive branch, however – they claim that the main motivation for the restored journal access was that, during the blackout, German scientists had been able to get hold of whatever papers they wanted anyway, either via international colleagues or by other means.

To assist journal editors in moving away from working under the big commercial publishers and subscription journals, and to set up new competing OA journals, Johan Rooryck set up the Fair Open Access Alliance. From his own experiences with *Lingua/Glossa*, Rooryck knew that a major challenge for the first years of each new OA journal was notably to secure enough funds and to obtain the trust from the science community. It was therefore a welcome development that certain funders and charities were willing to provide grants and other financial support for such mutineers.

Other initiatives have been taken to encourage editors of subscription journals to resign. In 2008, the Open Access Directory (OAD) set up a 'hall of fame' for those editors willing to issue a 'Declaration of Independence'– i.e. resign and launch an OA journal instead. The hall of fame was inspired by a similar project set up by SPARC in 2001 – the US organisation taking its inspiration from the US Declaration of Independence.

Breaking away from the system can be scary – but it is clear there is a strong and growing network of supportive peers to catch editorial rebels after they jump. Journal communities are loyal – and a journal itself is only as good as the contributors, editors and other creatives that contribute towards it. When Johan Rooryck flipped *Lingua* to *Glossa*, he did it with the help of his editorial board but also his long-standing authors and readers. As Mark Wilson concludes in his 2016 article 'What Happens to Journals That Break Away', it is increasingly evident that new OA journals tend to do better than their old, subscription namesakes.

2.19 Berlin take two: entering the lion's den

After the riotous success of OA2020, Robert-Jan returned to Berlin in the new year for the annual Academic Publishing Europe (APE) conference on 15 January 2019 (it is true: publishers hold an awful lot of conferences). Once again, Robert-Jan presented the Plan S initiative to stakeholders from across the academic publishing and communications landscape. He started his talk by correcting something the speaker before him had said.

Michiel Kolman, the senior vice president of Elsevier and president of the International Publishers Association, had preceded Robert-Jan's talk by telling stakeholders that 'the value of our business is built on copyright'. This, Robert-Jan knew, was not correct. 'The value of your business is built on the science community and its output,' he said – and with this the conversation turned heated, fast. Following criticisms over the income made by certain society publishers, AAAS's Rush Holt fervently defended using publishing income for his society's activities, and at one point Judy Verses, executive vice president of research at Wiley, compared Plan S to Donald Trump's Mexican wall.

The furore distracted from the exciting side event taking place during the conference: Wiley itself signed its first open science agreement with German institutions through Gerard Meijer's Project DEAL. Under the three-year deal, member institutions agreed to pay a fee based on the number of articles that their researchers published per year – with room for the price paid to be adjusted accordingly at the end of each term. Crucially, the contract allowed all researchers in Germany the option to publish their work through Wiley's open access journals at no extra cost.

At the APE conference, Horst Hippler from the Project DEAL steering committee announced the agreement as 'revolutionary'. It certainly marked a stark contrast between the consortium's relationship with Elsevier at that time – Germany had cut ties from the publisher the previous summer after a row over spiralling subscription costs became unsalvageable.

2.20 Latin America speaks out

It felt like a long time building but, on 10 February 2019, Plan S stakeholders finally heard from Latin America – and, with it, the Coalition received its first sharp criticism of the initiative for being too 'Europe-centric'. It gave pause for thought for Robert-Jan and his colleagues; this was exactly what earlier critics had warned might happen, but Science Europe organisers had hoped that the open door policy and consultation period would provide an opportunity for productive discussion with representatives from the region.

Arianna Becerril-García is executive director of the Redalyc network of scholarly journals and chair of AmeliCA, an open knowledge foundation for Latin America and the Global South. As a long-time observer of the changing academic publishing culture, Becerril-García explains that the main problem she saw in Plan S was that it would encourage the slow introduction of APCs where they did not exist before, in countries where researchers 'can't afford them'.

Admittedly, the root of this problem comes from the growth of the larger commercial players in the Global North, she explains. There are plenty of stories out there of long-standing journals being targeted by the likes of Elsevier, who see an opportunity to buy up the region's research system as its reputation in the Global North dwindles. A common fear about Plan S in Latin America, says Becerril-García, was that it would legitimise and accelerate this wave of commercialisation across Latin America, when in fact it was never in the Latin American research culture to publish scientific work commercially in the first place.

'The vast majority of our academic work is published in journals that are run by and funded by the universities or research institutions,' she explains. Most journals in the region, as documented by DOAJ statistics, are made possible through the diamond model: they are supported most often by government or institutional money, and are made open access by default, with no charge to the author or reader.

'This system has worked well for us, but now the culture is starting to change,' says Becerril-García. In fact, it is only in the past few years that governments in the region have clocked on to the idea that commercial publishers could step in to provide a source of income in place of public funding – which, in policymakers' eyes, has the potential to save them money. At the same time, universities have started to take notice of impact factors – the artificial measure of quality purported by the commercial publishing industry journals that features so heavily in the Global North – and an increasing number of journals in the Latin American region are becoming commercialised.

'It's very worrying that many of our journals are starting to charge APCs for the first time,' says Becerril-García. 'It's an imitation of a model they believe can be lucrative – but the effect of this is that many of the universities that were subsidising these publications are no longer doing that, because they believe journals can survive without it.'

This in turn means less public funding for the academic sector, and also more uncertainty, given that their journals are not well known enough in the global context to be profitable. Suddenly seen as 'failing', the journals also lose subsidies from the government – and face a choice of selling out completely to larger publishers or folding. 'It's an extortion of our system from multiple angles,' says Becerril-García.

Impact factor plays a major role in this steady decline, too, she adds: 'We are already seeing this is happening – at the same time that they started to evaluate the quality of journals with rankings, they started to take away grants for the journals that didn't make it into a global index. That's always going to be high, because the global indexes are run by the English-speaking world predominantly; around 87 per cent of the content published in Latin American journals comes from Latin American researchers, so it's a pretty self-contained system.

'Since impact factor began to be recognised in the last couple of years, more than 300 journals in Colombia stopped receiving funding from government and institutions, for example – so many of them are now very near dying. Some of them are being sold to commercial publishers to save them. The few that are being supported by the government continue to be OA, but they are now just

10 per cent of the previous total. Take all of this into consideration and we are killing our own ecosystem.'

AmeliCA was set up in 2018 in response to the 'financial sustainability crisis' that Becerril-García saw coming: 'Transformative agreements that are happening in other parts of the world to transform subscription agreements into another fee – another kind of payment – is also very threatening for our region. The APCs that are requested by journals in the Global North are sometimes half of our researchers' total grant.'

With support from public university money, her team devised their own Latin America-centric indexing system on the AmeliCA platform. 'We had to find another way of letting the academic publishing community know they are doing well without them following the commercial strategy – because that system will disappear in the near future,' she explains.

When Plan S came along, Becerril-García feared her hard work to defend the continent's strong tradition of diamond publishing might be jeopardised. She spoke out against Plan S and listed the strengths of her own initiative, partly to make the point that Europe was not the first to address the challenges facing global academic publishing. She felt the plan was designed 'by Europe, for Europe' – and was sceptical of the impact it might have for these reasons.

Upon hearing of her criticisms, Robert-Jan immediately got in touch with Becerril-García to urge that AmeliCA and Coalition S should not fight each other but join forces since they both were aiming for the same goal: making OA a reality. 'I should have reached out to them much earlier, but then again there was so much going on,' Robert-Jan reflects.

Today, relations between AmeliCA and Plan S are much stronger. But Becerril-García believes there is still a long way to go before the two initiatives are aligned – if they should be at all, for that matter. 'I do believe now that Plan S has really good intentions, and it is having a positive impact in Europe,' she says. 'But we think Plan S should be careful in globalising its strategies, because there has to be context. Our way of working has to be learned and understood before they come to implement a global strategy in every region. Otherwise, it is naive. And that's why we said that Plan S should focus as well on strategies to support diamond publishing – which is not exclusive to Latin America, it's worldwide.

'The diamond model should be strengthened because we believe this is one of the closest ways in which to achieve participatory and inclusive scholarly communications worldwide. I know there are commercial publishers and they have to deal with them, but I believe Plan S should put this model in the place it deserves. It deserves funding, it deserves recognition, it deserves strategies that can help guarantee that this model survives in the future and be competitive. If we only focus our attack on commercial publishers, we are guaranteeing income to them still … so we believe Coalition S is missing something important.'

2.21 Big interest from big players ... and another withdrawal

Interest in Plan S continued to grow from around the globe and, on 10 February 2019, Zambia's National Science and Technology Council became the first African agency to sign up to Plan S. It was an incredible achievement for the Coalition, which could now celebrate having members across three continents, with further support pledged by stakeholders in the Middle East and Asia, too.

At the same time as the Zambian announcement, the African Academy of Sciences (AAS) also expressed its support for Plan S and an intention to sign up fully in due course. Issuing a statement, Felix Dapare, president of the AAS, said the association commended the Plan S Coalition for its 'courage ... in offering a vision of the world in which results are distributed to be built upon for the benefit of mankind'.

What made the African support all the more special for Robert-Jan and his colleagues was that this was one of the regions that could benefit most from a globally coordinated mandate on OA. To have them on side was an indication that they were doing something right – that Plan S really could make for a fairer publishing landscape across borders.

The AAS had also recently launched its own Open Research Platform in April 2018 to great success.[105] The project had been launched with F1000 Research as part of an effort to reduce dependency on dominant subscription publishers in the Global North, and so there were valuable lessons for Coalition S to learn from them, too.

After the positive news from China and now Africa, India soon followed: in February 2019, Krishnaswamy VijayRaghavan, India's principal scientific adviser, announced on Twitter that his country's government would be joining Plan S as part of efforts to lower the costs of academic publishing and improve public access to it. 'India joining Coalition S, will optimise it to our benefit,' he said. 'Access of published research to all. Authors [will] be liberated from finding publishing [fees].'[106]

The sheer scale of public research in India presented another cause for celebration for Coalition members. By this moment in time, the country was well on its way to becoming the fourth biggest producer of scientific research in the world: figures from Elsevier Elsevier's SciVal database show that India

---

[105] Maincola E. *AAS Open Research turns two*. F1000 Blogs; 2020. Retrieved from https://blog.f1000.com/2020/04/27/aas-open-research-turns-two (accessed 14 March 2021).

[106] Twitter. n.d. Retrieved from https://twitter.com/PrinSciAdvGoI/status/1095266653930024960 (accessed 14 March 2021).

published 187,000 academic papers in 2019, an increase of 5 per cent on the previous year, and overtaking Germany for the first time.[107]

The Government of India funds over half of all scientific research undertaken in the country – so any public pledge to mandate open science would have a significant impact on the global scale of OA publishing overall.

But the celebrations were to be short-lived. By October 2019, enthusiasm from India had cooled and, during a public engagement talk on 25 October, VijayRaghavan announced that India would not be signing up to Plan S after all.

'We are not joining Plan S. Plan S is itself evolving, and the terms that we are trying to push is something that we will ask Plan S to push for in their format,' he told Indian news website *The Wire*. 'Since February 2018, some water has flowed under the bridge. We have done substantial work here and had consultations with government, individual scientists and the academies.'[108]

While India would not give up on pushing for OA, it was clear the government had decided to devise its own means of getting there, without the Coalition. Of course, any commitment towards OA was a success in itself in the eyes of Robert-Jan – Plan S or no Plan S. But India's decision was a warning sign to Coalition members – a reminder that for them to nurture the initiative's relations outside Europe, even when schedules were packed and European politics felt dominant.

The fact of the matter was that there were so many new developments taking place with Plan S across several continents; it was near impossible for such a small primary team to keep on top of international relations to the extent Robert-Jan would have liked. It was around this time, too, that the World Health Organization (WHO) began to express a serious interest in the initiative, and Robert-Jan travelled to Geneva to meet with its officials. In August 2019, the WHO became the first of the United Nations agencies to join Plan S.[109]

But, to this day, India's departure remains one of Robert-Jan's biggest regrets from his time as OA envoy.

---

[107] Bothwell E. India overtakes Germany on research output. *Times Higher Education*. 2020. Retrieved from https://www.timeshighereducation.com/news/india-overtakes-germany-research-output (accessed 14 March 2021).

[108] Mukunth V. India will skip Plan S, focus on national efforts in science publishing. *The Wire*. 2019. Retrieved from https://thewire.in/the-sciences/plan-s-open-access-scientific-publishing-article-processing-charge-insa-k-vijayraghavan (accessed 14 March 2021).

[109] Coalition S. *World Health Organization and TDR Join cOAlition S to Support Free and Immediate Access to Health Research | Plan S*. Coalition S; 2019 Retrieved from https://www.coalition-s.org/who-joins-coalition-s (accessed 14 March 2021).

2.22 The goodbye

In January 2019, Robert-Jan received the SPARC Innovator Award for his contributions to the OA movement with Plan S. Among the previous winners were the Bill & Melinda Gates Foundation, the World Bank and the Harvard University Faculty of Arts and Sciences – so the award was a huge honour.

According to Heather Joseph, executive director of SPARC, 'Plan S represents a sea change in the standards for the Open Access policies of research funders. The push for immediate access combined with full reuse rights is a tremendous signal that funders have grown impatient with embargoes and read-only research articles … Smits's willingness to step up and champion that move sets a new bar for the global research community, and drives home the fact that Open Access is here to stay.'

When news of the prize was announced, Commissioner Carlos Moedas was also vocal in his acknowledgement of the contribution Robert-Jan had made, adding: 'Smits was really the right person for this job. He was able to convene key players and stir a lot of interesting ideas and discussions around this topic. His long-standing leadership in science and innovation meant he had the credibility and the network to do it very fast. Now Europe has a clear roadmap to get this done and lead the way.'

Another unexpected honour came in the form of 'Nature 10', *Nature* magazine's annual shortlist of the top 10 people who matter in science. Both making it on the 2018 Nature 10 list and receiving the SPARC Award were pleasant surprises for Robert-Jan: 'I had not at all seen this coming, but of course felt very honoured, especially when I noticed who had received the award in previous years,' he says.

For him, it was a nice icing on the cake – especially given that two months later he would leave his position of Europe's open access envoy. That such generous praise of Plan S was trickling in now signalled to Robert-Jan that the initiative would continue to succeed in his absence; it was time for a new adventure.

Robert-Jan's term as open access envoy was linked to the term in office of President Juncker and his college of commissioners. This was due to come to an end on 1 November 2019. However, because of the European Parliament elections earlier that year, the European Commission effectively became a lame duck from 1 May, in the sense that its members could not introduce any new legislative proposals, only work on the negotiation and implementation of earlier ones.

'Although my move back to the Netherlands should not have come as a surprise to the members of Coalition S – I had informed them from the start that I would leave my post in Spring 2019 – it did,' he reflects. 'It took the Coalition therefore quite some time to advertise for my post, which was mainly due to the issue of finance: who would pick up the bill to cover the salary of the next open access envoy?' Robert-Jan's salary had been paid for by the European Commission, but, now that Plan S was established, it was up to Coalition S to take the baton. Finally, once the budget issue was sorted out, the post was published – and on 28 August 2019 Johan Rooryck was appointed.

With over 20 years' experience as an editor, and a track record as an OA advocate, Rooryck was the perfect fit to take over, and Robert-Jan felt confident that 'Plan S, this initiative that grew from just the spark of an idea into a global game changer almost overnight, was in safe hands.'

When Robert-Jan met with Rooryck for a handover, he passed him five messages:

1. Keep the European Commission on board at all costs. With its enormous science budget and prestigious programmes such as the ERC, it can make the difference in making Plan S a reality.
2. Pay lots of attention to consolidating Coalition S to keep the current members fully committed. It is not enough to just keep the core group together.
3. Reach out to like-minded initiatives such as AmeliCA and sign 'non-aggression pacts' with them, because they aim at the same goal: to arrive at 100 per cent OA. The last thing that is needed is a fight within the OA community.
4. Reinforce the Science Europe OA secretariat and back office to deal with the numerous requests for information coming in.
5. Remain visible in the media. For this purpose, set up a global network of Plan S ambassadors.

'Notably, the first point was especially important and not a given. Luckily, my successor at the European Commission's Directorate-General for Research and Innovation, Jean Eric Paquet, was very committed to Plan S and openly declared his intentions to safeguard and protect my legacy,' says Robert-Jan. 'That he kept his promise became clear from the success of his first international visits.'

Part Three

3.1 Changing the narrative

Robert-Jan has often likened Plan S to a stone thrown into the water – with rippling effects that have caused both bigger and smaller waves. Few will deny that the initiative helped to accelerate the number of transformative agreements taking place; it also incentivised the creation of new publishing platforms in the OA domain. But, above all, Plan S forced big commercial publishers to rethink their business models – some for the first time – and sparked a debate about the future of academic publishing that would make it impossible for the broken system to stay as it was.

Plan S forced universities to adjust their rewards systems, to step away from the trap of journal impact factor as the sole criterion to assess scientific output, and to develop new metrics as part of an open science agenda. Furthermore, the mandate was a wake-up call for the academic community not to let commercial entities gobble up the rights to their data in the same way that had happened with scientific publications. This latter point has become increasingly relevant with the steady shift seen by companies such as Elsevier to move away from presenting themselves as publishing companies, instead investing in data services – from the storage of data to data analytics – buying up the start-up businesses (for instance, Mendeley) that specialise in these fields.[110]

---

[110] Elsevier. *Social media guide for Mendeley*. Elsevier; n.d. Retrieved from https://www.elsevier.com/__data/assets/pdf_file/0007/96487/mendeley-social-media-guide-02161841.pdf (accessed 14 March 2021).

Data has rapidly become the new frontier, the new oil – and the last thing the research community needs is to have data sets that are generated with public money locked behind paywalls. There is work left to be done here, but it is undeniable that Plan S has helped paved the way for it – and that its impact reaches far beyond academic publishing alone.

In early 2020, just as Plan S was rumoured to be losing some traction (and criticism continued abound), the Covid-19 crisis hit. Almost overnight, researchers from around the globe joined forces in a race to develop a vaccine, just as global leaders were forced to work together to strategise against this new threat to humanity. This turn of events has changed the way we think about and act upon information, possibly forever. It has also reinforced the founding principle of Plan S: to make the sharing of both publications and data the new normal.

In this final section, we will reflect on some of the changes taking place in publishing since Plan S – and find out what experts really think about them.

1. Transformative agreements: a valid solution?

There is no doubt that Plan S has accelerated the use of transformative deals to facilitate the transition to full and immediate open access. As explained in Part Two, a transformative deal is one whereby the publisher and consumer (i.e. library or institution) agree a new contract – typically known as a 'publish and read' deal – which is signed on the basis that the publisher is committed to transition its content to full OA in return for the fees paid by the subscriber. For an agreement to be considered 'transformative', it must contain binding conditions or mechanisms that (1) guarantee the full transition to 100 per cent OA within a defined, short timeframe and (2) guarantee that the process cannot be easily reversed or cancelled at the end of the contractual period. The agreement should encompass all the publisher's titles and include OA to legacy content.[111]

After the successful negotiations led by Gerard Meijer and his team in the Netherlands and Germany,[112] on 15 January 2019 Project DEAL signed a three-year contract with Wiley.[113] Under the agreement, researchers at more than 700

---

[111] Definition provided by Frontiers. *Current transformative agreements are not transformative*. Frontiers; 2020. Retrieved from https://blog.frontiersin.org/2020/03/10/current-transformative-agreements-are-not-transformative (accessed 14 March 2021).

[112] More on this in Part Two, 'Berlin 2018: a radical intervention'.

[113] Jobmann A. *Meaning and opportunities of the DEAL-Wiley contract for the open-access transformation*. National Contact Point Open Access OA 2020-DE; 2019. Retrieved from https://oa2020-de.org/en/blog/2019/03/18/meaning_opportunities_wileydeal_openaccesstransformation (accessed 14 March 2021).

German academic institutions were granted access to Wiley's journal content – including back catalogues dating back to 1997 – as well as the right to publish open access across all of the publisher's hybrid and gold open access journal portfolio.

The publish-and-read fee for Wiley was calculated at €2,750 per article for publications in hybrid journals. Authors are still required to pay an APC for publishing in a gold access journal, but with a 20 per cent discount on the existing price set by Wiley. On 22 August 2019, Project DEAL signed a similar agreement with Springer Nature to begin a new, three-year publish-and-read contract starting 1 January 2020.[114] At the time of writing, the organisation is yet to agree a deal with Elsevier.

Similar progress has been seen in other European countries, too. Jisc is the UK's primary expert body for digital technology and digital resources in higher education and research, and a key part of its work is to assist in negotiating licences and digital content agreements on behalf of UK universities and libraries. In 2020, a transformative 'publish-and-read' deal was finally struck between the UK consortia and Wiley after several years of negotiation.

Under the agreement, as of 2 March 2020, UK-based corresponding authors are given the option of publishing open access in Wiley journals at no extra cost to them – the overall aim being to increase the publisher's open access content to 100 per cent by 2022.[115] 'As a result of that deal, the number of articles being published open access has shot up from 27 per cent to around 85 per cent, which is huge,' says Liam Earney, director of digital resources at Jisc.[116]

What is also interesting is that, since doing the deal, Wiley has received more submissions to its journals from UK authors than ever before – a 26 per cent year-on-year increase, totalling nearly 33,000 submissions in 2020. Part of that is likely to be driven by Covid-19 – journals saw a spike in submissions during the pandemic, not just in immunology and other biomedical sciences but

---

[114] Springer Nature. *Projekt DEAL and Springer Nature reach understanding on world's largest transformative open access agreement*. Springer Nature; 2019. Retrieved from https://group.springernature.com/fr/group/media/press-releases/springer-nature-and-deal-reach-mou-on-largest-oa-agreement/17090258 (accessed 14 March 2021).

[115] Wiley. *Open access agreement for UK/Jisc institutions*. Wiley; n.d. Retrieved from https://authorservices.wiley.com/author-resources/Journal-Authors/open-access-affiliation-policies-payments/jisc-agreement.html (accessed 14 March 2021).

[116] Source: Jisc. *Jisc, UK institutions and Wiley agree ground-breaking deal*. Jisc; 2020. Retrieved from https://www.jisc.ac.uk/news/jisc-uk-institutions-and-wiley-agree-ground-breaking-deal-02-feb-2020 (accessed 14 March 2021).

across the board[117] – but Earney is confident that the spike also illustrates how, 'given the opportunity to publish openly, authors will do it. And if you can allow people to publish in the avenues they have historically published in behind a paywall, they seem very keen on OA indeed.'

A Wiley spokesperson adds, 'In 2020, we saw a 25 per cent year-over-year increase in article submissions globally. Some of the increase can be attributed to the COVID-19 pandemic, with the largest growth coming from pandemic-related subject areas like clinical medicine and epidemiology, as well as from business growth. That said, we believe strong demand to publish is here to stay.'

A mixed reception

Perhaps the most miraculous thing about transformative deals is that, after decades of bitter differences, they are something that a lot of stakeholders can agree on – not everyone, mind, but in the past three years or so they have proven to be a popular solution for both library consortia and publishers.

In the eyes of Daniel Ropers, former CEO for Springer Nature, transformative deals are the only realistic solution. 'I think by far the fastest route to getting the value of open access to the world of research is allowing the existing journals to migrate and support open access – and by far the fastest, easiest and cheapest route for the system to do this is to create this corridor,' he says. 'Yes, you can expect publishers to be articulate about what they want to achieve, to drive demand for open access – but you can't force them to guarantee there's 100 per cent demand. The publisher is not creating the demand; that's the funders and the researchers themselves. Publishers can drive it, but you can't make the publisher responsible for open access migration without coordinating that the funds to get published via open access will be available.'

In short, transformative deals offer a solution to one of the major blockages to publisher compliance with OA: cash flow. It makes sense that, in order for a contract negotiation to work in this way, each party must deliver a degree of compromise. For the libraries and other subscribers, part of the price to pay for a transformative deal is trust that the publisher will indeed deliver on its promises to migrate to full OA over time.

---

[117] Several studies across different disciplines suggest evidence of increased research activity during the Covid-19 pandemic. Two examples: Bell ML, Fong KC. Gender differences in first and corresponding authorship in public health research submissions during the COVID-19 pandemic. *American Journal of Public Health*. 2020; *111*(1): e1–e4. DOI: https://doi.org/10.2105/AJPH.2020.305975; Squazzoni F, Bravo G, Grimaldo F, García-Costa D, Farjam M, Mehmani B. No tickets for women in the COVID-19 race? A study on manuscript submissions and reviews in 2347 Elsevier journals during the pandemic. *SSRN Electronic Journal*. 2020. DOI: https://doi.org/10.2139/ssrn.3712813.

It is part of the reason why some remain sceptical about the method. The Open Access Scholarly Publishers Association (OASPA), based in the Netherlands, has been vocal in its concerns that the signing of large-scale publish-and-read contracts perpetuates the existing monopoly of academic publishers' biggest players. This, they argue, would put the smaller and more vulnerable scholarly society and emerging OA publishers at a 'significant disadvantage'.

Publishing its feedback to the Plan S consultation guidance in February 2019, OASPA said, 'Many [publishers] are not even of sufficient size to make agreements directly with institutions. For a healthy, competitive market in the longer term, the needs of fully open access publishers must not be overlooked … smaller publishers, learned societies and innovative new platforms will be at a significant disadvantage unless they are properly considered and steps are taken to ensure they are able to compete fairly in the market.'[118]

Even after years of consultation and planning to smooth the transition, many of these concerns have not gone away. 'I haven't seen one transformative agreement that's going to work for everybody,' says Maria Leptin, the former director of the life sciences organisation EMBO. 'Yes, the current transformative deals seen by the big publishers are fine. But then where does that leave the small independent journals? And where does that leave small countries that can't negotiate with all the publishers?'

Martin Eve, who chairs the Open Library of the Humanities (https://www.openlibhums.org), also has his reservations about the transformative deals being made with the likes of Springer and Wiley: 'Where's the contract that says they'll do it, is the first question. What are the consequences if they don't commit to transitioning in time – are they legally obliged to do this?'

Regarding the UK's deal with Wiley, he points out that 'the rates that they are asking for to make the transformative agreements are extortionate compared to continuing with just the old subscriptions – a 3 per cent rise was one of the prices we were quoted to carry on with just the subscription model, or 10 per cent increase if we wanted to do the transformative agreement. We simply can't afford a 10 per cent rise at a time of immense financial crisis in the higher education sector, and library budgets forecast to be slashed by 20 per cent in the UK. So my real worry is that the rates publishers are asking for these transformative agreements are set up to fail.'

He continues, 'It's ironic that it's a time when the need for OA couldn't be clearer, due in part to Covid-19, and yet we have a budgetary situation that's a massive contradiction while the big players are still increasing their prices at three times the rate of inflation. It's a crisis brewing.'

Publishing a joint position paper in March 2020, a group of pure OA publishers including Frontiers expressed concerns that 'large-scale publish-and-read

---

[118] Redhead C, OASPA. *OASPA feedback on Plan S implementation guidance.* OASPA; 2019. Retrieved from https://oaspa.org/oaspa-feedback-on-plan-s-implementation-guidance (accessed 14 March 2021).

deals lack the transformative conditions that are necessary to bring about the transition to OA'. The signatories called out what they referred to as the 'weak transformative potential of these large-scale agreements', which they claimed too often 'lack binding commitments to a full transformation to OA', limit access 'to selected parts of a publisher's portfolio' and contain variable conditions across national borders.

The group also argued that such deals 'crowd out pure OA publishers from institutional or national agreement negotiations ... Agreements of this type tie up large sums of public funding, they do not provide full OA to all the publishers' content and they do not contain a binding commitment to do so within a defined period.'[119]

Speaking a year on, in 2021, Kamila Markram, CEO and co-founder of Frontiers, stands by that statement. 'I remember the optimism at the announcement of Plan S almost three years ago; there was a real sense that publishing was finally moving into the 21st century,' she says. 'There was a new emphasis on universal access, cost transparency, and the end of unreasonable commercial practices ... It was a systemic shift designed to improve the way we as a society manage knowledge and optimise innovation and well-being. Today, however, I am less optimistic.'

More than this, Markram suggests that the Plan S branding is in some cases being misused in order to promote what she believes are poor deals, even feeding the root of the problem: 'To use an analogy, subsidising subscription publishers to transform to open access with indeterminate outcomes using taxpayers' money is like awarding large public supplier contracts to traditional car manufacturers whose entire operation is pegged around fossil fuels. It's like asking them to start building clean energy engines while superior clean energy options already exist elsewhere. Imagine asking an innovative organisation like Tesla to wait in line with their fully electric cars and better value proposition, while organisations that have not invested in newer, cleaner technology are allowed to play catch-up, financed by taxpayers.'

Asked what she believes should be happening instead, Markram replies: 'More transparency and a level playing field in the publishing market. That would be the much-needed contribution of public policies such as Plan S.' And key to this, she adds, is empowering those who work in and contribute to the industry with more information about how the publishing system operates. 'Authors and libraries need the information and the freedom to choose the service that best fits their requirement,' she says. 'If, instead of having to carry the baggage of historical legacies and costs, they have the necessary information and budgets available to make better decisions.

---

[119] *Current transformative agreements are not transformative.* Frontiers; 2020. Retrieved from https://frontiersinblog.files.wordpress.com/2020/03/position-statement-transformative-agreements.pdf (accessed 14 March 2021).

'This requires two things: close monitoring of the effects of transformative agreements, and shifting funds away from outdated legacy deals towards budgets that can be used to pay for the service that offers the best value proposition. The transparency that has come to be expected of open access should be mandated throughout the publishing industry, giving fully open access publishers equal treatment, and allowing for greater public scrutiny of how public money is being spent.'

Of course it is possible that, from a business perspective, challenger publishers like Frontiers feel the pressure placed on them by transformative deals because they have the potential to make the OA market more crowded. Launching from the get-go as a pure OA model gave Frontiers a unique selling point – if traditional subscription-based publishers join them on the boat, will their unique appeal begin to sink?

Markram contests this theory: 'We see competition as the solution, not the problem,' she says. 'A full flip of the system to open access is the best possible outcome. Once this happens, the quality of services and their prices can be compared transparently and fairly across all journals and publishers. This transparency will determine where authors want to publish and where public funds should be allocated. We welcome competition because open science is in everyone's best interest.'

The problem is that, inevitably, not all market competition is 'fair', she caveats – and the rules of competition also vary between country and region. 'Unfortunately, in many countries extremely strict criteria are applied to new innovative entrants to the academic publishing market, while incumbents are protected through large publish-and-read deals,' she notes. 'This has created a separate class of new innovative players, whose margins are already small, while cosy big-deals protect the oligopolies of old. This problem will persist for as long as traditional publishing and open access publishing are treated as different markets and different standards are applied to them, which is not in the public interest.'

Finding a way to successfully merge the new and the old will therefore be the greatest and more important challenge in order to create a fairer marketplace. Many stakeholders feel there should be room enough in the sector for both these challenger OA publishers and older legacy publishers once they are transformed – and part of the solution here will be allowing the publishing process itself to evolve, says Johan Rooryck: 'Ultimately I think we should move to a system where payments are made on an article basis,' he says, 'but where the amount paid is dependent on the size of the institution or the country – a globally equitable system in which the payment is completely invisible to the researcher.'

Without sufficient movement, the publish-and-read deals being drawn up now risk becoming another halfway obstacle to slow to transition down, just like hybrid journals. This is another concern of Markram's, as she argues that 'traditional publishers can now offer options that comply with Plan S without radically changing their business. Plan S has opened new pathways to compliance by allowing hybrid journals under transformative agreements. This is a problem.'

Here again, she warns that publish-and-read deals contain hidden challenges, in that pledges made to transition will be difficult to police and monitor across international borders. 'Transformative agreements only cover the country they apply to,' she explains. 'Most countries don't have transformative agreements with all publishers, which means open access will not be a universal standard and conditions will vary, adding to the already problematic lack of transparency.'

But the key difference here is that transformative agreements have a strict deadline: full OA must be reached by 2024 in order for the deals to meet Plan S guidelines. The bigger question is, of course, how the actions taken towards meeting this deadline will be monitored.

'Transformative deals are far from perfect, and they are sometimes very expensive, but let's not forget that we are trying to move from a system from publishing deals to publish-and-read, and in the ideal case you want that to be cost neutral – you don't want shocks through the system,' says Rooryck. 'The deals are imperfect because you have to go country by country, consortium by consortium and, very slowly in the transition, reach OA. But once that is done you come to a system that people can live with and will invent new mechanisms for payment of publishing services.'

For Daniel Ropers, it is these kinds of reservations that further demonstrate the need for publishers to be clear on their intentions – and ensure their intentions run deeper than just individual contracts. 'I think all these things are now starting to move. People understand that there needs to be a certain pacing, that if you want an open access migration to be fast, you need to embrace the transformative publisher model – not just a transformative journal model – the transformative deals where a publisher says, "I'm going to do all these things and drive my whole portfolio". The ability to row in open access to offset the decline in income, or to get income via read-and-publish deals, it's an insanely risky thing for publishers, but it's necessary for them to do it to help drive the change.'

Kamila Markram believes the transition to a better system is within our reach – through the establishment of fair competition in the marketplace. 'We need to give authors the power to choose which partner will provide the best value for its services. This will significantly improve the way science is published and drive the virtuous cycle of innovation across all of society. Let's move beyond the "big deal" mentality and let taxpayers, administrators and scientists see openly how scientific knowledge can be disseminated in this 21st century.'

2. New publishing platforms

Since the rules on Plan S were laid out in earnest, new opportunities for innovation have been seized by the research and business sectors alike. The evidence for this can be seen in the number of challenger platforms and innovative start-ups being established. In 2018, Swedish researchers launched SciFree,[120] a journal search tool software connecting universities and their researchers to known and lesser-known OA publishing platforms across the world. It's just one example in a growing industry of researcher-led OA networks.

In November 2020, OASPA founded a new organisation designed to future-proof governance and funding structures for OA publishing. Its 'OA Switchboard' initiative is a not-for-profit collaboration between funders and institutions to provide essential infrastructure, standards and back-office service – which organisers hope will assist in the transition of the market towards open access.

'OA business models are becoming more and more diverse, some with or without individual publication fees, some through agreements, some through sponsorship models,' a statement from OASPA said. Part of the solution to coordinating OA efforts, therefore, is by having intermediary bodies: 'The OA Switchboard … is a central information exchange hub, connecting parties and systems, streamlining communication and the neutral exchange of OA related publication-level information, and ensuring a financial settlement can be done.'[121]

Such initiatives are all positive progress in the eyes of Plan S coordinators – they demonstrate not only researchers' appetite to reach full OA but also the desire from the stakeholder communities to assist in getting there.

'The great thing about Coalition S is that for the first time we have got funders working together on a common policy. And that's what makes a difference,' says the Wellcome Trust's Robert Kiley, who also holds the role of Coalition S coordinator. 'Before, we did things slightly differently, each in silo. And obviously, with a common policy, everyone's had to compromise a little bit. Not everyone's got exactly what they wanted, but basically we've ended up with a common set of principles and the publishers can make a choice as to whether they wish to publish research funded by cOAlition S funders or not.'

3. Copyright reigns supreme …

Arguably the most important legacy of Plan S is the implementation of its rights retention strategy (RRS). On 15 July 2020, the Coalition released a statement announcing the new mandate, which it said would give researchers supported

---

[120] See more at https://scifree.se/scifree-jst.
[121] Folan B, OASPA. *OASPA founds new organisation with future-proof governance and funding structure for the OA switchboard.* OASPA; 2020. Retrieved from https://oaspa.org/oaspa-founds-new-organisation-with-future-proof-governance-and-funding-structure-for-the-oa-switchboard (accessed 14 March 2021).

by Plan S funders 'the freedom to publish in their journal of choice, including subscription journals, whilst remaining fully compliant with Plan S'.

Under the new strategy agreement, Coalition S member organisations agree to facilitate this by changing their grant conditions to require that 'a Creative Commons Attribution licence (CC BY) is applied to all Author Accepted Manuscripts or Versions of Record reporting original research, supported in whole or in part by their funding'. In short, the mandate means that publishers no longer have the automatic right to keep the rights to the author's work upon publication.[122]

In Kiley's view, it is this principle that means any persisting argument that Plan S impacts on author freedom is rendered null. 'People's fear of losing their academic freedom comes from the idea that they won't be able to submit their article to their journal of choice, because they don't want to be in breach of the rules,' he explains. 'But that's why the rights retention strategy is so effective, because it doesn't matter what copyright conditions that journal puts in place, the agreement you have with your Plan S-compliant funder – that the work must be made open immediately upon publication – predates the publishers' demands.'

The worried author might well respond to this with the concern that the journal could decide to reject the author's submission on that basis, as is their right. But Kiley feels confident that this outcome is unlikely – after all, Wellcome is one of the largest funding agencies in the world. If the journal decided to reject all Wellcome-funded articles on the basis that they disagreed with Plan S and could not make the work OA, the journal would effectively be closing itself off to a large section of the world's best research. The concept works on a much wider scale, of course, when taking into consideration all the major funders that have signed up to Plan S.

'The publishers saying, "All this great content, I don't want to see it"? I just don't believe that will be the case. So does Plan S limit author freedom? No, I don't think so,' says Kiley. As ever, Wellcome is continuing to monitor the outcome of where its funded work ends up being published – and he is confident that, six months after Plan S is implemented, 'it will pretty much look as it always did. They will be publishing in all the usual places.'

In fact, the power of the copyright refusal has already been tried and tested by Harvard University for many years. 'And *Science* and *Nature* just accept it,' says Stan Gielen, president of the Dutch research council NWO until April 2021. 'If you submit your paper to them, you will not be asked to sign for copyright transfer because they know Harvard imposes the rule that you are the owner

---

[122] Coalition S. *Plan S Rights Retention Strategy | Plan S*. Coalition S; n.d. Retrieved from https://www.coalition-s.org/rights-retention-strategy (accessed 14 March 2021).

of your copyright. The publishers are not in a position to say, "Ok, we will not accept papers from Harvard anymore."

Martin Eve feels similarly enthusiastic about the RRS in that he believes it will help to 'normalise' the idea of academic authors keeping their copyright – eventually: 'Ripple effects take a long time so it's not going to change things overnight.'

To suggest that the new policy can fix what is an already broken system completely would be falsely optimistic, however. An unavoidable limitation of the rights retention initiative is that it only applies to new research being submitted. As Eve points out, one of the biggest challenges presented by the monopoly of the big five commercial publishers is that 'they already own the copyright to almost all existing research, which means it's very late to be putting the stopper back in the bottle.'

By EU law, nobody apart from the individual 'has the right to make their work public or reproduce it'. But, because academic authors have historically signed away any rights or ownership of the papers they submit to a journal to be published, commercial publishers typically own that copyright for 70 years after the last corresponding author has died.[123] 'For the foreseeable future, the vast majority of research copyright is owned by those big international corporations, and they can do what they like with it,' says Eve. 'They can make it OA, or withdraw access and take it offline – it's up to them entirely. OA models with open licences mitigate this to some extent because if it's a CC-CY licence then anyone can copy it and put it somewhere else, so it's quite hard for them to then take it away at any future point. But the vast majority of material is not openly licensed OA at the moment.'

What's shocking is that researchers are partly to blame for the lack of movement surrounding copyright in particular – at least from Eve's experience working with humanities scholars. 'There are cultural challenges around licensing,' he explains. 'The one historians always use, which is somewhat ridiculous to my ears, is that if we put things out under CC BY licences, bad people like neo-Nazis will take their words, alter them to make it look like they said something else, then put it out there. I tend to point out to them that neo-Nazis are likely to behave badly anyway ... The fact is that they are not great respecters of copyright law in the first place, so if you really think they've read the detail clauses of the licence and thought, "Ah, here's our opportunity," then you might be mistaken.'

---

[123] Your Europe. *Copyright in the EU: How to get copyright protection.* Your Europe; n.d. Retrieved from https://europa.eu/youreurope/business/running-business/intellectual-property/copyright/index_en.htm#:~:text=Nobody%20apart%20from%20you%20has (accessed 14 March 2021).

... But publishers won't give up copyright without a fight

Publishers, too, feel sceptical about the RRS – albeit for different reasons. Springer Nature's chief publishing officer, Steven Inchcoombe, is particularly vocal in concerns that 'the only purpose of having the RRS is to support green OA' – a route he believes 'undermines' the work that publishers do and forces them to keep investing in paywalled content. Given that the accepted manuscripts typically published on preprint servers are a 'work-in-progress version', Inchcoombe argues that 'free and immediate access to them by the public and general media could even damage trust in science'.

All this leads on to his reasons for distrusting the RRS: 'There is no point in having rights retention placed on gold OA, because the day the article is published it's immediately available to everybody with a CC licence. So why would you want to retain rights to a prior version – who on earth would ever use that?'

The claim that RRS protects the author is also false because it is near impossible for a journal to remove their work from the public sphere once published, he argues: 'The only thing a journal can do is to retract an article. And there it has to be for very legitimate reasons. So you can never retract an article for business model reasons and you can't, once you've published something CC, rescind that. So no, the only reason for RRS is to support green OA, and this is where it will really go very wrong.'

The RRS also ignores the work put into a published article by the editors and all those who work within the publishing chain, he says: '[RRS] means the authors are wanting to claim rights on this accepted version of a manuscript, which is a place where more than 50 per cent of the investment of publishers is taking place and where all that quality assurance occurs. Publishers can't just give that away, or they would be out of business. This is a major point of friction that I think will need to be resolved in the coming months.'

Those in favour of RRS point out that its existence alone offers much-needed reassurance to researchers that, whatever happens to their work, they won't lose their rights to it. Inchcoombe doesn't buy it: 'We have been talking extensively to researchers and they have been completely confused by it. There have been no significant numbers of active researchers asking for this – it's a mechanism that the funding bodies are trying to use as a stick to hit publishers with, but it's actually a means of confusing everybody and, if we are not careful, undermines the very progress that we are starting to make with genuine [gold] OA.'

It would be easy to accuse a spokesperson for one of the world's major publishing bodies of simply defending the company purse, but Inchcoombe insists his beliefs are led by the scientific community he works alongside: 'We have been consulting widely on it. If this is what scientists really wanted, we would have to find a way, but they are saying no, that's not what we want at all.'

He continues, 'We are not asking authors to transfer the copyright of the submitted article to us, we leave it with the author, so that's not what this is about. It's about claiming rights in and controlling access to the accepted version of the article, which is where the peer reviewers, the editors and the authors have all contributed and it's substantially different from the original submitted manuscript. And if it wasn't substantially different the funders wouldn't be interested in trying to claim rights over it or to take control over access to it.'

As a long-time spokesperson for Springer Nature and well versed in the publishing debate, Inchcoombe is a big character. He is known for being outspoken in his views and is no stranger to stirring up debate in the press. It feels worth noting that he and Jasmin Lange, Brill's director, are two very different personalities. And, yet, the two share similar views, which seems indicative that the RRS discrepancy will not disappear anytime soon.

'I was really disappointed about the RRS when it was published,' says Lange. 'We want to transition this system away from subscriptions towards open access but heavily marketing the accepted manuscript with a CC BY licence, I think, is completely unacceptable, as it doesn't appreciate whatsoever the right of publishers to get back the investments they made in getting the article to the accepted manuscript stage.'

Like Inchcoombe, she too views the presentation of the RRS as misleading: 'It was framed as if authors are getting back control, but actually what Coalition S has done is they have devised a blanket policy to [put] the rights of the author into the hands of the user – so I felt this was completely wrong. Authors understand that, with the CC BY licence on their accepted manuscript, all rights to their manuscript are with the user and not in their own hands anymore.'

One caveat we would add to this, for transparency's sake, is that the CC BY licence does require that original authors must be credited for the work if and when their research is reused in any form.

It is clear that the disagreements surrounding the RRS stem deeper, however. Since meeting with Robert-Jan very early on in the planning process for Coalition S, Lange has been heavily involved in consultation between the funders and small- to medium-sized business community. She has also been an active participant in price transparency workshops run with Plan S members to determine fair APCs for journals, among other things. That publishers were not consulted on the RRS feels like a personal slight, therefore.

'I feel the RRS was not presented correctly and I was disappointed about this. There was also no consultation going on whatsoever, which is something that they have done in the past really well,' she says. 'It was just thrown out there with a big press release and social media campaign with this [sense of] "now you publishers deal with it" ... and they probably have done it because they understand that no publisher could ever accept this, I mean, at least not if you believe in certain principles of publishing. That was their choice, but we're not going to comply with the CC BY request; that's really a step too far and I don't really understand what the vision behind it is.'

Both Lange and Inchcoombe have spoken publicly about possible alternatives and variations to the CC BY licence promoted by the RRS, for instance CC BY-NC-ND, which only allows others to download the published work and share it with others if the author is credited, and prevents the content from being changed or used commercially. In contrast, the CC BY licence lets others distribute, edit and build upon the authors' work, including commercially, as long as the original author is credited.

On 3 February 2021, a statement published by the International Association of Scientific, Technical and Medical Publishers (STM) and signed by a number of its members called on Coalition S to reconsider the RRS's approach. 'The Rights Retention Strategy ignores long-standing academic freedoms and will work against the shared objective of a more open and equitable scholarly ecosystem,' the statement read. 'It provides an immediate free substitute that eliminates the ability to charge for the services that publishers provide, whether via subscriptions or Article Publishing Charges. As such, the Rights Retention Strategy is not financially sustainable and undermines potential support for open access journals.'[124]

To this, Rooryck (now executive director for the Coalition) published a response with Robert Kiley saying that the statement 'continues to perpetuate a number of myths and errors' surrounding the RRS. 'While we do not underestimate the value that publishers add to the process, we point out that peer review is conducted on a voluntary basis by the research community,' they added. Counter to any claims the RRS impinges on academic freedom, Kiley and Rooryck argue it 'restores long-standing academic freedoms, in that it asserts the authors' ownership of their publication after peer review, to reuse and share as they please. It is up to the publishers to demonstrate the added value of the Version of Record [i.e. the article published in one of their journals], for which Coalition S funders are willing to pay.'[125]

Their response to STM also came with a warning: 'The Rights Retention Strategy is now a contractual grant condition for Coalition S grantees. It would be a matter of significant concern if we saw the publishers encouraging Coalition S grantees to violate their contractual obligations with their funder.'

The debate continues.

3.2 Reimagining publisher business models

Plan S has forced academic publishers big and small to rethink their approach to cost and profit. And, while the road for small- to medium-sized publishers in particular has not always been smooth, many have demonstrated that it is

---

[124] STM. *Rights Retention Strategy*. STM; 2021. Retrieved from https://www.stm-assoc.org/rightsretentionstrategy (accessed 14 March 2021).

[125] Coalition S. *cOAlition S response to the STM statement: the Rights Retention Strategy restores long-standing academic freedoms | Plan S.* Coalition S; 2021. Retrieved from https://www.coalition-s.org/blog/the-rights-retention-strategy-restores-long-standing-academic-freedoms (accessed 14 March 2021).

indeed possible to make the transition to OA even when working with much smaller budgets and resources.

For Jasmin Lange and the journals Brill works with, transformative deals are what makes this possible. 'We have made a lot of progress, closing three transformative deals in 2020–21,' she says. 'And that was in part because we felt the sense of urgency – for us this is the only way to be Plan S-compliant, so it's really important for us to close these deals, and I think librarians felt the same way, at least in the very proactive countries we work with like Sweden, the Netherlands, UK, Austria, Switzerland … I mean, these are really open access-minded countries.'

That's not to say the transition has been easy across the board, however. 'In other places there is no such development at all for small- or medium-sized publishers – in some countries, we're still waiting for the market to move and if there's no interest we can't really close any transformative deals,' she cautions.

Meanwhile, business is booming for Brill: the company increased its OA billing by 87 per cent in 2020, which Lange says is 'brilliant', pun unintended, but notes that 'the base from which we have increased OA is low compared to the bigger publishers'. As of February 2021, OA content in Brill journals sits at around 10 per cent, and its OA book publishing content is around 6 per cent of the total. The spike doesn't equate to high profits, either, not that Lange expected it to. 'The percentage of our total income coming from OA publishing was about 4 per cent in 2020 – we are doing fine, but compare this with Springer Nature or Elsevier and you will note that as a humanities and social sciences publisher we are lagging behind significantly.'

'Revenue increases have been very modest because we have lost a lot of print sales and, of course, if we do business in OA book publishing, we don't sell eBooks, for example – it's one or the other,' she adds. 'But the model is growing fast.'

Lange anticipates the number of OA articles published through Brill journals will continue to rise – albeit at a slightly steadier pace – and feels mostly positive about the transition so far: 'I expect OA revenue to grow by another 20 per cent maybe in 2021, which shows that activity is increasing enormously.' But it is early days, and it remains unclear just how resilient small businesses will be to the transition in the longer term.

'We're managing it while going our own way and trying to work with policies and mandates of all the funders,' says Lange. 'I would say it has triggered us to really be more proactive with transformative agreements and to continue setting up full open access journals, which is really positive – but it has not transformed the business yet. We're not just going to accommodate Plan S; we're trying to accommodate all the various funders and funding schemes which are out there … and sometimes we might have to say no if we think a particular policy is harming our business in the long term.'

The RRS already presents one such red flag – and Lange is open in admitting she has no intentions of adhering to the rule in its current guise. Time will tell how this particular conflict plays out, but it is clear that, as a humanities and social sciences publisher with relatively large international reach, Brill has a loyal community of researchers behind it that will help to secure its future to some extent. Smaller, independent and society publishers have a tougher time ahead since they will struggle to get a seat at the table to negotiate transformative deals, she notes.

'If I was a really small publisher with a diverse programme, I think I would try to look for some sort of corporation with other small publishers and go for these transformative agreements together – find, say, 10 publishers with a similar profile and similar customer base and then one external party who can work with you on that,' says Lange. 'In today's market you have to be creative on the publishing side; you can't expect others to solve these issues for you.'

Working together to form a collective was exactly what Robert-Jan had suggested to the society publishers when he met with them in London, at a meeting organised by Stuart Taylor, publishing director of the Royal Society. Not only would collaborating give them a seat at the table in negotiations; it would also allow them to cut costs by setting up a common printing service, he pointed out.

'But the reason why these small society publishers did not line up and cooperate was, in my opinion, that they were comfortable working in silos,' he says. 'They had simply been doing their own thing for hundreds of years, so why should they give up their traditional way of working?'

Taylor had arranged the meeting because he was very conscious of the worries some of the smaller societies had regarding the provisions of Plan S. The meeting also provided the Wellcome Trust with the opportunity to share information on their own project, set up to 'identify routes through which learned society publishers could successfully transition to open access and align with Plan S'.

'This was not the only occasion where the Royal Society played an important role with regard to Plan S and its implementation,' says Robert-Jan. 'At an earlier stage the society had developed its own "royal" route for becoming Plan S-compliant and made it known to many learned societies that compliance with the provisions of the plan was perhaps not easy, but still possible.'

The Royal Society had also reached out to Robert-Jan when Plan S was still on the drawing board, making a convincing case that, for monographs and books, outlets more often used in social sciences and humanities research, more time was needed beyond the 2020 deadline to transition to full and immediate open access.

The big five today: appetite for change?

Daniel Ropers left Springer and the publishing world in 2019, partly, he explains, because he saw a challenge ahead that would take many years to work through – years he had not factored in when agreeing to take the role of CEO in the first place. And yet Ropers feels positive about the changes in attitudes coming from the industry. He is less positive about the international coordination of transformative models, however. 'The problem is people always want to have the cake and eat it. So you could migrate all the US to open access, if the US research industry would be willing to pay the same amount for the publishing volume that they are paying for the subscription, right? And you could get all the other territories to agree that, although the US content is now open access, they would still pay the same amount for a subscription.

'But the latter are unlikely to do it. And, actually, the former are also unlikely to do it, because they'll be looking and saying, "Hey, but if I take the subscription payments from all of China and divide them by the number of Chinese articles, China might only pay €1,000 per article." If you do the same calculation on the US market, you might find out that Americans end up paying €4,000–5,500 per article that they get published. And yet it's the same work that's being done. So will America accept that it has to pay that much more than China? It's difficult.'

The public consultation on Plan S guidelines (contributions for which were collated in February 2019) gave publishers and stakeholders further opportunity to speak their minds with regard to the Coalition's proposals – this time in a public forum. As detailed in Part Two, the consultation was broad, attracting more than 600 responses from academic groups and publishers, representative bodies and individuals. For Marc Schiltz, president of Science Europe, the results of that consultation marked a 'very important milestone' in that he felt a sudden shift in attitudes from the major commercial players.

'There were concerns and some very valid criticisms, and we amended the plan accordingly – for instance by expanding the deadline for compliance to January 2021,' he says. 'Though I have to say, by and large, in those hundreds of responses there was an overwhelming agreement that we have to do something, make a big change to reach full OA. So, from the moment when we presented the revised version, I felt there was an agreement within the scholarly community and many publishers for the first time as well.

'I think at that time it became clear to what I call the legacy publishers that Plan S will not go away. They had resisted and brushed us off, but from that point in 2019 you could clearly see the shift in the course of communication – the attitudes from publishers changed from outright rejection to more of an acceptance. Still very critical – but kind of starting a dialogue. They began to take us seriously, realising they had no choice but to engage in the movement with us.'

Looking back to those first, exceedingly tense meetings between Robert-Jan and the larger commercial publishers before the launch of Plan S, it is clear the relationship between academics, publishers and indeed policymakers has improved tenfold. Nevertheless, it will take time for the culture wars – that 'them vs us' attitude – to subside completely.

'I wouldn't go so far as saying the relationship is friendly; that would be an overstatement,' says Schiltz. 'When even the key principle of protecting an author's right to intellectual ownership of his or her manuscript is challenged, what does that say about the publishers' attitudes? We agreed there are costs, we actually put money on the table to pay for it. But with conditions,' he adds. 'They come to us with their problems saying we have to pay all these professional editors, we do this and that … and I just say that's not our problem. There are new constraints; their customers have new expectations. In any other business, if you don't meet these expectations you are out of business. And that's something which is absolutely not accepted by some of the legacy publishers.'

Rooryck largely shares Schiltz's sentiments. He feels positive that 'publishers have really moved along, Springer Nature in particular I think has really changed. But Elsevier Elsevier is still lagging behind and looking increasingly concerning.'

This book has already illustrated through interviews across the field just how poorly many researchers feel towards the dominant commercial publishers. But, when Ropers joined Springer in 2017, he saw this conflict from the other side. 'My parents are both scientists, so that was I think part of the reason why I couldn't resist the opportunity to lead the second largest public research publisher in the world. I felt that this was a unique opportunity to help with what I believe to be one of the most important things in the world, which is fundamental knowledge creation and the dissemination of that knowledge to be used to improve the world.'

Another key reason for his decision to join was the impression that 'Springer Nature was by far the leader in open access. To me, it didn't take a lot of thinking to get to the notion that paying for content behind a paywall was an anachronism coming from the paper subscription age, and that actually if you could change this movement of payment from the output [i.e. readers paying for access] to the input [paying to publish] then there would be a huge amount of value created just as a result of it.

'The total amount of money spent would have been roughly the same, but the actual value – through accessibility of that content – would increase dramatically. You don't have to be a genius to understand that that's a great idea, and I haven't come across anybody in my two years at Springer Nature or in research that didn't feel that, if we could draw the whole system from scratch anew, we would probably do exactly that. No one would have to pay for using content or considering reading it.'

To meet Ropers is to witness a mind that works at 10 times the normal human speed; he went on to explain the complex and exacting mathematical formulas by which he had calculated how the shift to full OA could be possible for the company. His intention to help push the company towards full OA, and rapidly, was therefore pure – if a little naively optimistic. What he hadn't prepared himself for was the internal squabble taking place between the two sides of research.

'What I quickly discovered was that the number one reason for people to want open access was not to reduce costs – which I think will happen – or to expand their visibility … it was actually to kind of get even with the publishers that they felt for one reason or another have not done a good job in selling them over the past decades,' he says. 'I was shocked by it. To be honest, I thought I was joining this group of people who, by definition, are very smart people – if you choose a career in fundamental science and research, you must be interested in finding truth; you must be interested in understanding complex mechanisms and systems. And here I was talking to these people that had a career in science, and it was like a schoolyard fight.'

He continues, 'It was as if everybody had just ganged up on [publishing], to focus on the perceived unfair profitability or the perceived power of publishers. It was not about the value of open access at all. I was shocked by it, because it seemed so fundamentally irrational, and I believe this was one of the core reasons why open access had not been proliferating fast enough.'

It is true that OA is an emotive topic for many – and there are certainly a vocal minority who are of the opinion that such large-scale publishers do not deserve to exist at all. But, stripped back to its core, the bullish persona of the commercial publisher is arguably nothing more than the defence mechanism of a company fighting to remain consistent in its profitability and success – as any animal does. 'To me it starts more fundamentally,' says Ropers. 'Imagine you are part of a system, and there are tons of ways to improve the system, but the people you must do it with tell you that whatever you propose the outcome must be, then you can no longer exist. And even if part of this is emotional, and part of it is people saying this is down to your own actions of the past … if the end result of any new system must be that you don't exist anymore, it's just highly unlikely for this individual entity to then play along. It's highly likely they will do everything they can to stop the change.'

Time for another analogy: 'My parents wanted me to tidy my room, but this was not something I liked to do – my parents' threshold for thinking my room was untidy was way before I felt, as a kid, that my room was untidy. So there needs to be some kind of motivation to do it. If you tell a child to clean their room, and there's a reward if they do, or a punishment if they don't – then they're going to spend the next 10 minutes cleaning their room. Conversely, no one's going to say, "you have to clean your room, and once it's done we're going to put you up for adoption." This is not how you get people to agree on change.'

Steven Inchcoombe is used to being asked to defend his company's profits – it comes as part of the territory. But he believes that, when it comes to publishers' agendas, 'nobody now is trying to support the status quo. Even the most successful publishers are adapting and that means giving up some of their historic levels of success.'

While he insists that Springer's profit margins are 'nothing like some others' – i.e. Elsevier – part of the reason for that can be attributed to the company's efforts to transition to OA. 'We have been on this journey for the best part of 20 years and we have spent a lot of money on OA – which is one of the reasons we have become less profitable. But that is the path we chose to go down because we thought it was the future, and therefore we wanted to be ready for the future rather than end up playing catch-up and putting the sustainability of our business at risk.'

> ### Case study: University of California
>
> Jeffrey Mackie-Mason had been aware of the OA movement for decades, but became actively involved in campaigning for it when he took up his role as dean of libraries for the University of California, Berkeley, in 2015. With a background in economics, he had recognised the changes taking place in the publishing industry due to the rise in digital distributions. 'It was always clear to me it was better for science, the right thing to do as long as we could afford it, and the emergence of the internet made it feasible economically,' he says.
>
> UC is huge, stretching across 10 campuses and producing 10 per cent of all US academic research papers. The largest public university system in the US, UC's research activity gives the same clout and scale as the entire research system in some European countries. Here, Mackie-Mason saw an opportunity: what if he were to publicly challenge some of the commercial publishers on their subscription charges, leading the way for fairer contracts going forward?
>
> 'Scholarly communications is a responsibility of the library, so naturally it became strategic for me to push back on subscription publishing. Given that the University of California was one of the leading institutions in the US pushing for OA before that, it was a ripe environment,' he says.[126] 'I wanted to make a mark somehow for Berkeley and for scholarship in my role as a leader and it seemed like a great opportunity. It combined my expertise as an economist and my long history of being involved with digital information ... and we happened to be coming to the end of our contract with Elsevier. All these things came together.'
>
> Mackie-Mason put his idea to colleagues, the other deans of libraries at UC. 'I said to them, we don't like the contracts we have with the big publishers, we're not happy with the progress on OA. Why don't we just

---

[126] UC Office of the President. *UC terminates subscriptions with world's largest scientific publisher in push for open access to publicly funded research.* University of California; 2019. Retrieved from https://www.universityof california.edu/press-room/uc-terminates-subscriptions-worlds-largest -scientific-publisher-push-open-access-publicly (accessed 14 March 2021).

cancel our contract and use our buying power to put some pressure on them? And I was told I would be fired the next day.'

Colleagues worried that faculty members would 'revolt' if the contracts were cancelled and they lost access to their work – and the strong existing democratic governance system at UC meant that the faculty had the power to get Mackie-Mason fired from his libraries role if they deemed it necessary. 'But I said, "that's ok, I'm willing to take that risk".'

Mackie-Mason also had the advantage of tenure, which meant, even if he got fired by common demand from his librarian role, he would keep his job as professor. But his experience working as a faculty member meant he was also confident that fellow academics would do the right thing.

In February 2019, after two years of planning and six months of failed negotiations, UC cancelled its $11 million (USD) a year contract with Elsevier, sending shockwaves through the academic world. The decision meant that UC scholars were no longer able to access Elsevier Elsevier's vast troves of publications (legally, anyway) but, to the deans' and publishers' surprise, the university's 227,000-strong faculty reacted well to this, expressing their support for the UC library team – even more so than Mackie-Mason had anticipated.[127]

'UC is progressive,' he says. 'We have a very long history of pushing for OA – not just among the librarians but also among the faculty, which is very important because they are, after all, the ones who are writing the articles; they are the ones reading them. The other thing is that UC is a public university: that's common in Europe but not so much in the US. It's a public university which has a very deep commitment to its public role and sees itself as being here to promote the public interest – so there's sort of this political or social activism ethos to the university that means that between the administration and faculty and the librarians, we all sort of are aligned in our interests and our views, which enabled us to build a really strong coalition.'

UC was by no means the first to question its publishing deal with big commercial players – following on from Germany's example in its Pro-

(Continued)

---

[127] Baken P. University of California defiant as Elsevier cuts journal access. *Times Higher Education.* 2019. Retrieved from https://www.timeshighereducation.com/news/university-california-defiant-elsevier-cuts-journal-access (accessed 14 March 2021).

ject DEAL negotiations, several European consortia opted not to renew their contracts with Elsevier and others between 2018 and 2019. But the size of the US institution meant the move held gravitas and set a precedent for negotiations going forward.

'Cancelling contracts does cause disruption, there's no doubt about it,' Mackie-Mason admits. 'It's hurtful to the faculty and to the students. I often use the metaphor – not because I like it so much as people get it quickly – but it's like going to war. And in war you make short-term goals and long-term sacrifices. As in any well-run war you try to protect the civilians as much as possible but there is rationing … they can't get quick access to the journal articles they want and so they are unhappy. They have to believe in the mission and the long-term goal for the war to work, and we spent a lot of time preparing for that and getting people on board.'

Speaking in early January 2021, Mackie-Mason feels hopeful that the long-standing stalemate between UC and Elsevier may soon be over, however. Negotiations reopened in September 2020, and he is 'cautiously optimistic' that an agreement will be reached this time. What's changed to hopefully make this possible is publisher attitudes, he says: 'We have held our line steady throughout, there are no changes to our demands.' The fact that the university has successfully signed a transformative agreement with Springer Nature also bodes well. 'Basically, our position has gotten stronger and Elsevier Elsevier's has gotten weaker,' he says. 'They have seen we can withstand the cancellation: we are now two years in and we haven't fallen apart. And they are seeing their competitors signing deals with us. So we are feeling quite strong and demanding the same things we were two years ago.'

Sure enough, after two years of stalemate, on 16 March 2021 UC announced a landmark, four-year open access publishing agreement with Elsevier – the largest such agreement in North America to date. 'As of 1 April 2021, all research with a UC lead author published in Elsevier's hybrid and open access journals will be open access by default, so that everyone in the world can read it for free,' a statement from the university read. 'The agreement delivers on the University's two faculty-supported goals [https://senate.universityofcalifornia.edu/_files/reports/rm-jn-transform-scholarly-communication-declaration-2019.pdf] for all publisher agreements: securing universal open access to UC research and reducing projected costs by integrating library and author payments into a single contract.'

Commenting on the announcement, Mackie-Mason said the negotiations reached a 'turning point' when Elsevier came back to UC 'with an attitude of wanting to work with us to find common ground'.

> 'We had a terrific UC coalition with a really clear strategic plan,' he added. 'This was teamwork. We had a systemwide working group of 18 people — librarians, faculty and staff representing the whole system … We can now tell our colleagues that it's over.'[128]
>
> 'Our agreement with UC delivers a real win for the world-class researchers across the UC system, supporting them to publish open access in Elsevier journals and access high-quality, trusted research by others,' said Kumsal Bayazit, CEO of Elsevier. 'Both sides showed flexibility to reach a truly tailored approach, based on the needs of the research-intensive UC community, so we can test and learn from author choices and enable a sustainable transition to universal open access to UC research.'

The fall of publisher power

'I remember once someone came up to me at a meeting and said, "All you need to do is ban Wellcome researchers from publishing with Elsevier,"' Kiley recalls. 'And I said, why would I need to do that? If you don't want to publish with them, don't submit to them. It's not my job to ban it. I certainly don't want to put anyone out of business. It's just in the long term I would question whether we need 30,000 journals in an age where we can publish anything anywhere. I don't think we need so many.'

In the short to medium term, there can be no doubt that the dominant publishing companies will continue to hold a hugely disproportionate sum of academic money. And, while it is safe to say that few people truly believe publishers should go bust – or want them to – there is at least a growing awareness that, in fact, publishers need the academic community much more than the academic community needs them.

Following on from Germany's nationwide boycott of Elsevier journals during its Project DEAL negotiations, in April 2018 French institutions announced they would not be striking any new deals with Springer Nature. In May 2018, Sweden's Bibsam Consortium, representing 85 institutions, chose not to renew its contract with Elsevier on the grounds the publisher had failed to meet expectations in transitioning to OA, and in 2019 Norway followed suit.

But this time something had shifted; clearly the publishers were beginning to feel the vulnerability of their position and the bad press that had followed

---

[128] Read more on the University of California's announcement: https://news.berkeley.edu/2021/03/16/ucs-deal-with-elsevier-what-it-took-what-it-means-why-it-matters.

these high-profile cancellations. Elsevier in particular had been burned before in the stalemate between them and the University of California – and the group made the surprise decision to strike a publish-and-read deal with Norwegian universities one month later.

'For-profit publishing houses no longer have the authority they thought they had,' says Martin Vetterli, former president of the Swiss National Science Foundation's National Research Council, 'and in fact they never had it. For a long time, academics have worked under the assumption that publishers own them in some way – but in fact you can run a very high-quality journal that is essentially run in a not-for-profit method with a good editorial board and sound reviewers, at a lower cost.'

There is a place for journals – but it is not what publishers think it is, he continues. 'I do read *Science* and *Nature* every week in paper, so there the editorial content has value and I am willing to pay for this. What I am not willing to pay is this overhead for reading pure research papers where the peer review has been done pro bono by colleagues of mine. And people are waking up to that.'

Kamila Markram is less optimistic about the pace of change – again, she believes, as a consequence of the transformative deals taking place. 'The transformative journals scheme is [problematic] because compliance is entirely based on a non-binding promise by legacy publishers to convert their journals in three years without consequence,' she says.

'As a result of this watering down of Plan S, vast amounts of public money are being paid to the big legacy publishers to incentivise them to transform to open access, while the innovators and pure open access publishers are squeezed out of negotiations and asked to reduce costs. Considerable amounts of work have been dedicated to open science and there are signs of progress, but it is slow. We will only see a significant shift in the publishing paradigm if big funders are committed and demand change.'

Despite his decision to leave the publishing world, Ropers feels positively about the changing attitudes among commercial powers. He references the positive impact felt with communications between stakeholders with the joining of Kumsal Bayazit[129] (who joined as Elsevier's CEO in 2019) and a new senior leadership team at Wiley. 'I think there are some changes taking place at the helm – there's a lot of new blood, also across the board levels.'

He believes the heat from the campaigners' side has also mellowed: 'I think there's this growing understanding of the complex mechanism that we're trying to manage when we say something as simple as, "let's just make publishing open access". It is just very, very complex.'

Reflecting upon the attitudes taken by both commercial publishers and OA campaigners, however, it is clear his loyalty does not sit comfortably in either camp. 'It's easy for me to say now because I don't have any skin in the game,

---

[129] Elsevier was approached multiple times for interview during the period spent writing this book (2020–21) but no conclusive answer was ever given.

but, if you speak to people now, they actually do acknowledge that some of the logic, some of the arguments used [by either side] were false and needed to be replaced with something which is way more stable, which is way more constructive, without unnecessarily creating so much collateral damage. Because that might actually be bigger than the actual value that's being created by OA.'

3.3 The future of academic publishing

What, then, do the changes brought about by Plan S mean for academic publishing in the future? In opening the door to new possibilities and enforcing change, it seems inevitable that many stakeholders and observers of the academic research and publishing sectors are increasingly questioning the value and purpose of the entire publishing system as it stands. Given the opportunity to start afresh, what could a future publishing system look like? Will there come a time when journals no longer exist? Can we imagine a world without scientific articles at all?

These conversations have been bubbling away under the surface for some time, and are both intrinsically linked to, and independent of, thought from Plan S. As our perceptions of the publishing world – and what we deem as necessary and fair – change, many stakeholders are beginning to question what the academic landscape might look like in the not-so-distant future. The suggestions are as varied as the academic and publishing industries themselves – but one thread that remains consistent is that academic publishing will change dramatically from the traditional peer review and publish work system we see today.

Idea 1: Journals will be dead

Robert Kiley doesn't mince his words: 'We don't need journals. Journals were really useful in an age where we had to physically print things to distribute them. Since the 1990s, we've had something called the internet … what do we still need journals for?'

While some may argue otherwise, it is certainly true that the printed journal is very much a convenient luxury in the modern age rather than a necessity when digital copies can be created in an instant. But what about the concept of the journal itself, digital or not? The value of the curated document, Kiley says, is 'only to say this is the stuff worth reading. We certainly don't need the 30,000 or more journals that currently exist.'

If a new scholarly communications system were to be built from scratch today, Kiley believes it would look a lot like the repository model that's been built in recent years by Wellcome and the online publishing platform F1000. Of course, he would say that, coming from Wellcome – but he makes a convincing case.

What he proposes is to create 'a completely open repository where researchers can upload their research once they feel ready to share it – just like any preprint server. A publisher might run this service, it might not.'

He explains, 'The submission is looked at to make sure it complies with basic scientific, and ethical principles (i.e. text is not plagiarised, links are provided to underlying data, and it doesn't contain inappropriate images etc.), but after that it can go up online. Now here's the difference – the peer review happens on that preprint – so you still formally invite reviewers 1, 2 and 3 to review it, but those reviews are published openly, too.'

The advantage of doing this is simple: it takes the decision and control about whether a paper should be published out of the hands of the reviewers, and out of the hands of the publisher, because the version of record is already there on the repository. There is no need for internal politics to get in the way of a fair decision on how worthy each paper might be for publication – the reader can be left to decide for themselves.

'As a reviewer, the sole focus now is helping the author to improve the paper,' says Kiley. 'So they can say, you've missed this bit out, I'm not sure if this methodology is the best one to use here, whatever. And, in turn, the author can take on board those suggestions and make version two. And then version three, or however long it takes. At some point they might decide they are done with it – what's been worked on is ready to be left out there for judgement. Or they might want to keep reviewing and revising it until it's the best piece of work ever.'

This idea of making each step of the article publication process transparent has already been trialled and adopted by some younger, challenger OA platform publishers such as F1000 Research and *eLife*. Following a successful trial run, *eLife*'s editor-in-chief, Michael Eisen, announced in 2019 that the platform would start taking requests from authors to conduct reviews of preprints already published on the BioRxiv server – the reviews of which would be posted for everyone to read, regardless of the outcome.

Explaining the rationale behind this, Eisen expressed hopes the move would eradicate the 'submit–review–accept/reject–repeat paradigm' under which academics waste time and effort chasing journal editors for publication. He too expressed a desire to 'get rid of journals', describing them as an 'anachronism' – and Eisen and Kiley are not alone.[130]

Wellcome Open Research is already part of the way there with Kiley's vision – all that's missing is the curation element, traditionally provided by the journal. In this respect, he does believe there is still a place for publishing editors – just not in quite the same role they have now.

'We could – and already do – have a place where all the content is open, you can lose yourself to your heart's content, drown yourself in this reservoir of research. But what if you don't want to spend hours trawling – if actually you

---

[130] Link to twitter thread: https://twitter.com/mbeisen/status/1155286615721254912?lang=en-gb (accessed 25 February 2021).

want to know what's worth reading? Well, then you could subscribe to the publisher curator, or the Society of Neuroscience's curation service, even independent bodies and charities and funders – and they will tell you. It's a model that already works for other things like newspapers and retailers.'

Another benefit to such a system would be that research papers would not need to be owned by one particular publisher. Currently, whether a paper has a CC BY licence or not, it is highly unlikely to be picked up and shared by more than one reputable journal, because commercial journals rely on exclusivity and the ability to present new releases. In this utopia, a strong piece of research might have approval badges from *Cell*, *Nature* and *Science*, as well as smaller society publishers. 'It would only strengthen the value of that paper, and different badges would of course mean different things to different people.' That is, if the publishers can get past their long-held – sometimes centuries-old – rivalries.

Of course, it ought to be said that many perceptions of the traditional journal as archaic, redundant pieces of furniture are at least in some way influenced by the typical negativity felt towards the big five players that publish them. Brill director Jasmin Lange points out that, even if the printed record ceases to exist, a journal is so much more than the paper copy that sits on the library shelf – particularly in the smaller and more niche research fields.

'What a journal does is build community,' she says. 'It's a social thing, a platform for discussion which we as a publisher have put together with the editors and are continuously working on to improve by seeking out new authors and also new readers. One thing with OA is that we still need to look for readers for that community – because there is a huge information overflow, which makes it hard for people to find online the information that's relevant to them.'

With this in mind, she predicts that in decades to come the researcher community 'will still meet at conferences to present their work and invite people to OA journals to join the discussion to take place' – if anything, the community surrounding a journal will become even more important in ensuring that good-quality work gets promoted in a sea of information. The shift to OA will allow that community to grow further: 'It's not restricted by readership so much anymore. Likewise the community will not split dramatically away from the existing models of journal, because we are talking about very specialised communities that publish with society journals – subfields of subfields. And we need all of this rich tapestry to keep research diverse and moving forward.'

As former director of EMBO, a researcher-led organisation promoting life sciences that also publishes a select number of journals, Maria Leptin has a fair insight into the attitudes and behaviours of the research community. She believes that, even in decades to come, researchers 'will still be submitting articles for peer review in the same way as they do now', and has evidence to support this. EMBO ran a survey of its members in 2019 to ask how they would go about choosing articles to read in a field aside from their own. 'It was perfectly clear which options came out on top: they choose articles written by someone they know or have heard of, a highly regarded name in science – or they look to a highly selective journal,' she says. 'That says it all to me – people care. They need some kind of flag that says, "start here". Of course there's no guarantee those papers are good but they are at least well regarded. It matters to people.'

As for the suggestion that verification could be achieved in other ways, she is unconvinced. 'Post-publication commenting, badging and all that ... I don't see it, because the work that expert referees put into reviewing the papers makes them better and is already something that we use to judge papers on.' But, as she rightly points out, 'That's exactly the bit that costs money.'

Idea 2: Articles will be dead – well, almost

Jean-Claude Burgelman is another firm believer that the academic publishing structure is due a radical rewriting. But he takes this one step further by suggesting that it will not only be journals that are a thing of the past but articles too. In fact, neither authors nor publishers will have a choice in the matter, he says – the reasons for which all come down to the growing power of data. 'In the future, a publication will be a set of data and correlations and the article will only be the narrative to explain it,' he says. 'And with that goes a change in all the dynamics of science.'

'A lot of my generation see the article as the ultimate wisdom, whereas the way science is developing is becoming a continuous stream of updated knowledge based on data. And so this holy status of the article – that one piece of text can once and for all give the truth about something and that's the end of it – that's over.'

Marcus Munafo shares a similar vision of the future: 'You could imagine a world where you do a research project, you have a study protocol that generates data, then write up the results. You can imagine the modular parts of that all being shared as they complete on some kind of repository – either institutional or national – and that then forms a product, but it's a living product so when you do a second study you can link back to it so that the knowledge expands.'

F1000: a case study

F1000 (formerly known as Faculty of F1000) provides open research publishing services to organisations such as the European Commission, Wellcome, and the Bill & Melinda Gates Foundation, as well as to individual researchers directly. Set up in 2000 by the UK entrepreneur Vitek Tracz, who also founded a number of early scholarly sharing platforms including BioMed Central, F1000 was designed with the vision of taking a fresh approach to the existing publishing system. As such, the company pioneered the 'post-publication peer review' publishing model: its life sciences platform F1000Research is not just fully OA in terms of the papers it publishes but it also takes an OA-like view towards peer review, too. Articles are published first (as they would be on a standard preprint repository) and peer-reviewed after publication by invited referees, whose names and comments are made visible by default on the website alongside the research.

The data behind each article is also published open access and free to download. Crucially, the platform does not require the traditional written article structure for a piece of research to be published – F1000Research publishes both traditional research articles, but also single findings and snippets of information such as case reports, protocols and experiment replications. Importantly, it welcomes the publication of null or negative results – consciously shifting away from the culture of only publishing work deemed to be headline-grabbing or of mainstream interest.

According to managing director Rebecca Lawrence, F1000Research was established with four key aspects in mind in addition to the overarching goal of reaching full and immediate OA in science. 'First we wanted to address the serious delays in the length of time it takes between a researcher's initial discovery and when others actually get to benefit from it,' she explains. 'Typically that's at least months, but it can very often be years by the time an author has gone from journal to journal trying to publish something, perhaps because it has a negative result or it's not deemed as exciting enough. That's crazy if you think about it, because really any result should be out there as quickly as possible.

'Number two is the fact that most research is communicated without the supporting data being shared,' she explains. Asides from the obvious point that lack of background data sharing prevents others from reproducing the claims, it can impede on a researcher's ability to convince gatekeepers the work is worth publishing, too, she adds. 'So often you see the summary results and the claims, but actually, if you think about it, the peer reviewers and the experts that have assessed this piece of work can't see the data either – they have to take your conclusions as read.'

The third point Lawrence and her colleagues wanted to address was the flaws in the existing peer review process. 'That process of experts deciding whether the content is good or not is typically completely anonymous, and yet the reviewers are likely people working in the same field,' says Lawrence. 'Because it's so competitive and rivalries exist, there's a lot of temptation to reject an article, to push it back … as nothing is transparent you don't know who made the decision or why.'

(Continued)

Finally, she points out, there is a 'huge amount of research done that's good quality and never shared or published' – often for the reasons stated above. A well-known study by the epidemiologists Paul Glasziou and Iain Chalmers conducted in 2009 suggested that as much as 85 per cent of medical research is wasted one way or another.[131] The figure is frequently contested, and more recent estimates suggest a more conservative 50 per cent. But the authors stand by their findings even today and point out that 'we know from follow-up of registered clinical trials that about 50 per cent are never published in full, a figure which varies little across countries, size of study, funding source, or phase of trial'.[132]

Still, today, Lawrence agrees it is 'just really hard to get a journal to publish something, whether it's negative or null results or incremental findings that might not be some huge development but is still significant to the specialism … the journals want citations so they want big publications with big stories.

'And the net effect of that is that you see the publications of research where the results are positive, but because you don't see the publications where the results are less conclusive – maybe somebody's done the same thing and they found a negative result – you get this actual factual inaccuracy. That means you can't reproduce the findings because you can only see the positive results and it's not counterbalanced with the negative.'

Lawrence and colleagues do not call F1000Research a journal, and the platform deliberately does not have any kind of impact factor rating. 'It is a publishing model but it's a completely different way of publishing that really tries to rethink how we do research with the technology we have now.' When founding F1000Research, directors asked themselves the very question we've been asking interviewees for the purposes of this book: 'If we started again today with a clean slate, what would we do? What would publishing look like? Would you start again? Actually,' says Lawrence, 'the system would be a different thing entirely.'

---

[131] Chalmers I, Glasziou P. Avoidable waste in the production and reporting of research evidence. *Lancet*. 2009; *374*(9683): 86–89. DOI: https://doi.org/10.1016/S0140-6736(09)60329-9.

[132] Chalmers I, Glasziou P. Paul Glasziou and Iain Chalmers: Is 85% of health research really 'wasted'? *BMJ*. 2016. Retrieved from https://blogs.bmj.com/bmj/2016/01/14/paul-glasziou-and-iain-chalmers-is-85-of-health-research-really-wasted (accessed 14 March 2021).

Idea 3: New technologies will lead the way ...

As technology and industries become increasingly automated, experts believe the practical aspects of publishing will become increasingly managed using artificial intelligence software. According to Kamila Markram, this is already the case at Frontiers: 'Through innovations like our Artificial Intelligence Review Assistant (AIRA), we can automate many of the tasks previously carried out by humans, enabling more high-quality science to be published.'

Introducing an additional level of analysis by ARIA means 'quality control is managed with more efficiency and accuracy than it could be by humans, allowing our teams and editorial board to focus on the science itself,' she adds.

Such technologies can act as another tool in the armoury of large-scale platform publishers like Frontiers, which can come up against criticisms that they are simply too big, and publish too much research, to ensure everything that is published OA is of high quality.

'Quality and scale are not mutually exclusive, but you have to have the right technology in place to enable it,' she says. 'Frontiers was founded by scientists to make peer review constructive, to bring the best technology to the service of the authors and editors so that more high-quality fully open access science can be published.'

Reliance on machine learning technologies will also allow academic publishing to become more consumer-led. After all our discussions on the importance of freedom of access, that might sound capitalistic – whether it's a good or a bad thing is another debate. What it does highlight is how far the research publishing sector falls behind other industries.

As Kiley puts it, 'You log on to Amazon and it knows what you want to buy almost before you open the browser. Likewise, music streaming sites know what to recommend based on what you've already listened to ... so we've got all this tech which we can apply to trivial stuff like helping to find new music to listen to, and then we spend billions on research just to say, no, we don't want to use these technologies to mine the research.'

In other words, so long as journal paywalls are up – along with restrictive reuse licences – information about the latest discoveries cannot be drawn upon by AI programmes seeking new connections about the world around us.

... If data is made open

These days, Tom Callaway works as an open-source technologist for Amazon Web Services. Given his personal and professional experiences, he says he is 'a fervent believer that academic data should be open by default. The purpose of academic data is to be a foundation for additional research, and that data must be reproducible and verifiable. When data is hidden, obscured, or otherwise restricted, it calls into question any and all research which is built upon it,' he adds.

'One of the lessons of open source is that we can never predict what someone will do with the code we write. By making it open, we invite a universe of possibilities and remove the barriers from innovation. That same innovation may occur when the code is closed or restrictions are put in place, but they happen much faster without them. Open is an accelerant.'

It is not unusual to feel uneasy about the open sharing of data – for researchers, it means their entire processes are laid bare, exposing them in a way that a carefully worded written article from that dataset does not. For perhaps the first time, they are required to make the data publicly presentable and neat – which also takes time.

But Maria Leptin believes the culture is shifting in the right direction. 'Our editorial team spends quite a lot of time helping authors in terms of determining where to put the data and broadly how to structure it. We have a lot of guidelines,' she adds. 'So that does sometimes mean rules – don't do this, do that – but also supporting researchers in demonstrating what it all means and why we do it.'

She has also noticed significantly more investment from institutions to provide training to researchers on how to share their data, something that has been helped by an upsurge in hiring data stewards: 'people employed by an institution to support researchers in thinking about how to deal with data, its storage and how to structure it. So it's improving a lot,' she says. 'Not all our researchers feel comfortable with sharing their data yet but the attitude is definitely shifting. It's becoming more the norm to share data and more publications are asking for it too, which speeds the process up.'

For Leptin, it is crucial that data transparency goes hand in hand with the opening up of other steps in the publishing process too, including peer review. 'What we try to do is ensure everything that's published through one of our journals is published alongside the data needed to share the methods,' she explains. 'So that's the other thing we have to really support the authors on, making sure they detail what they did to produce the data – otherwise how as a reviewer or indeed as a reader and a user do you really know what's happened and how to make your own judgement on the work?

'It's difficult because you know, if you only tackle one aspect of it, it kind of doesn't make sense. You have to say, ok, this is what we're trying to do and this is really where we're trying to get to and I think researchers see the benefit of it. Yes, it can be a bit more work sometimes, but you see the benefits on the other side – I can't tell you the number of authors who have said to me that by showing their data, they found collaborators they never would have found before. They realise there are a lot of upsides.'

As Marc Schiltz sees it, 'everyone knows data is the asset of the future'. But, more than this, open science has the power to turn traditional research practices on their head. 'There is so much data generated now, we are seeing this paradigm shift in science,' he explains. 'We used to be hypothesis-driven – so you have the idea and you go and collect data to test it out. Whereas now we have this huge amount of data available and it speaks for itself. The hypothesis is found later. It's an entirely new approach to research which is really exciting.'

Idea 4: Attitudes towards cost will change ...

It is clear that, in order to make the transition to full OA, publishers will have to change their business models. And, as illustrated above, there is already plenty of evidence of this happening by way of transformative, read-and-publish deals. But, for the most part, APCs will continue to play a major role in the financing of publishing journals – and inevitably continue to pose a point of resistance for many.

For the most part, researchers in the affluent Global North (or, indeed, their funders or institutions) have grown accustomed to the charges associated with publishing open access. But what counts as reasonable is still very much open to debate. In November 2020, after much anticipation, Springer Nature announced its APC for Nature-branded journals would start at €9,500 in January 2021. The publisher also announced a pilot project in which authors could pay a non-refundable fee of €2,190 in return for an assessment of which Nature title might suit their paper best. If a match is found and the paper meets all the editor's publishing requirements, the author is required to pay the remainder of the publication charge for OA. Acceptance is not guaranteed, however.[133]

It's an interesting experiment that draws into question just how much money authors are willing or able to pay for the privilege of having a top brand of journal on their CV. That aside, Bodo Stern, chief of strategic initiatives for the Howard Hughes Medical Institute (HHMI) feels confident that, as more journals transition to OA and state their article processing charges, publishing culture 'will go in the right direction'. What he means by that is that authors and their financiers will only stand for so much.

To explain his theory, he breaks down one of the main problems with APCs: 'In an OA model, the publisher is being paid once at the time of publication,' he says – unlike a paywall, that is, which charges readers for the opportunity to reap the benefits of those services, indefinitely. 'You can interpret the APC as a service fee, but it lumps together all the services that the journal executes into a publication fee that covers not just services on the articles they publish, but also

---

[133] Kown D. For a hefty fee, Nature journals offer open access publishing. *The Scientist*. 2020. Retrieved from https://www.the-scientist.com/news-opinion/for-a-hefty-fee-nature-journals-offer-open-access-publishing-68181 (accessed 14 March 2021).

on all the articles that the journal rejected. This explains why highly selective journals like Nature, which may reject up to 90 per cent of submitted articles, have very high APCs.'

So how does this make for a fairer system? 'Now my argument is, I don't think it's a great idea to charge $10,000, but there is going to be a transition period where that will happen. What will happen in the longer term is scientists will be irritated if they have to pay that much for an article, and so those journals may no longer attract the best science.'

And so the playing field will level out. Or, you might cry, the elite journals will simply become more elite in status, available only to the wealthiest of scholars with the most generous backing. 'Yes, that is probably what will happen initially,' admits Stern. 'In fact, it already happens because experimental revisions for highly selective journals take a lot of time and money; something only well-resourced scientists may be able to afford. Well-resourced researchers may also say, "I hate the high APCs but I'm going to cough up the thousands because it helps me in my career or my trainees' career." But, in the whole ecosystem, it's not going to work. It's neither sustainable nor equitable. And publishers know that. They understand it's not attractive. And so I think what will happen over time is that they will realise that we need better open access business models.'

... And journals will have to get creative ...

Could a publishing system exist without APCs? 'By moving to OA, it should be directional in the sense that it pushes quality publishers away from subscriptions but eventually also away from the APC model – because both models are flawed,' says Stern. Of course, however the publishing system is organised, whoever foots the bill, someone somewhere still has to pay it.

What Stern is hopeful for is a more transparent breakdown of the costs. 'What we should end up with is a system where publishers get paid directly for their services, like peer review,' he says. To this end, scholarly publishing 'should move towards a model where scientists and their funders pay for services, like peer review. If a paper gets rejected but it is peer-reviewed, there is a service already executed. Of course, the journals do get paid for that time; it just gets lumped together with the publishing fee for the winners. So there isn't really a difference – it's just that it becomes more explicit.

'Now, a high-quality journal could say "we are elite, we provide extra good service, and are charging more for the peer review than someone else" ... and I think initially that would be fair enough. Of course, over time what will happen is every journal that charges for peer review will have to show proof that it is conducting high-quality peer reviews, and so we will reach a time when outcomes of peer reviews have to be published as standard procedure.'

Open publishing of peer review is indeed already happening among the likes of F1000Research and trialed by others including *eLife*, for the reasons stated by Rebecca Lawson above. But the first journal believed to have begun posting peer review reports and reviewer names alongside published articles was *BMC Biology*, published by BioMed Central (part of Springer Nature). In January 2019, the journal took its experimental efforts to reduce waste in the editorial process a step further by implementing a 'portable peer review' policy. *BMC Biology* would allow reviews of papers that had been rejected to be passed on to other journals, free of charge, except in cases where the research had been deemed scientifically unsound, its chief editor, Mirna Kvajo, announced. The aim of this was to 'provide better service to authors, whose papers will reach the community faster, and via a process that aims to be less stressful' while also reducing 'time and effort which are going to waste'.

Dr Kvajo expressed hopes that other journals might do the same, regardless of publishing house, but her comments sparked some debate. Russell Foster, professor of circadian neuroscience at the University of Oxford, told *Times Higher Education* at the time that often, when a paper is rejected by one journal on the basis that it 'requires a more specialist journal', it is 'usually just code for it being no good', he added. 'I would be reluctant to take on someone else's report as I like to look at a paper with an open mind.'[134]

There are even more innovative things being trialed, too. In December 2020, the editorial board of *eLife* announced that, as of July 2021, the platform would only consider manuscripts for review that had already been published as preprints. Announcing the move in the form of a scientific article on the *eLife* website, editor-in-chief Michael Eisen and colleagues said the company would also 'focus its editorial process on producing public reviews to be posted alongside the preprints'.[135] It is clear the tide is turning on closed peer review – and the mysteries historically associated with selecting papers for publication altogether.

... But not all will survive

We have already read the warnings detailed by interviewees in this book about the precarious position many smaller publishers find themselves in, faced with the push to transition their business models. The situation may be worse than many people realise, says Steven Inchcoombe. Through his work with the STM association, he says there is evidence to suggest 'the vast majority of publishers don't make much profit at all. Once you get to medium and small ones they are

---

[134] Pells R. Journal shares peer reviews of rejected papers with rival titles. *Times Higher Education*. 2019. Retrieved from https://www.timeshighereducation.com/news/journal-shares-peer-reviews-rejected-papers-rival-titles (accessed 14 March 2021).

[135] Eisen MB, Akhmanova A, Behrens TE, Harper DM, Weigel D, Zaidi M. Implementing a 'publish, then review' model of publishing. *eLife*. 2020; 9. DOI: https://doi.org/10.7554/eLife.64910.

likely in debt. It's not clear they will be sustainable, given the costs and risks of transitioning to OA. So I expect many to sell out at this stage – and the only organisations big enough to buy them are the commercial publishers that have the resources to do so.'

Here lies a contradiction, then, if smaller independent journals continue to be eaten up by the big five commercial players. The big five, inevitably, hold an even greater monopoly than before. 'I think there is going to be a further wave of consolidation,' says Inchcoombe, 'which is one of the unintended consequences of the transition to OA. It's not what Plan S wanted, but it is going to be a consequence because there are costs and risks of transitioning.'

Where the internet and other digital tools provide opportunities, there is a flipside to the fact that OA is fundamentally possible because of digitisation. 'Digitisation, as we've seen in every other sector, hugely rewards scale,' says Inchcoombe. 'Individual journals and learned societies just can't generate the scale, so they end up struggling to compete – the large organisations get larger and the small organisations either fold or – and I think this is the more likely outcome – they will liquidate their position by selling their journals to be able to turn those assets into funds that they can then use for their other purposes.'

In drawing up Plan S, Robert-Jan was open from the start in saying he always knew there would be some casualties. It's been one of the biggest concerns for him, his successors and key organisers at Coalition S, and is also the main reason behind the expansion to the timeframe for Plan S implementation.

Less anticipated, perhaps, was the threat to journals already consolidated under the big five publishers. Koen Vermeir, co-chair of the Global Young Academy and a researcher with the CNRS in Paris, took up editorship of a longstanding humanities title in his field after becoming increasingly interested in the OA debate taking place with Plan S.

Vermeir says he 'wanted to better understand the inside workings of the academic publishing world' and had the ambition to flip the journal with Wiley's support, but the support didn't come. So he began to fundraise independently.

'It's interesting because we were thinking of basically buying out the journal from Wiley and making it open access with an OA publisher, and then potentially working with funding that is in the system,' he explains. 'Then, only two weeks ago, Wiley told me that they're planning to shut down the journal.'

Vermeir says Wiley did not want to give an explanation, and the situation is still a mystery. 'At 70 years old, this journal is one of the oldest in the field,' he says. 'It's doing really well, and on all the metrics and its missions it's doing much better than a few years ago. But now the publisher says financially it's not interesting.'

Vermeir speculates that the changing OA context, and Plan S in particular, may be the reason. Despite the transformative deals Wiley has agreed to since, a specialist journal like Vermeir's just was not worth the money or the hassle of flipping to OA – and so it was not worth the publisher's time continuing it at all.

'In a sense it feels ok,' he adds, 'because now we don't need to have a fight with Wiley about buying the journal – they will just shut it down and we can start a new one in an open access format elsewhere. But again, it's a sign that for these smaller disciplines … the OA transition has an effect.'

Vermeir's journal will hopefully survive the flip – because it had been planned out months ahead, and because the journal has a loyal group of supporters to help it transition. But the same won't be said of all journals, particularly the smallest ones. The danger for niche titles is that if the publisher no longer sees it as profitable, it can no longer be sold as part of a subscription package – a bundle of many small titles from the same publisher – which would previously have got the journal into libraries by default. But if the journal is not part of a subscription bundle, and it only has one or two dedicated readers per university or research institution, it is unlikely the librarian will spend money ordering it directly. A negative cycle ensues: the journal makes even less money, and the likelihood of its survival deceases.

3.4 Navigating the data-led future

As highlighted in Parts One and Two, a quiet race is under way in the publishing world to dominate the next currency in academic publishing. 'Publishers are smart,' says Martin Vetterli. 'They know that the traditional publishing of journal papers itself is not going to grow as fast as they would like. So they merely look for the next step, which is the added material that realises open science – data, code and so on.'

Asides from the ethical dilemma presented by the commercialisation of academic data, it also presents new challenges for researchers and consumers of that research, too, as Callaway points out: 'I think we should be concerned about data ownership. If I independently reproduce a dataset in an experiment, do I owe Elsevier money?'

But, to him, an even bigger concern is that corporations will go out of their way to 'hide data that could be used to benefit others. The majority of pharmaceutical studies result in failure, but often the results stay locked away. When data is published in the open, it minimises the need for repeating processes and tests and can assist people who are trying to solve different problems.'

'I hope that data ownership does not become the default, but I suspect that is the path in front of us,' he adds. 'I am encouraged by the popularity of services like Kaggle, an independent platform for sharing data openly (even if not strictly meeting the letter of open data). My kids are growing up in a world where the internet puts everything at their fingertips, and I hope that their generation will choose to use that power to share and collaborate rather than hoard and restrict.'

When it was drawn up, Plan S did not explicitly mention the openness of data – and this has been a point of criticism from even some of the initiative's most loyal fans. As Kurt Deketelaere, secretary-general of LERU, puts it: 'Everyone knows that open science is here to stay, but saying the same for OA data – suggesting within the next year or so it will be not only full OA but full OA data – it is certainly not going to be the case.'

Robert-Jan explains that the decision to exclude data from Plan S was a deliberate one, however. 'The reason for this was that the debate on OA data was just starting and it turned out to be even more complex than OA publications. Therefore, if I would have integrated a plan for OA data as well, I would have never been able to develop Plan S on time and to stick to one of my key principles: keep things simple. Kurt Deketelaere is right when he says that it will take in any case much more time before OA data is realised.'

Marc Schiltz reasons that the open data mission is much more diverse in its considerations, too: 'When it comes to the particular obstacle of making data open it is a little bit more nuanced because there are some data that you simply can't make open – personal data, covered by data protection regulations. There may be data as well where there is an IP exploitation strategy behind it. The quandary has been addressed in the European Commission with the now commonly referred to catchphrase "as open as possible, as closed as necessary",' Schiltz says, 'which is fine, but of course you have to ask what does it mean? Which data will we make OA and which can we not make OA? Even if data cannot be made OA, are there ways we can make it accessible on request, for instance? There are many practical questions still to answer.'

The role of funders and institutions

One thing Plan S has highlighted is that the discussions taking place around OA articles are already out of date. What comes next is determining how to manage data outputs. As emeritus research director at CNRS (the French national centre for scientific research), Anne Cambon-Thomsen has roots in the debate around open science and open data from its earliest days in the 1990s. She believes Robert-Jan made the right choice in starting with publications and working backwards – in that the published article is really the final step of the research process. 'I think that Plan S has by default resulted in a huge push for data to become more open,' she says.

But there is far to go: 'I think that's good for publications and facilitating access to the results of research, but now we need a second Plan S to cover OA across the whole chain of research: access to research protocols, access to methods, sharing equipment as it already exists through infrastructures. Philosophically speaking, we need to realise the whole chain of knowledge as the published article, and not just the end point, which is the written paper. I would love there to be a sort of general framework for OS with different tools for different steps. But make it a framework that follows general logic.'

Another reason why Cambon-Thomsen agrees that starting with OA to publications was the right thing to do is that, put simply, 'data is messy – it's far easier to start with the articles and hope that it grows from there'. It's something she knows from experience – she herself was once part of a group that attempted to create a traceability system for biobank use. A biobank, for the uninitiated, is a collection of biological samples with data attached. The idea was that, in tracing where the resource they established had ended up being used, researchers would be able to see the gain in sharing their data, not just the burden of organising it for accessibility.

But the platform was difficult to manage and the incentive difficult to enforce. She came up with an idea for a biobank impact factor (BIF), to quantify the use of a biobank: the concept was similar to that of a journal or citation impact factor and, she hoped, might incentivise researchers further to share their work for due reward. 'We transformed it afterwards to be called an "impact framework" not "impact factor", she adds, 'since impact factor now has connotations and is truly a source of hatred for many researchers and because it was not just an index but a set of tools to facilitate citation and traceability of the various uses.'

A perfect solution is yet to be rolled out, therefore. And, while the questions surrounding data ownership are not new, they are becoming more and more urgent with the rapid changes taking place within research and publishing. The more publications become open, the less value they hold in the eyes of commercial publishers looking to sell a product – and the more valuable data becomes in their place.

As Gielen puts it, 'How and what are we going to do with data and data analytics on all the papers, how the content of the results of all that become available – that's the future.' He has a very clear idea about how to tackle it: as of 1 January 2021, the NWO is mandating not only OA publications – in line with Plan S – but also that researchers make their data publicly available on a trusted repository. It is a bold move that has undoubtedly ruffled feathers. 'There is a discussion now on what sort of data should be made available. My point of view is that you should make all the data available that belongs to the dataset that you used for your publication. So that means that other scientists should be able to reproduce your data based on what you made available. It's research paid for by public money, so the data should be made available too.'

As discussions centre increasingly around the reproducibility of results – in recent years especially in social psychology, but also epidemiology and, in part due to the pandemic, virology and immunology too – scientists and the journals they publish in are being held increasingly accountable for the validity of data behind their published findings (more on this in Part One). 'In order to prevent these irreproducible studies, we should make data publicly available and make other scientists do the replication studies based on the same data,' says Gielen. 'There is an issue on privacy in data, especially in, say, social sciences and medical data. But there are pretty straightforward solutions for that.'

The solutions posed include one suggestion that researchers should be so confident in their data at the time of submission that the data is made open by default, with researchers made to apply for an exception to the rule only under certain mitigating circumstances.

A challenge here is that presenting data in an accessible format – refining notes, uploading text, files and so on – places an additional burden on researchers. That's why the sharing of data cannot be left as an afterthought, says Gielen. 'Once the paper is published, the author moves on. They don't care about the details and descriptions of their data.'

Gielen believes this should be taken into account when (and he says 'when' not 'if') the existing reward system for researchers is rewritten: 'If we, the funder or the institution, require that you publish your data we should, for example, give credit if many other scientists end up using your data.' Above all, it is another reason why data management needs to be supported by the employment of extra staff members in universities and research institutions. 'I think it's extremely important that we have what we call in the Netherlands "data stewards", who make sure the data are on a repository with all the requirements. We have provided funding for universities to appoint them and I think that's very critical because there's a large amount of pressure on scientists already.'

The hiring of data stewards and similar roles is steadily growing in popularity among individual universities, research institutions, academic societies and other scholarly groups. Increasingly, employers are realising the importance of supporting their employees in making the transition.

'It is clear there is not enough awareness among researchers that they are signing so much of themselves away to publishers, particularly when it comes to data,' says Cambon-Thomsen. 'That's part of where the education and training is needed.' Here, having some independent institution for data stewardship – externally but also within individual workplaces – could help keep data open by preventing authors from unintentionally giving away the rights to data: 'Big publishers have these astoundingly complex contracts ... so having someone who is able to compare different contracts and give some explanation of what it means, in terms that a researcher would understand, could really help – because sometimes labour terms are convoluted. They don't always have a concrete meaning for people. This is something that universities and research institutions could do more of to help their researchers.'

Managing academic data

There is a school of thought that simply in making more academic research open in its entirety – data and all – the community becomes increasingly self-regulatory. But, on the other hand, some fear that opening the system up also opens it up to more potential fraud – individuals are free to copy or steal one another's work, their misdeeds hidden by the vast expanse of the internet.

Jean-Claude Burgelman believes the latter is a misconception. 'First of all, mischief has always existed,' he says. 'Of course, it's now more obvious in its manifestations because the scientific population has quadrupled over the past 50 years. But, secondly, openness is the best guarantee to detect mischief.' Once again, the academic reward system could have a role to play here. 'Imagine I get rewarded for keeping myself busy trying to find mistakes in data crunching, imagine that that also counts as a scientific product. That's what we should do.'

For others, the very notion of data sharing conjures fears of security breaches, of privacy invasion, even the data-leaking scandals of the past decades. 'But if we are really going to tackle the serious issues we as a society face – whether that's climate change, epidemic preparedness, food security, whatever it is … we need to make more of academic data,' seconds Kiley. 'There are huge challenges ahead; we need to use all the tools at our disposal to help us do that. We fund research to help answer those questions. We now need to deploy all our learning and get machines to help read and understand and spot associations. Machines can't do that if the first thing it comes across is a paywall. That's no good to it – the machine needs to be able to "read" the article, and the machine really needs to know that this article is licensed in a way that allows this machine to use it.'

The value of data mining is that it allows a computer algorithm to sort through data at a rate that is several thousand, even millions of times faster than a human could manage. There are plenty of misconceptions around the motivations behind this – much of the time, it is researchers themselves seeking new solutions to gaps in our understanding of technology, or for the average outcome of a chemical formula that would take hours of practical time in the lab to conduct themselves.

'We are talking millions of articles that could be mined here. PubMed uploads something like 200,000 a year, and that's just in the life sciences,' says Kiley. 'If you make it broader there's probably between 5 and 10 million articles a year. We need to make sure they are all open and I think probably then it gives us a better chance of addressing some of these huge societal problems.

'Maybe we will still mess up the planet, maybe we will still have climate change issues, but given that we are spending money on trying to address these challenges, let's ensure we maximise our chances by using existing research to find solutions. Whether it's a new vaccine for Covid-19, or whether it's developing a new battery which means we can all give up our fossil fuel cars because we can actually drive to the supermarket without having to plug in again. There's so much we need to do, and research is obviously a key part of it, but research is only half done if you don't make that research open.'

Europe's role in protecting academic data

Burgelman, on the other hand, does not feel so concerned about the path to open data – and certainly not about the apparent land-grab for data ownership from the large commercial players. 'It's not worrying per se, on the condition we make sure there is not unintended abuse,' he explains.

His confidence on this can be attributed to his involvement with the European Open Science Cloud: an initiative that claims to provide a solution to the threat of a data-led arms race by larger players. The EOSC is effectively a storage solution for academic data. Burgelman calls it a 'governance solution for research data in Europe, to be governed according to the principles European member states wants to prevail.'

Its policy initiative is motivated by a wish to develop a culture of 'data stewardship' with the academic community, whereby researchers are incentivised to take care of the data they generate through research projects.

In practice, this means reinforcing the message to researchers that they have a duty to present data in a way that is translatable and readable for others. It also means the data should be carefully checked for the removal of errors and noise – as the biological psychologist Marcus Munafo put it neatly in Part One of this book, messily listed variables might make sense to the scientist who has been studying them intently for months, but the likelihood is neither they nor anyone else will be able to make sense of them months or years later.

'One way of realising this is by making the development of data management plans (DMPs) a requirement as part of the grants that funders provide to the science community,' explains Robert-Jan, who helped to design the EOSC with Burgelman during their time together at the European Commission. 'Scientists should in this way be forced to think about what they will do with the data they generate through their research project, in what repositories will the data be stored. Furthermore, these data should respect the FAIR principles: Findable, Accessible, Interoperable and Reusable.'

Another strand of the EOSC is related to the development of European repositories, sometimes called e-infrastructures, where the data could be stored. In this context, the European Commission supported the setting up of individual initiatives such as Elixir, Clarin and Dariah – web-based tools for particular scientific disciplines. All of this helps to avoid the event that valuable data is left on the individual researcher's computer to rot.

The cloud is designed as a confederation of the existing data infrastructures and practices in Europe – on which billions of euros have already been spent. With this in mind, Burgelman describes the EOSC as 'a safe haven for European research data – nothing more than that. It's to guarantee abuse doesn't happen, and usage is done according to European principles.

'The easiest metaphor is if you take the aviation industry. You have airports in every country, you have different companies and they all fly. If you would do that unregulated, it would never work. So you have air traffic control determining the rules – where can you fly, where are the corridors, what kind of planes can go, what kind of training the pilot needs. That is just like the EOSC: the air traffic control of research data.'

'As it is a distributed design, the data stay where they are but they are stored and made accessible in a format that allows you to use them in an interoperable way,' Burgelman says.

As Burgelman writes in his own paper describing the evolution of the EOSC – in which he likens the story to a 'Greek tragedy' – the fact the cloud's launch accelerated in 2018 is no coincidence. 'That year the EOSC idea got indeed the "oracle of Delphi" type of unexpected, unplanned but highly convincing support from a series of data misuse scandals,' he wrote, noting the Cambridge Analytica scandal, in which a British consulting firm was accused of providing analytical advantages to political campaigns and interfering with elections such as the US presidency and the UK Brexit referendum.[136]

That a cloud system should exist while incorporating some form of 'air traffic control' makes perfect sense – but the scheme is not without its critics, many of whom have questioned the authority of one European body to control academic data in this way. Others believe data should not be locked away in a cloud at all, but be much more open to allow for third-party use and data mining where appropriate.

'Of course we need some coordination and harmonisation within Europe on open science issues. But there are very different views on this,' says Stan Gielen. 'So far, it is not clear to me what the aim of EOSC is.'

Part of the rationale behind creating a coordinating body like the EOSC was as a response to growing awareness among European policymakers that very different activities and practices were taking place with regard to data management – varying widely between fields, cultures and disciplines. 'In my view, the conclusion that there are differences in open science initiatives and repositories between different scientific communities is correct,' says Gielen. 'I would interpret this as a very positive sign: without any support from universities and government, scientists in various scientific communities took the initiative to sit together and to design a structure for storage and exchange of their data. Obviously, the type of data is very different in fields like computer science, medicine, neuroscience, psychology and, therefore, these communities came up with different designs and structure to store and exchange data (and software). I would say: this is great! It illustrates the need for repositories and it illustrates the motivation of scientists to facilitate exchange of data according to the FAIR principles.'

But he cautions: 'Is the variety of initiatives a compelling argument for strict top-down coordination to ensure identical formats, protocols and repositories? I don't think so. Of course harmonisation and similar protocols are necessary. But if we bring these active and enthusiastic researchers together and facilitate changes towards harmonisation, that will work better than top-down coordination.'

Gielen personally believes that the EOSC should operate that way – relying on the goodwill and creative thinking of the European research community, but led by a broader range of representatives from different subject areas to make it work. 'It should recognise the differences in data, protocols and procedures in different disciplines and it should try to achieve a common environment to allow different scientific communities to merge their infrastructure

---

[136] More on the evolution of the EOSC can be read in Burgelman's own words here: Burgelman J-C. Politics and open science: How the European open science cloud became reality (the untold story). *Data Intelligence*. 2021; 3(1): 5–19. DOI: https://doi.org/10.1162/dint_a_00069.

into the EOSC,' he says. 'It is like the motorway system in a country – it should be accessible for all vehicles, be they VW, BMW or Mercedes.'

Burgelman admits that some confusion exists around the EOSC's purpose – in part because it is still a new concept, 'but also because there are a lot of misconceptions there. People don't understand the mission of the cloud ... it is a bit abstract. It's much easier for them to see the cloud as a huge building in Brussels where billions of data are collected and an army of bureaucrats control it. First of all, this is not feasible, and it is absolutely not desirable.' Furthermore, the data cloud is not the same thing as having a data regulator: that is not the EOSC's remit (although Burgelman and many others agree such a regulator should exist).

Cambon-Thomsen agrees the EOSC is 'a good idea' but believes it should be built up with caution, and a 'step by step approach'. That way, she says, coordinators 'will come across the inevitable problems one by one, on a smaller scale, rather than discovering we've created some catastrophe too late'. The cloud should also be rolled out under pilot schemes in different disciplines, she suggests: 'We are setting the tone now for something that is going to exist hopefully for generations. That's why democratic governance is important. You can't guess the problems in advance but you can set up systems that will be able to take into account the problems of the time when they come – for instance by opening the project up to consistent review, transparency in decision-making and so on. All these things will take some time, but I think it's important.'

Like Gielen, Cambon-Thomsen feels strongly that the EOSC should be a democratic entity, and monitored to ensure the level of control over the data stored does not exceed what is reasonable.' The fact it is the community putting their data there means they should be involved in either electing representatives or there should be some democracy in the way the cloud is run,' she notes, 'Not just people nominated by the European Commission somewhere – such platforms require a certain level of democratic representation in the governance system which should allow to take into account different voices. This would be my answer to this worry about controlling data, which is very real.'

The impact of Covid

In the months after Robert-Jan's departure from his role as OA envoy, plenty of movement was happening around Plan S – albeit at a slightly slower pace than before – with the details of its implementation taking further shape through 2019. What Coalition S coordinators hadn't anticipated was the acceleration brought about by the global pandemic.

While both a tragedy and crisis, none can deny the unexpected publicity boost provided by Covid-19 in convincing the public and private stakeholders of the value of open science. And, in February 2021, senior researchers into the Covid-19 genome published an open letter calling for the data on the virus found by researchers across the world to be made open.

But first, a recap. On New Year's Eve, 2019, as millions around the world celebrated seasonal holidays and all the promise that comes with the dawn of a new decade, reports began to fly in to world health authorities about a mysterious new illness spreading across Wuhan, China. What followed over the coming months would devastate communities – and the economy – the world over.

The spread of Covid-19 around the globe made the sharing of both publications and data a necessity in the race to develop a vaccine. Within one month of it first being reported, the virus had spread across 19 countries; within six months, the pandemic had caused half a million deaths, with a total of 12 million cases recorded worldwide. It is thanks to the principles of open access that researchers have been able to speed up the process of working on treatments and cures.

By summer 2020, more than 80 trials were under way to find a Covid-19 vaccine – an unprecedented global effort that was only made possible thanks to the quick action taken by Chinese researchers to share the virus's genetic coding online. Funding bodies across all continents have made their latest findings on the novel coronavirus free and easy to access through open access – many suspending existing paywalls in the process. Making the secrets of this problem open allowed vaccinologists across continents to begin work on their own solutions to the pandemic, and ultimately embark on one of the largest-scale global collaboration projects the world has ever seen.

The Covid-19 crisis has shone a spotlight, therefore, on the importance of cooperation within the scientific community to share publications and results. It would be false to suggest that nobody knew a global health crisis was coming – international organisations such as ONE, the World Health Organization and the Coalition for Epidemic Preparedness (CEPI)[137] had all warned of the threat of viruses and, more pressingly, our lack of readiness to tackle them, for years ahead of the Covid-19 outbreak. The Ebola virus proved to be an example of that.[138] But, in late 2019, nobody in the publishing policy world at least could have predicted the Covid-19 pandemic – or the impact it would have in terms of opening up research.

The first outbreak of the new coronavirus in China prompted Jeremy Farrar, director of the Wellcome Trust, to call for medical findings to be shared freely and widely to prevent the spread of the disease and improve treatments for patients. 'Access to the most up-to-date information based on the most robust data possible helps countries understand the likelihood of future spread of the

---

[137] https://cepi.net/.
[138] Dahn B, Mussah V, Nutt C. Yes, we were warned about Ebola. *New York Times*, 7 April 2015. Retrieved from https://www.nytimes.com/2015/04/08/opinion/yes-we-were-warned-about-ebola.html (accessed 13 March 2021).

virus,' he said, reiterating the stance already firmly in place by the funder. Not only did publishers agree to take down their paywalls for the good of public health, they practically fell over themselves to do it, recognising the opportunity to shine their public image.

'What Covid has shown us is basically that publishers have conceded on OA,' says Robert Kiley, head of open research at the Wellcome Trust. 'They have recognised the value of openness, and virtually every article on Covid is open. In doing this, they've given themselves away – because they recognise that work has to be open for it to be its most valuable … but if it's ok for Covid, why not for malaria, or for stroke or breast cancer? It doesn't make sense.'

According to Maria Leptin, former director of EMBO, the answer to that question is that it is 'simply not sustainable,' at least in the short term. 'It's important that everyone does their bit to help with Covid but you can't just expand and expand on that without a cost plan in place,' she argues. 'Anyone can give some stuff away for free for a while – whether it's farmers giving their produce to food banks, whether it's newspapers offering free access to their Covid coverage … it's good and it's interesting. But it doesn't mean that the farmer can give away all their food for free. It has to be paid for somehow.'

The big question for stakeholders now will be whether those paywalls start to creep back up again once the pandemic ends. Kurt Deketelaere is for one not convinced that the positive action seen will stick in the long term – and his scepticisms stem from the attitudes he has witnessed expressed by universities, not commercial publishers. 'It's clear that a lot of people have been using the Covid situation now as a kind of stimulus to promote OA data and OA publications, and I think this has been a good thing. At the same time as publishers doing this, we have seen that universities are happy to make an exception on giving free access to publications and data immediately.

'In this one very specific case it works because obviously societal need is so high, societal pressure is so high, everyone is looking at those in power to see how they will react … and so a lot of universities have been willing to give early access to data, to publications, to what they probably otherwise would not grant access to. My feeling is that they were prepared to do this now for Covid, but that they are not so flexible or willing to do it in a general way.'

Rooryck agrees that paywalls will likely go back up once focus eventually dissipates away from the pandemic: 'That is exactly our fear.' At the same time, he has reason to feel positively that Covid-19 will have a lasting impact on the attitudes towards open science by publishers. 'The whole situation is a poster child for OA – never has it been more evident that we need this, and the fact that even publishers like Elsevier have made a certain number of journal articles open for some time is a triumph.'

'At the same time, by doing that you also see the limits of the approach, because those papers that are open cite other papers that are not. So you very quickly run into difficulties that you did not anticipate,' Rooryck notes. 'This entire crisis is really the biggest argument in favour of OA – things have to be available immediately so that other people can build on that. No paywalls, no embargoes, and of course Plan S funders are willing to pay for it. We are not suggesting this should be free.'

For Kiley, 'one positive thing, I really hope, is that Covid has changed the way we all live – whether it's the way we work, where we shop, interact with friends and neighbours, everything. But it's also shown that we can do scholarly publishing in a different way and I hope that one of the lasting legacies of this dreadful pandemic is that scholarly publishing changes,' he says.

There is already evidence to suggest that the pandemic has had a positive influence on the attitudes of researchers themselves, if nothing else. In October 2020, Frontiers surveyed around 25,000 researchers from its publishing network on the impact of the pandemic on their work. Of those who responded, 44 per cent said they were now more likely to publish in an OA journal than before Covid, and 45 per cent said they were more likely to share their data. Some 29 per cent said they were more likely to publish their work on a preprint server as a result of the changes seen during the pandemic.[139]

'In the immediate future, we may see a behavioural shift in the way researchers choose to publish,' says Kamila Markram. 'What the survey results suggest is the more aware the research community becomes of the benefits of open access to society at large, the more publishing will shift in favour of greater scientific cooperation and sharing.'

The pandemic has demonstrated what the university and research sectors are capable of achieving in a short space of time. That researchers were able to find a vaccine within a matter of weeks, when it would usually take years, is proof of the power that government support and plentiful funding can provide. But, more than this, the fact that universities were able to shift their undergraduate teaching, staff meetings, collaborations and research conferences online almost overnight surely reveals the ability of a culture to shift itself urgently when called for.

'The disruption of things like the pandemic are interesting,' says Munafo. 'One vice-chancellor of a university told me they had a 10-year climate plan to reduce emissions that they managed to achieve in about four weeks, because everyone suddenly had to start working from home. It just goes to show these radical changes can happen quickly if there's the will to do it – or some kind of external stimulus. But people resist that kind of rapid change because it feels uncomfortable.' All it takes is that external push.

'Scholarly publishing is currently undergoing a rapid period of transition and I do not expect the pace of this disruption to slow any time soon,' says Markram. 'We have seen more turbulence in the last 20 years than there has been since publishing was conceived in the 1600s, and I expect the industry will continue to evolve in line with technology. It is technology that creates the right conditions for innovation, and innovation underpins market disruption.'

---

[139] https://www.frontiersin.org/articles/10.3389/fpubh.2020.621563/full.

Putting power back into the hands of experts

The closing reflections for this book are being written at a curious time for science; the Covid-19 pandemic has triggered alarm bells over an apparent distrust of experts and scientific knowledge. Munafo believes this simply highlights how archaic the academic system still is – and how urgently the entire community needs to switch its outlook in order to regain the trust of the public. 'The culture of academia is still very much rooted in the 19th-century model, where independently wealthy people went after findings because they were interested in them and because they tended to come from a certain social background,' he says. 'The sub-text was: "You can trust us." And science is still very much built on trust. You read the results of a paper and you can't see the data or lab books or what went on behind the scenes, you just have to trust that it's being reported accurately. And you've no way of knowing or checking.'

Phrases seen in the media during the first waves of the virus outbreak appeared to suggest that politicians in particular were falling out of love with experts. On a very basic level, the science simply didn't support the mandates many governments wanted to implement or maintain: think Donald Trump's ill-advised public musing on drinking disinfectant as a cure, or the UK government's refusal to enforce public lockdowns until long after their chief scientific experts advised it.

Munafo believes scientists are 'not particularly comfortable' with the weight of trust placed on them either. 'What's interesting with the pandemic is it's really laying bare all of these issues,' he adds. 'Nothing new is happening, but all of the usual problems are being compressed into a much shorter time frame.' A few days before Munafo was interviewed for this book in late 2020, a leaked government report warned of a projected worst-case scenario of 85,000 new deaths during the UK winter. 'Reports said this was a leak by a scientist because they themselves felt uncomfortable that the current model wasn't being subject to sufficient external scrutiny because it was all being done so secretly,' says Munafo.[140]

'So the point about transparency is that it just allows for greater error checking – more pairs of eyes. And whether that's transparency through OA or through FAIR data or through pre-registration of study protocols, transparency has a role to play as an error checking mechanism or a quality control mechanism. But if we only focus on OA we could have openly available low-quality work because we have only addressed one element of the issue.'

---

[140] Roach A. Leaked Sage report 'warns of 85,000 deaths in Covid second wave'. *Evening Standard*. 29 October 2020. Retrieved from https://www.standard.co.uk/news/uk/leaked-sage-report-covid-deaths-second-wave-a4573352.html (accessed 14 March 2021).

3.5 Plan S as a continued source of debate

Despite its enormous contribution to the OA movement, Plan S remains today a controversial topic of debate. This was something Johan Rooryck felt particularly strongly when he took over from Robert-Jan as Plan S Champion in August 2019.

'Robert-Jan's parting words to me were: "keep the Coalition together", he recalls. 'I definitely felt both a bit daunted and excited when I took over, as it's never easy to follow in the footsteps of a trailblazer like him, but it's been remarkably straightforward so far. It was really nice to find a set of people who are leaders of their own organisations, both for OA but also simply as leaders for the funding organisations who are so dedicated to this cause, and who think alike and who are extremely respectful of each other in making decisions. It was a really pleasant surprise, and it's very gratifying and rewarding for me to work with them.'

Rooryck recalls wanting the job because the principles of Plan S were so much in line with his own – as demonstrated through his work helping to design the principles of the Fair Open Access Alliance, an organisation set up between OA publishing representatives and open libraries with the aim of coordinating efforts toward sustainable OA publishing. 'I asked Robert-Jan if he thought it was a good idea, me applying for the role – I wasn't sure, given my tumultuous history with Elsevier Elsevier and so on. But he said, "Yes, of course, you have my support."'

He is not blind to the fact he has his critics, however – since Robert-Jan retired from the initiative, underlying grumbles have resounded from many members of the community that progress to expand Coalition S has been slow. Rooryck does not have the extensive network Robert-Jan had coming from the European Commission; it takes time to settle into any new job, and let's not forget he has to balance several others, including his editorial role at *Glossa*. The Covid-19 pandemic has not helped matters, to say the least.

Rooryck's task was first and foremost to try and find new members for the scheme. 'But Covid presented challenges,' he says, 'the main one being that we could not travel so much, which makes it much harder to talk to people and convince them in a personal way that they should join Plan S.' His difficulties were also furthered by the natural slowing down of enthusiasm that happens with the reception of any new project, he adds: 'I think at first it's easy to get the people who were already convinced of it to sign up. The people who did not want to join at the beginning, I think, still have those same reasons not to join.

'On the other hand, the pandemic has really changed their priorities, which are now to make sure there are enough resources there to research these things and coordinate that research, and I do understand that. But, again, the Covid situation has slowed things down.'

Critics have attributed the slowing down of signatories to Plan S as a marker that the Coalition is under-resourced, or lacks authority. But Marc Schiltz brushes these statements off quickly: 'I don't see it like that, even when Plan S was in its early days there were just four people working on it,' he says. 'Countries haven't signed up for various reasons – sometimes it's political: they have their own initiatives, they don't want to be led by Europe, for example.' Others are playing it safe, he reckons, having waited until after the implementation date to see how others manage it before following suit.

In the end, he admits, it 'doesn't matter so much whether everyone has signed up' – which may sound like an admission of failure, but in fact it is the opposite: 'So long as they are implementing the same or similar principles, which many countries now do, that's what matters. We have still achieved our goal. Plan S is much more now a kind of set of references, a guideline to get to OA,' he adds. 'If a country decides to implement these principles without implicitly calling it Plan S, that's ok.'

The legacy itself is enough to justify its existence, therefore. The fact that funders and research communities across the world know what Plan S is, what it entails and what its motives are signals progress in that 'OA is being talked about more'.

No silver bullet

'A failing in Plan S was that it developed a one-size-fits-all solution for every academic discipline, and didn't understand or didn't appreciate soon enough that in fact the culture in different areas of academia are quite different – that the plan would land in a different way in different subject areas and people would have different reactions,' says Paul Ayris, pro-vice-provost (UCL Library Services) and former president of LIBER, the Association of European Research Libraries. 'I don't think there is one system for everybody – that's a misunderstanding of what the future of open science is.'

Ayris refers to the eight 'pillars' of open access as defined by the European Commission: the future of scholarly publishing, FAIR data, the EOSC, education and skills, rewards and incentives, next-generation metrics, research integrity and citizen science.[141] 'My personal view is that there are a number of possible ways forward in each of those pillars,' he explains. 'What we need is a variety of options that individual universities and individual subject areas can choose from, rather than being told there is one model and that's that. Because that's not going to work. Having a number of options which you can choose from, that deliver on your long-term objective of 100 per cent immediate OA – I think that's a model which is more likely to work.'

The need for flexibility is a point that has been argued loudly by some and grumbled about quietly by many more since the early days of Plan S. But it's

---

[141] LERU. *Press release – open science and its role in universities: A roadmap for cultural change*. LERU; 2018. Retrieved from https://www.leru.org/news/open-science-and-its-role-in-universities-a-roadmap-for-cultural-change (accessed 14 March 2021).

clear to see from the many interviews undertaken for this book that there are just as many people who feel the opposite – that it is only by delivering a broad-brush, inflexible mandate that full OA will be reached.

'It could be as always said that there is no one-size-fits-all solution – well, that's exactly what Robert-Jan wanted to do,' says Vermeir. 'I mean, really, it's one clear set of principles and it should fit everyone. Which is great because it simplifies the discussion and the situation and the policies are relatively clear. Of course there's ambiguity at first, and we all took issue with the vagueness of the principles when they were first announced – but that's why the consultation and the implementation guidelines were the next step.'

Marc Schiltz agrees: 'In years previously, we have seen all kinds of national OA policies and institutional OA policies with varying focus, but they weren't good enough; they didn't work. The reality is we all have diverging approaches to what we think should happen. Really, the biggest asset of Plan S is that it is a uniform set of principles. There is still sufficient freedom in implementing them, but these are a set of principles we can all get behind – that way it's clearer and easier for compliance.'

The counterargument to having a strong set of principles in place, of course, is that flexibility will always be compromised. From the beginning, Robert-Jan was clear in saying he didn't want to make any exceptions on the Plan S principles for humanities or social sciences, for example, after representatives of such disciplines argued their publishing system was far separate from that of the life sciences. No matter how accommodating individual funders might be, there will always be some parties for whom the principles do not work well for.

While not every small journal or publishing group can be saved, efforts are being made to monitor the extent of the casualties that may occur during the Plan S-driven shift to OA. Koen Vermeir is part of a task force being created with Coalition S to gather information on how different groups are being impacted by the changes, with particular focus on vulnerable parties such as smaller societies and research communities in less affluent areas of the world such as eastern Europe and the Global South.

'I don't think you can just say "oh well" if some disciplines disappear or some individuals cannot publish,' he says. Addressing this is part of his role as a representative of the Global Young Academy, but it is also personal, and even more so since his own humanities journal was dropped by Wiley: 'My perspective is that we really need to look out for those who fall out of the system and we cannot make it worse for them.'

Work on the official Coalition S monitoring taskforce began in autumn 2019. An early draft of the monitoring framework includes an agreement to take in to account factors including impact on the community and the need to reform the evaluation system. 'The latter is especially important for early career researchers,' says Vermeir.[142]

As Plan S members work to enforce and monitor open access practices across their communities going forward, it will be just as important for Coalition

---

[142] See appendix for full draft.

leaders to be sensitive to the needs of those who fall outside that system, and in developing countries in particular, says Lars Bjørnshauge, director of the DOAJ. 'To some extent, our challenge now is to respect different publishing cultures. We cannot expect all countries to have the same publishing culture and do the same things in the same way as us,' he warns. 'But at the same time we are really putting a lot of effort in trying to persuade publishers in all countries to adhere to what we call best publishing practice, and transparency, most of all – since we believe this is the best way to make the process fairer for the most vulnerable research communities.'

Changing the culture in academia with each new generation

According to Bodo Stern, the main barrier to enforcing OA through mandates continues to be the concern felt for young and early career researchers. A survey of HHMI-employed researchers undertaken by the Center for Open Science in autumn 2019 found that, while almost all were in favour of OA in principle, support dropped off a cliff when participants were asked how they felt about a funder mandate that may limit choice of where they could publish. Support for a mandate sat at 47 per cent among principal investigators, while trainees were slightly more in favour (57 per cent). 'What was interesting was that 47 per cent of the PIs were either in favour or opposed. There were few neutral voices in the middle – many had a strong opinion,' says Stern.[143]

Another interesting factor in the HHMI survey is that all the PIs questioned on the topic faced little to no personal jeopardy as a consequence of the changes – they were already at the height of their career, with secured tenured jobs with the institution. Their fears were expressed on behalf of the newer generations they mentored or worked with – more so than the trainees themselves. 'The one concern that stood out was that trainees may have a harder time in their career if they cannot publish where they want,' says Stern. 'That's why our OA policy tries to achieve OA without limiting journal choices too much.'

At the same time, he acknowledges that effectively it doesn't matter if the trainees are unable to publish in *Nature* or *Science* – it only matters to the researchers if it matters to the institution, i.e. the seniors above them in charge of hiring and promotions and reward and recognition ('if we don't care then

---

[143] In autumn 2019, the Center for Open Science conducted a survey of HHMI-employed scientists, their postdoctoral associates and graduate students, and a cohort of HHMI grantees who were early career scientists. The scientists surveyed represent more than 245 leading academic and non-profit research labs in the United States. Link: HHMI.org. *What HHMI scientists think about scientific publishing*. HHMI; n.d. Retrieved from https://www.hhmi.org/content/what-hhmi-scientists-think-about-scientific-publishing (accessed 14 March 2021).

they don't care either'). And so a big responsibility lies on HHMI, and other employers like it, to spread the message of substance over journal title.

Does he personally believe that restricting publishing options for trainees could limit their career progression? 'We don't know this. It's premature to conclude that the shift to OA will have this effect. We all recognise that the system is totally flawed to rely on journal name in hiring decisions. So in some ways having people not try to publish in prestigious journals or not being able to is already pushing the system in the right direction. There could be a positive outcome on that as well, that funding and hiring committees will put less emphasis on where something got published, as they should.'

But, he muses, 'it's a little bit dicey to use that argument when talking to trainees to reassure them – because then if you say, well, we don't want funding and hiring committees to make decisions based on where something is published, and this policy may push in that direction, then the trainees would say, "Well, don't play this out on our backs." So it's hard to really be sure that it isn't impacting their careers when change requires many actors to push in the same direction.'

In short, there will never be a solution to satisfy all parties completely. 'I've come to believe policies and mandates are never really perfect, they are always directional. You just want to make sure that the policy goes in the right direction. And so in this particular case directional also means that an OA policy down the road could have an impact on culture and how we publish.'

The academic community, meanwhile, is not entirely innocent in its tendency to get stuck on the finer details of Plan S, 'losing sight of the bigger picture', Ayris believes. But an important step for the continued success of Plan S – and of the OA movement overall – will be to ensure researchers are included at every step of the way. 'What we need to do now is concentrate not so much on the statements but on the implementation,' he says. 'The way you implement change in any academic organisation is not enforcement – that's the wrong word, because it feels top-down and something that is being done to a particular community. What you need is a bottom-up approach, where you are working with the academic community to show them the benefits of what the change will mean for them. And then you take the community with you and they will start to spread the message for you and to deliver on the agenda that you set.'

Example of the UCL Press

Launched in 2015, the UCL Press was the UK's first fully OA university in-house publisher. Ordinarily, it takes decades for a new publisher to build its reputation, but UCL has successfully established itself as a

(Continued)

high-quality press in a short amount of time, with 13 OA journals and more than 175 open access books to its name.

'As you can imagine, starting a new publishing activity in a very commercial environment where there are many global, well-established publishers wasn't the easiest thing to do,' says Ayris, who oversees the operation in his position as pro-vice-provost (UCL Library Services). The secret of its success, he says, is partly down to the fact it was designed with the UCL research community each step of the way. But it is also down to the emphasis the university placed on communicating to its academic body the real-time benefits of publishing OA – specifically to the humanities and social science researchers, who were much more used to working to a subscription model environment.

'The real reason for success was that we were able to identify what the benefits of OA monograph publishing were,' he explains. 'The first point of interest was that the books that we published got many more downloads and were consulted much more often than if they had been published commercially. If you publish a research monograph on arts and humanities and sell 200 copies of that book, it's quite a small number but on the whole you would say that was a good outcome. Now if you look at the number of downloads that our books were getting on UCL Press, it was beyond compare.'

The most downloaded book from UCL Press to date is authored by a group of nine people including Daniel Miller, a professor of anthropology at UCL. The book, *How the World Changed Social Media* has been downloaded more than 300,000 times all across the world, according to UCL Press figures.[144]

'The moral of the story is that OA publishing changes the impact that your research has by making it more available to more people in more countries. It's important that we communicate that message to our authors, and it's why more researchers now want to publish with UCL Press over subscription or hybrid journals – because they see that those are the benefits,' says Ayris. 'The data are all online so they can see in real time how many people are downloading it, which is a nice reward after spending years writing an academic monograph.'

---

[144] UCL Press. *Statistics* [search: 'How the World Changed Social Media']. Retrieved from https://www.uclpress.co.uk/pages/statistics (accessed 14 March 2021).

Money remains a sticking point

The financial aspect of OA is another part of the Plan S debate that is not set to disappear anytime soon. It is Maria Leptin's opinion that many intelligent researchers still confuse two very separate economic aspects of publishing – and that's a problem. 'People have muddled these two things – the exploitation going on in publishing and the question of who pays for open access science,' she argues. 'Whether publishers should be able to make so much money and exploit scientists is one thing. Then at which end the money goes in is another.'

Jean-Claude Burgelman makes a very similar argument: 'The scientist who thinks that publishing should be for free makes two mistakes. Consider travelling to a conference: first of all, when you catch the flight, you still have to pay the ticket. Secondly, you have to pay the people who fly the plane for you. The same goes for publishing. It is simply ridiculous to think you can get rid of commercial publishing and do it on top of the salaries of academics, because, if it was that simple, it would already have been mainstream.'

Still, today, stakeholders in the OA movement tend to fall into two categories: those who are adamant that the best (or, sometimes, only) argument for Plan S and OA more broadly is financial, and those who are not. It frustrates Deketelaere, for example, that more has not been made of the argument that Plan S could save institutions money. 'If universities could see proof that there is a major financial saving to be made here, certainly the support would be much higher than it is today,' he says. For example, Germany's research funders' decision not to participate in Plan S, Deketelaere says, was purely driven by the fact that 'German rectors say the bill will be higher at the end of the day than what it is now'.

Others, including Burgelman, feel strongly that the more important argument to be made for OA is that it is 'good for science'. He believes that bringing costs into the equation, and specifically attempting to curb, monitor and sanction the costs involved in the publishing industry, was the Coalition's biggest mistake. 'The friction Robert-Jan and I had on this, and which we still have, is that I think that Plan S and the Coalition should not get into the messy issue of price costing, because they simply don't have the tools to understand it in a robust way,' he says.

'My view was, let's not get into the pricing because as a funder you pay it anyway. Instead, let's concentrate on the mandate of OA and go for a pricing structure solution via an economic regulatory mechanism, not via a science policy regulatory mechanism. Pricing is not a science issue, it's an economic issue. Of course the two are related and it has an effect, but as a science policymaker you have no instruments to determine prices.'

Burgelman's approach from within the European Commission ('and here I was completely unsuccessful') was to try and get the discussion of cost out of the scientific discussion once and for all. 'Better to create a regulatory board overlooking the prices, on condition that the hybrid model is finished. Otherwise it's relatively easy for publishers to say they agree but in the meantime continue on with the reductive hybrid model.'

He continues, 'My proposal was to create a regulation policy for the prices just like we have regulatory boards on consumer matters and so on. Then you can say, this is a reasonable price and this is not.' Another advantage of having a regulatory body would be that open science is better protected, he argues, although he cautions against mistaking the need for OA with the need to kill off commercialisation altogether. 'The right to make a profit should not be confused with greed and monopoly. But that applies to everything, not just publishing – if there was no regulatory control, the price of bread would go up as well.'

Rather than see these conflicting positions, or 'finances vs ethics', as a problem, we can view the fact that two sides exist so passionately as a positive. The argument one favours is arbitrary – the fact that the case is being made for OA from multiple angles only strengthens the argument that the need to push towards an open world is urgent and wanted.

The final word on hybrids

It is curious to look back on the hybrid debate – a principle Robert-Jan never dreamed would become the root of so much aggravation and dispute. Through the nature of negotiation and consultation, it was in many ways inevitable that Plan S would have to soften on certain principles. But the hybrid policy has stood firm.

As Robert Kiley puts it, 'If Plan S is one thing, it is that we do not support hybrid OA. That is the single thing which differentiates Plan S from a million other policies, and it's the thing which has caused most debate.'

This grief came to a head in July 2020, when the governing Scientific Council of the European Research Council (ERC) – an independent body of researchers that sets the strategic direction for the ERC funding body – announced it would be dropping out of the Coalition, removing its support from Plan S with immediate effect.

Releasing a statement, the ERC said, 'During the past six months, the ERC Scientific Council has intensified its internal debate and reached a unanimous decision to follow a path towards open access implementation that is independent of Coalition S activities. Therefore it has decided to withdraw as a supporter of Coalition S.'

The decision came as a huge shock – and, to many of those involved, indicated deeper issues of internal politics at the ERC, following a crisis of management at the organisation: Mauro Ferrari, chief of the organisation for just a few months from 2019 until April 2020, was forced to resign following criticisms he had neglected his responsibilities there.

The ERC has cited its dedication to supporting early career researchers as a primary driver for its choice not to participate in Plan S. But Eve believes this is hypocritical, to say the least: 'Organisations always go on about how the real equality issue is that junior researchers won't be able to get jobs if they can't publish in top-tier journals, if they can't publish wherever they like, or if they are faced with a fee to do so. But it's like the mafia – every time they say early career researchers won't get jobs, what you need to do is put on the end of that sentence: "because we won't give them jobs if they publish anywhere except where we've said". If the people in authority control the appointment processes and the criteria they use, and they still have a problem with it … it drives me mad.'

Relatedly, others understand the ERC's decision to leave the Coalition was largely based on the hybrid issue. 'The ERC's stance is that they support OA, they want research to be open, but they think the only way to do that while publishing with the big publishers is to pay APCs. So that is why they walked away from Plan S, because they want to continue to use EC funds to pay hybrid OA fees from January 2021,' says Kiley.

Robert-Jan called the ERC's decision to distance itself from Plan S 'most unfortunate' and proof of the leadership vacuum that existed. He also pointed out that the provisions on OA in the grant agreement used by the ERC are defined by the European Commission, and not by the ERC itself.

The real tragedy of the ERC's decision is that there is now an even bigger divide between them and the funders their members wish to work with. 'Whereas to other funders Plan S will apply to grants awarded from New Year's Day 2021, and for some it will apply to any calls they make after that date, for Wellcome and Gates and a few others it applies to any papers submitted,' says Kiley. 'And the rules are straightforward: no embargo; everything CC BY licence. The only asterisk against that is if you think there's a really, really good reason why your research should not be fully open, you can apply to us and ask for an exception. Then we will consider whether to publish CC-ND (no derivatives).'

For Wellcome and others, the debate remains non-negotiable – albeit with an asterisk. 'Publishers will tell you a different story, but the hybrid model was always predicated on being a transition route to move from a subscription world to an OA world,' says Kiley. 'I remember talking to many publishers really early on – and Wellcome was one of the biggest cheerleaders on hybrid. We have spent millions on funding OA payments over the last 15 years or so. We were always supportive of it – the idea was to give publishers this parachute, this safety net, so they could gradually transition their model from a subs to an OA model.

'Of course, what we've seen is that 15 years later, the number of subscription journals which have flipped is miniscule. So this sense that it's a transition model to help publishers move from A to B hasn't happened. And the only way we've got publishers to the table and got them to engage in these sorts of transformative arrangements is by making it clear: we ain't paying anymore. And if you don't like that, that's difficult really. Because that's our policy.'

Looking beyond the APC model

In early 2020, Coalition S commissioned a study into non-commercial (aka 'diamond') publishing platforms, with the aim of identifying ways to support diamond publishing initiatives going forward. This was a significant step in that it signalled to stakeholders the Coalition's intention to explore non-APC models as a tangible long-term alternative to gold, which remains popular among European publishers. It also reflected the original intentions set out by Robert-Jan in the very early days of Plan S.

The Diamond OA Journals Study was funded by Science Europe and published in March 2021 by OASPA. Its findings drew from analysis of around 29,000 journals, the majority of which (60 per cent) were in the humanities and social sciences. The work was undertaken between June 2020 and February 2021 by a consortium of 10 organisations (including OASPA) led by OPERAS.

What the analyses uncovered may not have come as a surprise to those with a vested interest – but the report has helped to formalise challenges that may once have been seen as difficult to pinpoint, and allowed experts to outline the steps needed to support diamond OA going forward.

Particular concerns highlighted include the issue of copyright licences and content preservation, as well as the financial challenges involved in running diamond OA journals, which still rely heavily on volunteering (at least in Europe and North America). The report highlights 'a need to develop infrastructure and to increase funding to support their operations'.

A set of recommendations – to libraries, universities, research funders and governments – was also published in line with the report and the objectives of Coalition S. This was put together by AmeliCA's Arianna Becerril-García and the DOAJ's Lars Bjørnshauge, among others.[145]

'The OA Diamond study highlights the importance of the many thousands of OA journals published without charging authors and their institutions for publishing,' says Bjørnshauge. 'It is highly overdue that these stakeholders put much more financial support in that direction. OA Diamond is a much more inclusive and cheaper way to provide access for all authors to participate in a truly global scholarly communication system.'

Will the US make a move on OA?

After the initial excitement felt during the Coalition's trip to the US in October 2018, US funders have been admittedly less receptive to the prospect of joining Plan S. Two years later, the same sticking points remained for US parties, namely politics – it being much more difficult to get motions passed in the states at a federal level, but also the fact that policymakers were gearing up

---

[145] https://zenodo.org/record/4562790#.YMXOuTb0nDI.

for the 2020 presidential election, not to mention a major global health crisis in the form of Covid-19 – all these things meant attention was understandably focused elsewhere.

But, after two years of stagnation, OA campaigners in the US began to see some movement once again. On 1 October 2020, the Howard Hughes Medical Institute announced it would be implementing a new, Plan S-compliant OA policy coming into place from 2021, with the new publishing rules effective from January 2022. Releasing a statement, the institute confirmed the new policy 'will require all HHMI laboratory heads to publish in a manner that makes their research articles freely available on the publication date under a Creative Commons Attribution License (CC BY)'.[146]

With more than 2,300 employees, HHMI is the largest private biomedical research institution in the US, with an annual spend of more than $750 million. The news it was joining Coalition S was therefore a huge cause for celebration. So what took the HHMI so long?

'The reason was, it's complicated,' says the HHMI's Bodo Stern. 'OA is complicated. If you keep it at a very high level, everyone is for OA and everyone understands why it's important. But as soon as you dig in, you realise that it's a complex net'. Where a funder like Wellcome can impose a rule on its grantees that only impacts on the money they give out, HHMI employs its scientists, Stern explains, and the HHMI policy covers not just research supported with HHMI money but also research supported by other funding sources. 'So it's more complicated.'

Robert-Jan had already tried to convince HHMI to sign up to Plan S in 2018 when he spoke to senior management at the agency, and, although he noted a strong interest and indication of support, he was told that HHMI needed more time, notably to convince more of its own researchers.

As such, HHMI does not strictly say it has joined Plan S, rather that its policy is fully aligned with Plan S principles. 'There are some differences to Plan S. We've decided to define the work that is subject to this policy as major contributions – so where our scientists are either first, last, co-first, co-last or corresponding authors. Articles to which our scientists made minor contributions are not subject to this policy.'

In November 2020, the world shifted in its outlook once again, following the highly anticipated US election. When Joe Biden took the majority after a long and very drawn-out vote count, liberals rejoiced the world over. At the same time, some expressed fears that the change in administration was unlikely to result in any rapid change towards science and research policy; to expect it would only be cause for disappointment – take, for example, the lack of power Barack Obama held in that area without the backing of Congress.

---

[146] HHMI.org. *HHMI announces open access publishing policy*. HHMI; 2020. Retrieved from https://www.hhmi.org/news/hhmi-announces-open-access -publishing-policy (accessed 15 March 2021).

Heather Joseph, executive director of SPARC, is confident that the Biden administration is excellent news for the OA movement, however. 'Actually we're really optimistic, and SPARC will be pushing for this and offering our consultation services wherever they are wanted,' she says. How quickly Biden will be able to move on OA is one challenge, but the question of whether or not he will is not a concern for Joseph or those in the industry. In 2015, when Biden was vice president under Obama, his eldest son, Beau, died from an aggressive brain tumour. While his son was being treated, Biden became intimately involved in trying to understand the latest research and potential experimental treatments that Beau could receive.

'He dug into the notion that the doctors at the medical centre where he was being treated sometimes didn't have access to the latest article – and well, he was infuriated by it,' says Joseph. 'In seeking out options, some of the data was transferred from the medical centre here in Washington, DC, to an experimental cancer centre in Texas. Biden was enraged when it took them 48 hours to reformat the data from one centre to another.'

After the tragic death of his son, Biden channelled his efforts, becoming a champion for open access to cancer data and articles, and establishing a research initiative known as the 'cancer moonshot' in the US.[147] Part of the requirement of receiving funding through the initiative is that all research funded by the NIH and the National Cancer Institute must be published with a zero embargo period and be made openly available from the moment it is published.

Even if its central federal funding bodies never explicitly join Plan S in writing, it is hoped the US will see more of the same kinds of initiatives and mandates going forward – which ultimately lead towards the same goal. 'Biden's top priority coming in as president is threefold,' Joseph says. 'One is getting a handle on the pandemic and preventing another one from happening. Second is beginning to address climate change. And the third is infrastructure: rebuilding the economy centred around science and research. For that we're going to focus on public universities that are the centrepiece of the American education system, because, really, what will drive recovery is investment in scientific research.'

Again, Marc Schiltz makes the point that whether or not the US signs up to Plan S in full is neither here nor there. 'I think we have come far enough to make the goal of reaching OA a reality,' he says. 'It's being heavily discussed in the US and that may take a bit more time – we will see; maybe the new US administration will move things quicker now. But those who criticise Plan S in saying, "well you haven't even got the US federal funders on board", I would say no – in fact they have an even larger coalition with similar principles to this one. That's what I saw after 2013, that all funders were independently setting

---

[147] National Cancer Institute. *Cancer MoonshotSM public access and data sharing policy*. National Cancer Institute; 2017. Retrieved from https://www.cancer.gov/research/key-initiatives/moonshot-cancer-initiative/funding/public-access-policy.

good intentions. There should always be more, yes, but that has become a rather weak argument. And I think most publishers also know that.'

3.6 Open science: the new normal

The founding idea behind Plan S was always that it should be set out as part of an overall open science policy by the European Commission. In 2014, the commission organised a public consultation regarding trends in science and the academic system more broadly – around that time there had been strong indications that the research system was undergoing big changes, both in the ways it was undertaken and presented. Respondents to the consultation confirmed this almost unanimously, citing the exponential growth of data, the availability of digital technologies to mine these data, the enormous growth of the global science community and increased opportunities for collaboration as key drivers of this change.

There was also, notably, increased demand from the surrounding academic community for better transparency in science publishing, while stakeholders wanted more bang for their buck. The respondents called for more openness and better cooperation. In short, they called for open science, or 'science 2.0' (a term that was later dropped to avoid confusion with 'industry 4.0' – another key driver of the changes to working life).

When asked about the possible advantages of open science, the respondents to the consultation mentioned among others: a faster circulation of new ideas, better use of public money, increased mutual respect and understanding, less scientific misconduct, more transparency, more support and ownership in society and more funding for research.

The respondents were also quite clear about the priorities of an open science agenda: open access to scientific publications, open access to data, and more global cooperation notably on grand societal challenges as outlined in the UN's Sustainable Development Goals. Research integrity, citizen science, a new reward and recognition system in academic organisations, the development of new metrics to assess the output of research and training, and training and education on open science: suddenly a scientific utopia seemed within reach.

In the period following the public consultation, clear strategies were identified for each of these priorities, Plan S being of the most noticeable, along with the European Open Science Cloud to facilitate OA data, an update of the European Code on Research Integrity and a proposal for Horizon Europe with greater emphasis on global science cooperation. A high-level committee, the Open Science Policy Platform, was set up to advise the European Commission on the further development and practical implementation of an open science policy and agenda.

Johannes Vogel, president of the Natural History Museum in Berlin, was appointed as chairman of the platform, and has provided sage advice to the

European Commission on its behalf since 2016. Sadly, the Open Science Policy Platform's final meeting took place on 5 February 2020, following the departure of Moedas and the appointment of a new European Commissioner for Research.

It is Robert-Jan's strong belief that the all-encompassing policy approach to open science was, and still is, essential for Plan S to succeed: 'Without alternative metrics to measure the quality and impact of research as an alternative to the journal impact factor, and without alternative metrics to recognise and reward scientists for their work as an alternative to counting citations in so-called high-impact subscription journals, it would be extremely difficult to get full support for OA within the academic community,' he says. Unfortunately, progress on both themes has proven to be extremely slow.

3.7 Taking stock of the legacy

On 1 January 2021, Plan S rules were finally implemented by its member bodies. And the headlines generated would hardly have been believed even a year previously. At the time of writing, 160 journals published by Elsevier are now registered as Plan S-aligned transformative journals. The majority of Springer Nature's 1,700 journals are also committed to transitioning to full OA and adhere to the Transformative Journal Framework.[148] This follows progress from Wiley and Cambridge University Press,[149] among others.

'With Plan S going into its implementation stage, universities will be forced to adjust their rewards and recognition systems and this time to take this seriously,' says Robert-Jan. 'No longer can the number of publications in subscription journals such as *Science* and *Nature* be used as a sole metric to measure academic output, since Plan S prescribes that all publications should appear in high-quality OA journals or on high-quality OA platforms.' It is true that thousands of universities and individuals from around the globe have signed the now-famous Declaration on Research Assessment (DORA), by which they commit themselves to improve research assessment practices and promise to move away from using journal-based metrics like impact factor. 'But in practice there are only a few that have walked the walk,' says Robert-Jan.

---

[148] Springer Nature. *Transformative journals | Open research*. Springer Nature; n.d. Retrieved from https://www.springernature.com/gp/open-research/transformative-journals (accessed 15 March 2021).

[149] Coalition S. *Over 200 Cambridge University Press journals become Plan S aligned transformative journals | Plan S*. Coalition S; 2020. Retrieved from https://www.coalition-s.org/over-200-cambridge-university-press-journals-become-plan-s-aligned-transformative-journals (accessed 15 March 2021).

Even in the summer of 2021, Liverpool University in the UK – one of around 2,200 organisations signed up to DORA at the time of writing – came under fire for introducing some archaic measures for assessing researcher performance. Struck by financial challenges, the university announced plans to cut 32 posts from its Faculty of Health and Life Sciences. But to fight to keep their jobs, academics were asked to demonstrate how much income their research was worth, along with a "substantial contribution" in other areas, for instance by producing "world-leading" publications.[150]

DORA commented that it was in private discussions with Liverpool about the issue, but at the time of writing, the industrial dispute remained unresolved. In an editorial piece for *Research Professional News*[151], DORA's Stephen Curry reflected: 'One lesson is that the declaration's authors did not consider redundancy as a possible outcome of research assessment, focusing instead on hiring, promotion and funding decisions. However, in my view, redundancy processes should not be delegated to crude metrics and should be informed by the principles of DORA.'

'That said,' he added, 'it is not DORA's job as an organisation to intervene in the gritty particulars of industrial disputes. Nor can we arbitrate in every dispute about research assessment practices within signatory organisations.'

Still, today, in many universities researchers are assessed and rewarded on the basis of the number of publications in so-called high-impact journals. They are not assessed on what they publish but on where they publish. Neither are they rewarded for the quality of their teaching, the number of start-ups they generate, for science communication or providing scientific support to policymaking. The reward system only turns around one single metric: the number of publications behind paywalls. 'From that point of view, the academic world is extremely conservative – old habits being utterly persistent,' says Robert-Jan.

It would be easy to lose heart when taking these persistent challenges into consideration. But there is also plenty of evidence of a change in the research culture, too. Schiltz for one, is understandably proud of what has been achieved so far, and optimistic for the future. 'Let's imagine for a moment that we do not achieve full OA – and I think we will, but suppose for a moment we won't,' he says. 'One of the interesting things that was really triggered by Plan S, and is still so important, is that we are now in a place of reassessing the reward system in science.'

That the need to readdress the research culture was included within the Plan S documentation from day one has really made the changes felt possible, he reasons: 'In acknowledging that the scientific reward system was setting the wrong incentives, we also committed funders to take that problem into their hands and agree to change it. In Science Europe, this is our top priority, the

---

[150] https://www.nature.com/articles/d41586-021-01991-z.

[151] https://www.researchprofessionalnews.com/rr-news-uk-views-of-the-uk-2021-9-how-should-dora-be-enforced/.

same as the European Commission, and so it's still the thing I am particularly proud of.'

In this regard, Plan S has far exceeded his expectations. Did he ever think the Coalition would get this far? 'No, I didn't,' he laughs. 'I don't know what Robert-Jan's told you but there were moments where I think both of us were really worried. There were various times when I certainly felt we were close to complete failure, but Robert-Jan kept saying, "No, let's go, let's move forward" – even when things were very difficult.'

'I remember in one of our very first meetings we said clearly to each other, we will not go for another empty statement of principles. I didn't want to see one more declaration of intent. We agreed immediately that if we wanted to make a difference, Plan S must be more than that. And I won't say we were walking into the dark but, well, almost. It was very intense in the early months for all of us. But I greatly enjoyed working with Robert-Jan, in a sense we completed each other well.

'I wouldn't have expected it to be so successful, actually, and the spill-over on questioning the research cultures, the reward system – that's just wonderful. That's the root of the problem and we have managed to bring that discussion to the table. It's the best outcome of all.'

The final reflections for this book come at a curious moment in science; we are on the cusp of a data revolution that will transform the way we live, work, learn and study forever. It is true that the Covid-19 pandemic has caused much damage to society, but, like any disruptive force, it has also paved the way for new opportunities to start afresh.

We are facing a complete rewrite of the systems through which science is communicated – in part sparked by the shared global mission of fighting Covid-19 and indeed preventing future pandemics, and in part thanks to the disruption started in 2018 by Plan S. Key to making OA work in the longer term will be nurturing a kinder working environment for scholars, supported by funders but also publishers, societies and independent stakeholders alike.

As we are finalising this book, the Portuguese Foundation for Science and Technology (FCT) has joined Coalition S, bringing the number of full members to 26. And in the US, after intense negotiations, the University of California and Elsevier have finally signed a four-year transformative agreement, whereby the university's researchers can publish open access papers and read content across Elsevier's extensive journal portfolio.

In terms of European progress, the Netherlands appears to be leading the way, with the percentage of publications made fully OA by Dutch universities growing to an estimated 75 per cent in 2020. The remaining 25 per cent will most likely be realised over the next three years as part of a number of transformative agreements with commercial publishers. The Dutch government remains committed to reaching 100 per cent OA.

In June 2021, a report published by the European Commission confirmed that 83 per cent of all publications resulting from research grants under Horizon 2020 were published open access.[152]

And, finally, Robert-Jan admits the 'S' in 'Plan S' did not stand for science, shock, solution or speed... It was in fact the name of the file that he created on the day of his appointment as open access envoy: Plan Smits.

---

[152] https://ec.europa.eu/info/news/new-report-confirms-positive-momentum-eu-open-science-2021-sep-06_en.

Epilogue

Seven Lessons Learned

Robert-Jan Smits

Plan S was without doubt one of the most challenging yet rewarding assignments I undertook during my Brussels career. What was supposed to be a sabbatical year in anticipation of my return to the Netherlands turned out to be a year-long, non-stop rollercoaster of events. It was exhausting and at times frustrating, but I learned a lot too – and I would not have wanted to miss the opportunity for a second. Would I have done things differently? Do I have regrets? To me, it makes no sense wondering 'what if'. That's not my style. I did what I had to do and what I could do.

Plan S was a stone thrown in the water: it rocked the world of scientific publishing off its feet and accelerated the transition to full and immediate open access. But there is still a long way to go.

For the journey to be completed, leadership is required from science policymakers, the funders of science and the science community itself. Furthermore, flanking measures are necessary – new metrics must be continuously developed and expanded upon to recognise and reward researchers working in the academic sphere in a much fairer and more rounded way. We must move away from journal impact factor as an urgent priority – the system cannot wait for the slow, natural progression made with each new generation of researchers.

How to cite this book chapter:
Smits, R-J. and Pells, R. 2022. *Plan S for Shock: Science. Shock. Solution. Speed.*
  Pp. 197–200. London: Ubiquity Press. DOI: https://doi.org/10.5334/bcq.e.
  License: CC-BY-NC

As long as the careers of scientists are determined mainly by where they publish (which is not necessarily identical to what they publish), and as long as scientists are not sufficiently rewarded for their teaching, knowledge transfer to industry, the commercial ideas and start-ups they create, the science communication they embark upon or the expertise and support they provide to policymakers … the transition to full OA will be hard to complete. This all makes the open science agenda so important.

And, dear members of the science community, let's not repeat the mistakes made for scientific article publishing when it comes to data. We must avoid at all costs the possibility that one day, research data that are generated with the support of the public purse are locked behind paywalls, inaccessible for further research. The Covid-19 crisis has shown us the importance of sharing both academic publications and research data. Let's not stop here with Covid – let's make this the new normal. It will help us to tackle some of the other major challenges we are facing, for instance cancer, climate change, energy transition and food security.

Reflecting on my time as OA envoy, I can see there were seven key lessons learned in the process of launching and nurturing Plan S – lessons that I believe could provide a reliable blueprint for others seeking to positively disrupt existing systems by robust policy initiatives. They are as follows:

1. Make a plan

Define a vision, based on a strong rationale, and make a plan (and roadmap) to realise the vision. Keep these simple. Adhere to the KISS principle ('Keep It Simple, Stupid').

2. Seek out allies

Mobilise the best and strongest networks and allies: you just can't do this by yourself. Create a coalition of do-ers. This will also allow you the space required from time to time to consider the challenges from a distance, and think critically and creatively about the next steps.

3. Listen to your peers

Listen to the advice of your peers, of those who are respected in the community and have credibility and influence. These might often be individuals who do not represent a particular organisation or institution, but are considered to be experts and respected for who they are as a person. Be willing to follow their advice without compromising on Lesson 1. Make them your allies and your advocates.

4. Communicate, and stay in the news

Communicate both inside and outside your organisation and be visible to the press. Stay in the news ... even if this requires putting out confrontational messages and bold statements. Someone's upset or disagrees? At least they're talking about it.

5. Engage with your opponents

It is important not to dismiss the concerns of your critics. Try to understand their concerns and address them. Stay serene in your exchanges with them, but firm in your conviction that you are doing the right thing. Adopt, where possible, some of their ideas without compromising on what you want to achieve. Make cease-fire deals, with those who have the same vision but want to follow different routes to realise the vision. It is the end goal that matters, after all. Beware of 'friendly fire': most often, the strongest opposition does not come from the outside but from within your own organisation, from those who you believe to be on board, on your side, who did not speak out. Remember that silence is not synonymous with consent.

6. Learn to be resilient

Each big new initiative should start with a bang – and hopefully there will be plenty of hype around it. But this will not last. Be aware, and be prepared that, once the hype is over, there will be moments of doubt and despair. At times, things might get rough or ugly, possibly even resorting to personal attacks and comments from opponents that hit below the belt. In such difficult times, be persistent and stay calm. Once again, be prepared for friendly fire coming from within your own organisation, too.

7. Know when it is done; plan an exit

Exit your initiative at the right moment – recognise when success has been achieved and your initiative is ready to go mainstream. Determine the moment of this exit yourself but make sure that, by that time, your initiative is fully embedded in the system, so that it can continue to flourish without you. It is therefore crucial that you set up and leave behind enough people, structures and partner organisations to ensure continuity. And, if you cannot help but feel you are in a dead-end street, first think about Lesson 6 and then, but only then, let go. It is necessary to do this in order to avoid your initiative (and, with it, you yourself) disappearing into a swamp.

***

Very soon after my return to the Netherlands, these seven lessons were put into practice at the Eindhoven University of Technology, where I joined as president upon leaving my post at the European Commission. One of the first decisions that my two colleagues on the executive board and I took concerned a robust gender equality plan: the Irene Curie Fellowship Programme, aimed at boosting the number of female staff at Eindhoven.

The plan was simple and robust: vacant posts at our university would only be opened up to female candidates. The rationale for this measure was crystal clear: in Europe, the Netherlands sits at the bottom of the list as regards the number of female researchers employed by universities. Within the Netherlands, the Eindhoven University of Technology was way down the list, which was frankly embarrassing. We had to do something about this!

Once announced, the plan went viral and triggered a debate around the globe on gender quotas. It was a controversial plan – a kind of Plan S for gender equality – and was heavily criticised just as we had expected. And, yes, there was plenty of friendly fire from within the institution, too. Despite the criticism, we stayed resilient and within 10 months were able to show with conviction that the plan was successful: 63 top female talents were recruited within that time frame from around the globe.

In 2020, inspired by what we had done, the Dutch government announced a bill that called for a gender quota of 30 per cent for the supervisory boards of listed companies. Yes, that made us feel proud. There is also an exit plan for the radical gender policy measure at our university: once we have successfully reached a minimum female ratio of 30 per cent, the measure will be phased out. Of course, the challenges involved are nuanced and will take some care to manage over the coming years. But the point here is to demonstrate that the seven lessons really do work, regardless of topic or challenge.

Plan S and the lessons I learned from that amazing year as Europe's OA special envoy are still with me – will always be with me – and continue to help me in my job. My parting advice from the experience: if you really believe in something, just go for it!

Index

A

AAM. *See* author accepted manuscript
AAS. *See* African Academy of Sciences
academia, culture of   178
academic authors   5, 12, 62
  idea of   141
academic community   16, 54, 58, 60, 63, 78, 79, 100, 131, 153, 172, 183, 191, 192
academic conferences   22
academic content   7
academic data
  Europe's role in protecting   171
  managing   170
  purpose of   161
academic freedom   88, 101, 108
  attack on   113
academic groups   147
academic institution   8, 12, 20, 36, 51, 133

academic journals   2
  subscription model for   3
Academic Publishing Europe (APE) conference   123, 124
academic publishing/publishers   5, 115, 124, 126
  future of   131
  in Europe   28
  market   47
  monopoly of   135
  practices   88
  predatory vs. reputable   91
  structure   158
academic research   26
  Brussels   43
  era for academic publishing   36
  European campaign   36
  Finch Report   42
  history repeating   iii, 29
  internet and OA   32
  publishing becomes big business   30

slow progress   46
Wellcome Trust and Gates
    Foundation for OA   37
academic researcher   31
academic reward system   170
academic scholars   xiii, 3, 26
Academy of Finland (AKA)   99
access
  burden of negotiating   4
  journals, subscription-based
    model of   31
  research papers   51
  to journals   20
active researchers   142
African Academy of Sciences
    (AAS)   127
African Education Research
    Database (AERD)   25, 111
African Library and Information
    Associations and Institutions
    (AfLIA)   26, 93, 111
African researchers   26
African-based academics   25
Amazon Web Services   161
AmeliCA   188
American Association for the
    Advancement of Science
    (AAAS)   39, 58, 101, 105, 124
American Astronomical Society
    (AAS)   34, 35
anachronism   148, 156
APCs. *See* article processing charge
article processing charge
    (APCs)   8, 43, 52, 53, 71, 72,
    75, 81, 83, 85, 90, 101, 104,
    105, 108, 109, 163
  and quality debate,   110
  model   188
  price of   85
  regulation of   8
article publishing charge
    (APCs)   144
articles

for business model   142
publication process   156
submissions   134
Artificial Intelligence Review
    Assistant (AIRA)   161
artificial intelligence software   161
Asamoah-Hassan, Helena   26,
    93, 111
ASAP (Aligning Science Across
    Parkinson's) foundation   25,
    50, 54
Association of European Research
    Libraries   73, 180
attitudes   163
  commercial powers   154
  of researchers   xiii
  publishers   113, 147, 148, 152
  towards cost will change   163
audiences   22, 23, 26, 32, 82, 89, 96,
    97, 98, 100, 102, 121
author accepted manuscript
    (AAM)   116
Ayris, Paul   97, 180, 183, 184

B

Bayazit, Kumsal   153, 154
Becerril-García, Arianna   124, 125,
    126, 188
Benzer, Seymour   55
Beretz, Alain   78
Berlin Declaration on Open Access
    to Knowledge   36, 40
Berlin Open Access
    Conference   120
Bermuda Principles   37
best value proposition   137
Biden, Joe   189, 190
BIF. *See* biobank impact factor
Bill and Melinda Gates Foundation
    39, 104, 106, 107, 129
biobank impact factor (BIF)   169
Bjørnshauge, Lars   8, 9, 53, 92, 94,
    182, 188

BMC Biology   165
Bogaert, Cynthia   67
books   7, 20, 24, 28, 48, 87, 88, 101, 112, 146, 184
Boyce, Peter   34
Bratislava Declaration on Young Researchers   108
Brill Publishers   145, 146, 157
  community of researchers   146
  journals   145
bureaucracy   25
Burgelman, Jean-Claude   13, 45, 46, 47, 75, 84, 85, 158, 170, 171, 172, 174, 185
business models   37, 39, 44, 49, 50, 52, 70, 74, 76, 101, 105, 106, 112, 131, 139, 142, 144

C

Callaway, Pam   1, 2, 4, 18, 22, 23
Callaway, Tom   161, 167
Cambon-Thomsen, Anne   168, 170, 174
Cambridge Analytica scandal   172
Cambridge University Press   68, 192
career progression   85, 183
career researcher groups   110, 116
CC BY licence   9, 75, 141, 143, 157, 187
CEPI. *See* Coalition for Epidemic Preparedness
chemistry journals   84
CNRS   166, 168
Coalition for Epidemic Preparedness (CEPI)   175
Coalition S   87, 99, 108, 112, 114
  agreement and key principles   86, 117
  associates and supporters   97
  grantees   144
  implementation task force   116
Collins, Francis   103, 104

commercial publishers/publishing   xiii, 11, 22, 25, 32, 34, 44, 48, 50, 51, 53, 55, 68, 71, 75, 92, 99, 100, 109, 112, 123, 125, 126, 141, 147, 148, 149, 150, 154, 169, 176, 185, 194
commercialization   186
  Latin America   125
  of academic data   167
communications system copies   155
compromises   84
Conference on Open Access Scholarly Publishing (COASP)   101
connectivity   24
copyright   3, 7, 13, 21, 52, 62, 84, 86, 87, 114, 117, 124, 140, 141, 188
Córdova, France   104
Covid-19   xii, 11, 24
  crisis   132, 175, 198
  form of   189
  genome   175
  global mission of fighting   194
  journals   133
  lockdowns   24
  vaccine for   171
Cox, Brian   30, 31
Creative Commons Attribution License (CC BY)   9, 75, 86, 87, 117, 140, 143, 157, 189
credit rating agencies   101
cultural change   58
Curry, Stephen   58, 193
cyberchondriac   23

D

DASH. *See* Digital Access to Scholarship at Harvard
data hugging   100
data management plans (DMPs)   172

data mining   9, 46, 171, 173
data ownership   167, 169, 171
data regulator   174
data services   131
data sharing   159, 171
data stewardship   162, 170, 172
data transparency   162
data, open sharing of   162
databases   9, 17, 20, 35, 40, 53, 94, 127
data-leaking scandals   171
de Rijcke, Sarah   54
de Vries, Saskia   73
Declaration on Research Assessment (DORA)   10, 41, 57, 193
Deketelaere, Kurt   80, 81, 82, 97, 167, 168, 176, 185
Dekker, Sander   45, 46
Diamond OA Journals Study   188
diamond publishing   126, 188
Digital Access to Scholarship at Harvard (DASH)   20
digital content agreements   133
digital distributions   150
digital literacy   25
digital object identifier (DOI)   90
digital technologies   133, 191
digitisation   36, 62, 65, 166
Dijkgraaf, Robbert   44
Directory of Open Access Journals (DOAJ)   8, 46, 53, 92, 93, 94, 125, 182, 188
DMPs. *See* data management plans
DORA. *See* Declaration on Research Assessment
double-dipping   52, 72
draft implementation guidance document   116
Droegemeier, Kelvin   103, 106
Dutch Research Council (NWO)   15, 75, 87

E

Earney, Liam   18, 133, 134
editorial rebellions   122

editorial writings   49
Eisen, Michael   115, 116, 156, 165
Elbakyan, Alexandra   41, 51, 52
electronic subscription   4
eLife   *25, 156, 164, 165*
Elsevier   4, 11, 26, 32, 47, 49, 50, 52, 54, 59, 60, 73, 74, 100, 101, 115, 119, 120, 122
  and Project DEAL   123
  anti-OA campaigning   50
  business models   101
embargoes   81, 129, 177
EMBO   135, 157, 176
EPSC   65, 66, 67
Eurodoc working group   82
Europe
  coordination and harmonisation within   173
  data infrastructures and practices in   172
European Code on Research Integrity   191
European Commission   43, 44, 45, 46, 65, 66, 68, 71, 74, 75, 82, 84, 87, 94, 96, 99, 129, 130, 168, 172, 174, 180, 191, 192, 195, 200
European consortia   152
European OA initiatives   89
European Open Science Cloud (EOSC)   171, 172, 173, 174, 180
European Research Council (ERC)   41, 77, 87, 95, 186, 187
European research funding programme   99
European Universities Association (EUA)   47, 115
EuroScience Open Forum (ESOF)   95, 96
Eve, Martin   10, 24, 55, 91, 115, 141
external funding   29

F

F1000 Research   127, 155, 156, 158
FAIR principles   172, 173
Farrar, Jeremy   107, 175
federal funders   106, 110, 190
finances vs. ethics   186
financial sustainability crisis   126
Finch Report   42
Foster, Russell   165
funders, role of   168
Fyfe, Aileen   28, 29

G

Garfield, Eugene   53, 54
Gielen, Stan   15, 22, 62, 75, 76, 113, 114, 140, 169, 170, 173, 174
Ginsparg, Paul   33, 34, 35, 92
Glasziou, Paul   160
Global Challenges Research Fund   25
global economy   30
Global North   111, 124, 125, 126, 127, 163
Global Young Academy   166, 181
Greek tragedy   172

H

Haange, Rem   74
Harvard University   7, 20, 105, 129, 140
HHMI. *See* Howard Hughes Medical Institute
higher education
  and research   133
  sector   135
high-impact journals   54, 59, 62, 193
Hippler, Horst   124
historical texts   21
Horizon Europe   99, 117, 191
Howard Hughes Medical Institute (HHMI)   163, 182, 183, 189
humanities research   24, 146
hybrid journals   53, 71, 84, 90, 101, 107, 110, 113, 133, 137, 138, 184
hybrid policy   186
hybrid publishing   103, 108, 110

I

impact factor, obsession with   53
impact framework   169
Inchcoombe, Steven   50, 142, 143, 149, 165, 166
inclusiveness   24
India, public research in   127
individual contracts   138
individual research articles   57
innovation, barriers from   162
institutions
  reduced-rate access for   25
  role of   168

J

Jisc   18, 133
Joseph, Heather   34, 49, 104, 129, 190
journals
  academic   2, 3, 5, 7, 27, 31, 34
  access to   6, 20, 123
  and publishers   8, 36, 121, 137
  APCs for   125, 143
  Brill   145
  editors   57, 58, 123, 156
  Elsevier   26
  gold vs diamond access   9
  hybrid   41, 52, 53, 71, 84
  level of quality   93
  papers, traditional publishing of   167
Juncker, Jean-Claude   65, 67, 68, 97, 129

K

Kamila, Markram   136, 138, 154, 161, 177
Karliczek, Anja   88
Kavanagh, Mary   102, 103, 105
key performance indicator (KPI)   100

Kiley, Robert   37, 38, 139, 140, 144, 153, 155, 156, 161, 171, 176, 177, 186, 187
Kolman, Michiel   124
Kratsios, Michael   103, 106
Kuster, Stephan   87
Kvajo, Mirna   165

L

Lange, Jasmin   69, 70, 71, 72, 143, 145, 157
Latin America   xiii, 9, 40, 124
Latin American journals   125
Lawrence, Rebecca   159, 160
Lawson, Rebecca   165
League of European Research Universities (LERU)   78, 80, 81, 82, 97, 167
legacy publishers   137, 147, 154
Leptin, Maria   135, 157, 162, 176, 185
LERU. *See* League of European Research Universities
LIBER   73, 95, 180
libraries
  academic   11, 31, 73, 98
  public   10, 29
  universities   4
library consortia   71, 134
literature   4, 7, 11, 21, 28, 32, 40, 48, 55, 92, 111, 116
Los Alamos National Laboratory   33
Luchtmans, Jordaan   28

M

Mabe, Michael   68
machine learning technologies   161
Mackie-Mason, Jeffrey   150
manuscript   8, 16, 142, 143, 148
  author accepted manuscript (AAM)   116
Max Planck Society (MPG)   36, 40, 119

Maxwell, Robert   30, 31
medical research   19, 22, 107, 160, 189
Meijer, Gerard   118, 119, 120, 124, 132
misconception   8, 93, 170, 171, 174
Mitchell, Rafael   25
Moedas, Carlos   66, 67, 96, 99, 192
monograph   86, 87, 88, 101, 118, 146, 184
Munafo, Marcus   16, 17, 158, 172, 177, 178

N

Nature Publishing Group   69
nature-branded journals   163
non-academic content   7
non-academic readers   4, 7
non-APC models   188
non-disclosure agreement (NDA)   4, 115
non-open access journals   7

O

OA. *See* open access
'OA Switchboard' initiative   139
OAD. *See* Open Access Directory
Obama, Barack   42, 102, 189, 190
Office of Science and Technology Policy (OSTP)   50, 103, 105, 106
O'Neill, Gareth   82, 83, 84
open access (OA)
  articles   72
  book publishing   53, 71, 145
  business models   70
  campaigners   42, 69, 154, 189
  commercial publishers   92, 104, 123
  cost of publishing   7
  definition of   40
  demand for   134

diamond   8
domain   22, 131
economic sense   11
envoy and delegates   68
financial aspect of   185
for lay readers   4
gold   42
green   87, 89, 96, 108, 142
Incentive Fund in 2010   22
initiative   40, 44, 70, 81
migration   134
models   141
pillars of   180
platform publishers   156
principles   xiii
principles of   40
privilege of publishing   8
public interest   18
quality and trustability of research   16
research process   14
transition to   53, 68, 114, 121, 136, 145, 149, 163, 166, 198
value of   134
Open Access Directory (OAD)   123
open access envoy   65
  European tour   77
  forming plan   67
  gaining allies   75
  impact on smaller publishers   70
  support from universities   80
  warning bells   72
Open Access Scholarly Publishers Association (OASPA)   135, 139, 188
Open Library of the Humanities   135
Open Research Platform in April 2018   127
Open Science Policy Platform   191, 192
openness of data   167
OSTP. *See* Office of Science and Technology Policy

P

paid-for distribution   3
paper, pay-per-view basis   4
paywalls   2, 3, 4, 7, 13, 15, 19, 23, 24, 36, 47, 51, 53, 60, 81, 97, 101, 114, 134, 148, 163, 171, 176, 177
peer review   11, 13, 28, 31, 60, 72, 88, 91, 98, 110, 144, 155, 157, 158, 159, 161, 164
personal anecdote   20
Phil Trans   27
Philipp, Tobias   89, 90
physical libraries   24
Plan S
  APC model   188
  APCs and quality debate   110
  appetite for change   146
  article processing charges, 163
  as continued source of debate   179
  at EuroScience Open Forum (ESOF)   95
  attack on academic freedom   113
  attitudes towards cost will change   163
  common criticisms to   108
  coordinators   110, 139
  copyright   139
  criticism of   83
  Europe's role in protecting academic data   171
  F1000   127
  financial aspect of OA   185
  future of academic publishing   155
  global awareness/coordination   112
  guidelines   138, 147
  hybrids   186
  impact of Covid   174
  implementation guidance   111, 116
  key principles   84
  managing academic data   170
  mixed reception   134

national funding agencies   85
navigating data-led future   167
new technologies   161
OA2020 in Berlin   120
power back into hands of
  experts   178
prospect of joining   188
provisions of   99, 146
publishing platforms   138
radical intervention   63
reimagining publisher business
  models   144
role of funders and
  institutions   168
silver bullet   180
stock of legacy   192
trade press   107
transformative agreements   121,
  122, 126
transforming narrative   121
UCL Press   183
PNAS   25, 26, 55
predatory journals   87, 90, 92, 93
printing   7, 15, 27, 28, 29, 67, 146
Project DEAL   122, 123, 124, 132,
  151, 153
public funding   xiii, 9, 10, 24, 41, 53,
  78, 103, 110, 125, 136
public libraries   29
public money   35, 88, 103, 114, 132,
  154, 169, 191
public policies, contribution of   136
public research in India   127
public university   126, 150, 151, 190
public volunteers   21
publications   xiii, 3, 11, 14, 16, 22,
  27, 29, 31, 32, 38, 41, 44, 46,
  55, 62, 72, 81, 86, 88, 89, 90,
  91, 102, 104, 112
'publish and read' deal   121, 123, 132
publisher power   153
publishing/publishers   3, 4, 5, 6, 11, 14
  academic   xii, xiii, 2, 5

and researchers   23
attitudes   147
bodies   25
business models   3, 8, 39
demands   140
economic aspects of   185
ecosystem   6
forms of   111
journals and   137
market   97
OA model of   120
open access content   133
platforms in OA domain   131
portfolio   136
principles of   143
traditional   137
PubMed   171

Q

Quinn, Geoghean   44

R

radical intervention   63
radical rewriting   158
rate of inflation   135
Reller, Tom   101
Research Works Act   49
research/researchers
  burden on   169
  community   48, 50
  copyright   141
  generation of   82
  institution   3, 8, 13
  on personal blogs and social
    media   23
  papers   2, 3, 14, 15, 18, 19, 22, 29,
    31, 32, 33, 37
  protocols   168
  publishers and   23
  resources and public funding
    for   24
  reward system for   170

resistance to change   61
reward system   59, 170, 193, 194
Richardson, Peter   109
rights retention initiative   141
Rights Retention Strategy
  (RRS)   139, 140, 144
Rooryck, Johan   57, 58, 59, 60, 61,
  62, 73, 123, 130, 144, 148, 176,
  179
Ropers, Daniel   69, 134, 138, 146,
  147, 148, 149, 154
Røttingen, John-Arne   78, 116
rules of competition   137

S

Schiltz, Marc   76, 77, 87, 102, 147,
  148, 162, 168, 179, 181,
  190, 193
Schmitt, Jason   59, 99, 100
scholarly publishing   28, 34, 115,
  164, 177, 180
Scholarly Publishing and
  Academic Resources
  Coalition (SPARC)   34, 38,
  40, 49, 104, 106, 123, 129, 190
science, impact and relevance
  of   22
scientific community   32, 35, 44, 74,
  76, 106, 107, 142, 175
scientific paper   4, 53
scientific publications   63, 67, 86,
  96, 119, 131, 191
Scientific, Technical, and Medical
  Publishers (STM)   31, 49, 56,
  68, 70, 144, 165
SciFree   139
Sci-Hub revolution   14, 51
shareholders, financial interests and
  demanding   47
Sheckman, Randy   25, 50, 54, 55, 58
shifting funds   137
smaller publishers   70
  impact on   70

smaller-scale publishing   71
Smits, Robert-Jan   xiii, 45, 51, 53,
  57, 65, 66, 67, 68, 69, 70, 71,
  72, 73, 74, 75, 76, 77, 78, 79,
  82, 83, 84, 85, 87, 88, 89, 96,
  97, 129
  determination   46, 79
  impatience   71
SNSF   89
  decision makers   89
  preliminary analysis by   90
  strategy division   89
society journals   49, 108, 112, 157
SPARC. See Scholarly Publishing
  and Academic Resources
  Coalition
Springer   30, 50, 58, 69, 135, 146, 148
Springer Nature   11, 14, 47, 50, 52,
  54, 69, 101, 121, 133, 134, 142,
  143, 148, 153, 163, 165, 192
stakeholders   xii, 13, 16, 23, 41, 45,
  46, 47, 57, 58, 74, 80, 82, 116,
  118, 120, 121, 123, 124, 127,
  134, 137, 139, 147, 154, 155,
  174, 185, 188, 194
Steel, Graham   19, 23
Stern, Bodo   163, 164, 182, 189
Strohschneider, Peter   88
Suber, Peter   7, 14, 15, 16, 20, 23, 32,
  33, 36, 38, 39, 48, 105
sub-Saharan institutions   25
subscription   3, 4, 10, 30
  costs of   31
  journals   3, 4, 5, 41
  model   3, 31
  paying for   72
  paywalls   24
  publishers   37
  to closed-access journals   25
  towards OA publishing   36
subscription-based journal   3
Swart, Marcel   59, 84, 113
Sweeney, David   79, 80, 81, 102, 116

Swiss National Science Foundation's National Research Council 62, 154
Swiss OA 89

T

Taylor & Francis 11, 47, 68, 115, 122
Taylor, Stuart 146
TDM. *See* text and data mining technologies 47, 161
Tennant, John 49, 115
Tesla 136
text and data mining (TDM) 46
traditional journals 157
traditional publishing 37, 73, 112, 137, 167
traditional research practices 163
transformative agreements 36, 110, 116, 121, 122, 126, 131, 132, 135, 137, 138, 145, 152, 194
transformative deals 132, 134, 135, 137, 138, 145, 146, 154, 166
Transformative Journal Framework 192
transformative models, international coordination of 147
Trump, Donald 104, 106, 124, 178

U

UCL Press 183
UK Brexit referendum 173
UK Research and Innovation (UKRI) 78, 79, 80, 87, 96, 116

universities 13, 17, 28, 31, 42, 51, 57, 62, 78
and research community stakeholders 80
growth of 29
libraries 4, 14, 29, 63
rewards systems 131
UN's Sustainable Development Goals 191
US federal funding system 103

V

van der Stelt, Wim 69
Venezuela 20
Vermeir, Koen 166, 167, 181
versions of record (VoR) 116
Vetterli, Martin 62, 63, 154, 167
Vogel, Johannes 191
VSNU/UKB study 22

W

Walport, Mark 78
Wellcome Open Research 156
Wellcome Trust and Gates Foundation 187, 189
Wiley 11, 30, 47, 58, 68, 105, 115, 119, 121, 122, 124, 132, 133, 134, 135, 154, 166, 181, 192
World Health Organization (WHO) 128, 175
World Wide Web 6, 26, 32, 34

Z

Zambia's National Science and Technology Council 127

www.ingramcontent.com/pod-product-compliance
Lightning Source LLC
Chambersburg PA
CBHW061254230426
43665CB00027B/2945